The Welsh Border

Archaeology, History & Landscape

The Welsh Border

Archaeology, History & Landscape

TREVOR ROWLEY

TEMPUS

First published by Michael Joseph Ltd 1986
This revised edition 2001

PUBLISHED IN THE UNITED KINGDOM BY:

Tempus Publishing Ltd
The Mill, Brimscombe Port
Stroud, Gloucestershire GL5 2QG
www.tempus-publishing.com

PUBLISHED IN THE UNITED STATES OF AMERICA BY:

Tempus Publishing Inc.
2 Cumberland Street
Charleston, SC 29401
1-888-313-2665
www.arcadiapublishing.com

Tempus books are available in France and Germany
from the following addresses:

Tempus Publishing Group
21 Avenue de la République
37300 Joué-lès-Tours
FRANCE

Tempus Publishing Group
Gustav-Adolf-Straße 3
99084 Erfurt
GERMANY

British Library Cataloguing in Publication Data.
A catalogue record for this book is available from the British Library.

ISBN 0 7524 1917 X

Typesetting and origination by Tempus Publishing.
PRINTED AND BOUND IN GREAT BRITAIN

Contents

List of illustrations

Text figures

Colour plates

Preface and acknowledgements

This book first appeared under the title *The Landscape of the Welsh Marches* in 1986. Since then there have been major advances made in the archaeological investigation of the region. There has also been important new work in the study of place-names and this completely revised volume takes into account some of that work. Over the last 20 years there have also been considerable changes in the housing market, particularly in rural areas. Shropshire and Herefordshire have become desirable areas in which to live, and new building and housing renovations are to be found throughout the region and as a result there are now no truly derelict areas left in the Welsh Marches.

Thanks are due to Hilary Groves for preparing the typescript and the index and to Esther Paist for proofreading. I am also particularly grateful to Peter Kemmis Betty for encouraging me to revise the book.

The author is extremely grateful to a number of institutions and individuals for agreeing to supply illustrations for this book, all of whom retain copyright to their images: Aerofilm (**14, 37, 84, colour plate 6**); CADW (**35, 36, 41, 47, 48, 49, 52, 59, 62, 64, 65, 68, 74, 81, colour plate 11**); Cambridge University Committee for Aerial Photography (**3, 4, 5, 10, 12, 13, 17, 19, 21, 23**); Clwyd-Powys Archaeological Trust (**colour plates 22, 31, 33 & 36**); Colourmaster International (**colour plate 12**); English Heritage (**colour plate 14**); National Monuments Record (**16, 20, 28, 31, 32, 43, 46, 50, 55, 58, 60, 73, 75, 78, 80, 82, 88, 92, 94, 95**); Rowley's House Museum, Shrewsbury (**24**); Museum of Wales (**27**); Professor Barrie Jones (**9, 11**); Richard Muir (**6, 7, 87, 89**); Gareth B. Thomas (**colour plate 20**).

The extract from Poem XXXI from *A Shropshire Lad*, published by Jonathan Cape Ltd, is reproduced by permission of the Society of Authors and the translation of *Caratacus* are reproduced by kind permission of the translators Mary Beard and Chloe Chard.

Introduction

The borderland between England and Wales became known as the Welsh Marches following the Norman Conquest. It was so named in order to distinguish it from English land in Norman hands and Welsh land in Welsh hands. The term 'march' comes from the Anglo-Saxon word *mearc*, which simply means boundary. Politically and legally the Marches were distinct from both England and Wales, and operated as a separate buffer territory, but under Norman control. The official recognition of this separate character of the Marches confirmed a geographical and historical reality that had been apparent from at least the time of the prehistoric hillforts, which indicate that the Marches formed a border region as early as the Iron Age. It was recognised as a boundary by the Romans in their attempt to conquer Wales between AD 48 and 84, at which stage the Marches formed the north-west frontier of the whole of the Roman Empire. A few centuries later the political domination of the western fringes of Mercia by the Anglo-Saxons was marked by the building of Offa's Dyke — a substantial linear bank and ditch which divided the Anglo-Saxon kingdom of Mercia from Wales. This great earthwork was, as the physical manifestation of the border, to become a symbol of the Marches across which the English (and Normans) traded, intermarried and fought with the Welsh.

Although the geographical Marchlands extend from the estuary of the River Dee in the north to the Severn estuary in the south, this book will primarily be concerned with the central Marches — Shropshire and the pre-1974 county of Herefordshire. Both counties take their names from the premier towns which sit on their watery lifelines: Hereford on the gentle River Wye and Shrewsbury on the River Severn. These two counties, which only assumed their modern shapes in 1536 at the time of the Act of Union with Wales, reflect ancient political and cultural territories that can be traced back to before the Roman occupation. The hillforts, linear earthworks and castles tell of periods of violence and oppression, while fine churches, elegant country houses and market halls tell of periods of peace and prosperity.

The tranquil and largely unbruised Marcher landscape is still essentially rural in character — its towns almost visibly grow out of the surrounding countryside which, for most of their history, they have served. Agriculture remains the dominant activity, although only a minority of workers in the region are still employed on the land. Only in relatively recent years has the industrialisation of farming begun to take its toll and to 'sterilise' areas of the Borderland, just as post-war urban development has succeeded in sterilising many historic town centres, making one indistinguishable from another, in many parts of the country.

The traditional isolation of the Marchland, however, has largely protected it from the extremes of post-Second World War redevelopment. The 'forgotten' broad belt of

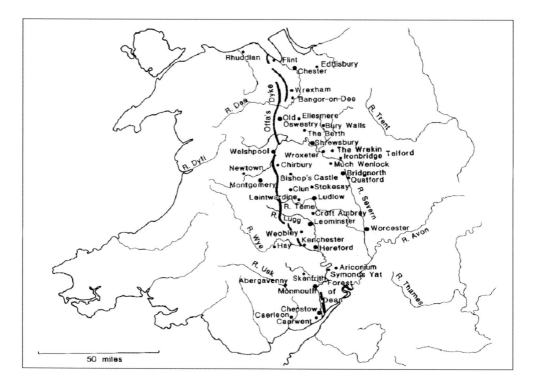

1   Main towns and historical sites in the Welsh Marches

countryside, which mainly lies between the River Severn and the Welsh mountains, is thinly populated in comparison with most other parts of Britain; the Industrial Revolution started here, but moved on before inflicting the visual damage it was to do elsewhere.

It is a nostalgic landscape of deeply engraved leafy lanes, which over the centuries has inspired many and has produced more than its share of creative artists — William Langland came from the Marches (either Ledbury or Cleobury Mortimer) and wrote of the Malverns in the fourteenth century. Five centuries later John Masefield, the Poet Laureate, was also born in Ledbury. The dramatist William Wycherley (1640-1716) was born at Clive, a few miles to the north of Shrewsbury; Wilfred Owen, the First World War poet, was a native of Oswestry, while A.E. Housman (1859-1936), who was originally from Worcestershire, was to produce the most evocative of Welsh Border writing in *A Shropshire Lad* and is now buried under a cherry tree in St Lawrence's churchyard in Ludlow. Shrewsbury's greatest son, Charles Darwin (1809-82), was first inspired to investigate natural history by the Marcher landscape.

The Marches also inspired Mary Webb (1881-1927), writer of novels based in the Shropshire countryside, Sir Edward German (1862-1936), author of *Merrie England*, Sir Edward Elgar (1857-1934), and Ralph Vaughan Williams (1872-1958). In the nineteenth century a parish priest of Bredwardine, a little village on the Herefordshire Wye, Francis

Kilvert, produced a wonderful diary describing his life and work set in the Border landscape of the 1870s and captured the atmosphere of the region perfectly:

Monnington on Wye, Tuesday, 6 April 1875

When I awoke a woodpigeon was crooning from the trees near the house and the early morning sunshine glinted upon the red boles of the gigantic Scotch firs in Monnington Walk. I rose early and went out. The morning was fresh and bright with a slight sunshiny shower. Flying hard by the church porch and on the western side of it I saw what I knew must be the grave of Owen Glendower. And here in the little Herefordshire churchyard within hearing of the rushing of the Wye and close under the shadow of the old grey church the strong wild heart, still now, has rested by the ancient home and roof tree of his kindred since he fell asleep more than 400 years ago. It is a quiet peaceful spot.

1 The making of the Marches

The Welsh border landscape is one of the most richly varied in the whole of Britain. Within a relatively small area there is plain, upland and mountain, and it is precisely this close juxtaposition of high and low land that has made the region a political and cultural boundary area for the last 2000 years at least. Moving from east to west, in the northern Marches the Cheshire plain gives way abruptly to the Denbigh moors and the Berwyn mountains. In the middle Marches between the River Severn and the River Teme the change is less abrupt, but nonetheless scenically dramatic with the Clee Hills, Wenlock Edge and the Stiperstones leading on to the Clun Forest, which forms the eastern edge of the solid Welsh massif. To the south the undulating Herefordshire plain abuts onto the aptly named Black Mountains and the bleak Radnor Forest region; further south still the uplands of the Forest of Dean span the southern Wye valley.

The Marches contain some of the oldest rocks in the world in the form of the Precambrian strata found in the Long Mynd and the Malvern Hills. Yet in geological terms the face of much of the Border region is relatively recent, the result of scouring by the Pleistocene ice sheets and the subsequent deposition of their debris, which has given rise to the meres of the Shropshire plain and the gentle lush landscape of the northern Hereford plain. The Marches can be divided into smaller distinct geographical regions, running from north to south.

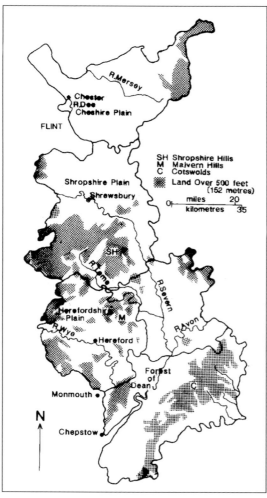

2   Physical relief of the Marches

3 *Aerial view of the Ellesmere 'lakes' in north Shropshire*

The Cheshire and Shropshire plains

The northern Marcher plains lie between 250ft and 350ft above sea level and are made up of a mixture of glacial drift and fluvio-glacial deposits, which in turn have produced soils varying from light sands to heavy loam. In many places these have been obscured on the surface by peat and valley marshes. During the last glaciation, southern Cheshire and northern Shropshire were occupied by two ice sheets, the most significant of which came down from the north by way of the Irish Sea and the Lancashire plain, while the lesser had its source in north Wales. Erratic rocks such as slate, volcanic lava and flint derived from both source-regions are to be found deposited on the plains. On the Shropshire-Cheshire border at Whixall, moss-peat is still commercially extracted, giving rise to an obvious conflict between commercial interests and concern for the conservation of the natural environment. In the Ellesmere area there are some three dozen meres and pools of glacial origin. The Ellesmere 'lakes' were formed at the time when the main glaciers retreated and large lumps of ice were left behind, buried in the glacial debris. As this ice melted, it in turn left behind sizeable depressions which eventually became water-filled lakes. Apart from man-made field ditches most of the meres are fed and drained by slow percolation through the drift on which they lie. This poor drainage, together with indifferent soils, has limited agricultural activity in the area historically, but the small lakes, often surrounded by woodland and low glacial hillocks, are most attractive and provide unusual lowland beauty spots in a region otherwise better known for its upland scenery. Despite the wide variety of rock types found in this area

4   *Lowland meets highland in the Tanat valley in north-western Shropshire*

there is little natural building stone, and the vast majority of buildings are half-timbered or built of brick.

To the north-west, in the region of Oswestry and Wrexham, the geography changes dramatically, with steep sloping hills and valleys heralding the nearby mountains of north Wales. These are made up of carboniferous Ordovician and Silurian rocks which in the area of the Berwyns are reinforced by extensive igneous intrusions. To the south the Shropshire plain gently gives way to the Severn valley, whose own broad flood plain has traditionally provided easy access to the heart of central Wales. It is believed that before the last glaciation the Severn flowed northwards to the Dee or Mersey or eastwards to the Trent. As the ice retreated the material left behind impeded the river's former course and eventually the Severn re-established itself, flowing southwards through a narrow gorge cut by glacial meltwater under pressure across the line of the limestone escarpment of Wenlock Edge. Hence below Shrewsbury as far as Buildwas the Severn flows in a wide plain, but it then enters the steep-sided Ironbridge gorge, flowing through it for several miles.

Across the southern central section of the Shropshire plain there is an outcrop of low hills made up mainly of New Red Sandstone (Keuper marls, siltstones and sandstones). Steep-sided sandstone outcrops such as Grinshill, Hawkestone Hill and Haughmond Hill contrast strikingly with the rest of the flat Shropshire plain and over the centuries they have provided a valuable source of building stone for places such as Shrewsbury Castle, Shrewsbury Abbey and many local parish churches. Elsewhere on the plain the traditional building material has been timber. However, since the sixteenth century brick has been extensively used and today, together with Welsh slate, it dominates the modest towns and villages. To the east, the acidic lower Keuper marl sandy soils gave rise to extensive areas of former heath land, particularly around Hodnet, to the east of the Tern valley.

The Wealdmoors

The Wealdmoors form a distinctive low-lying sub-region to the east of Shrewsbury, although geologically they are similar to the north Shropshire meres and mosses. They consist of a basin in which peat has accumulated since the disappearance of the Pleistocene ice sheet. From the late sixteenth century landowners began to enclose and improve thousands of acres which were largely given over to livestock fattening. In the nineteenth century large-scale drainage operations undertaken by the Duke of Sutherland finally transformed the area and divided it up into large, regular, arable fields. Today the Wealdmoors present a deceptively tranquil rural landscape, which effectively masks the treacherous and inhospitable reputation this region enjoyed in antiquity: then, it was dangerous to stray from the few well-established pathways that crossed the marshes.

The Wrekin and the Shropshire coalfield

The Shropshire coalfield formed the basis for the only extensive industrial area in the Marches apart from the Forest of Dean. The coalfield forms a triangle, extending from Lilleshall in the north-east to Coalbrookdale and Broseley in the south-west and from Wrockwardine in the west to Oakengates in the east. It is a relatively small area made up of valleys and escarpments, where settlement and landscape have been heavily influenced by piecemeal mining over the centuries. The ancient volcanic wedge which forms the Wrekin, reaching up to over 1000ft, provides the focal point of this region. It erupts out of a relatively low-lying area and appears to be higher than it actually is; its highly distinctive hogback profile makes it a dominant feature and one which has acted as a symbolic landmark for inhabitants of the central Welsh Marches over the centuries. In antiquity the greater part of the region appears to have been relatively uninhabited, although in the area close to the Severn, which cuts southwards, there has always been a concentration of settlement on the sand and gravel of the river terraces. The area has always been well-wooded, but heath and moorland are found on the spreads of boulder clay and carboniferous deposits. The post-Second World War new town of Telford now occupies much of the area, but evidence of its important industrial past is contained in the flourishing Ironbridge Gorge Museum, now designated a World Heritage Site.

The Silurian hills of south Shropshire and northern Herefordshire

Wenlock Edge

This area displays considerable geographical variety. The most impressive feature is one of the best-known escarpments in Britain, Wenlock Edge, today a wooded scarp running from Much Wenlock in the north-east to Craven Arms in the south-west. This remarkably straight cliff, unbroken for many miles, is formed by an outcrop of a richly fossiliferous Silurian limestone. The Edge has been a frequent haunt of geologists, and the area has yielded significant fossil discoveries which have helped in the understanding of the geological and tectonic history of central Britain. The Wenlock escarpment, which historically consisted of woodland and moorland, barely reaches to 1000ft, yet the bare grey crags of the heights can prove to be very inhospitable.

Corve Dale and the Clee Hills

Running parallel to this ridge often less than a mile to the east is a similar ridge made up of another sort of limestone known as the Aymestrey. Between the two ridges is a discontinuous hollow, Hope Dale, which passes into Corve Dale, a beautiful broad fertile valley connecting Much Wenlock with Ludlow. These beds have been (and still are) extensively quarried. The gentler eastern dip slopes, based on the shales, are much more fertile, and are often cultivated almost up to the crest of the scarp. Both in Corve Dale and in Ape Dale there are many small villages built mostly of the yellow-grey Silurian stone, which does not weather at all well.

Rising eastwards out of Corve Dale is a great stretch of undulating country, with many fields of heavy red soil marking an outcrop of Old Red Sandstone, which is the underlying rock of a large tract of the central and southern Marches. Standing out above it are two quite distinctive flat-topped hills, Brown Clee and Titterstone Clee. The Clees are capped by a layer of resistant dolerite giving rise to the craggy north-west face which makes their summits such prominent landmarks in the country to the east of Ludlow.

Where so many rocks are available there is naturally a great diversity of building materials. Yet half-timbered and brick buildings are still abundant, notably in Much Wenlock and in Ludlow, where the red tiles, weathering to a deeper tint than the bricks, provide the dominant colour. Ludlow Castle is built of the yellow-grey Silurian stone, while in the Onny valley near Horderley the main building material is a local Ordovician sandstone which is quarried in blocks of a variety of shapes and sizes and often has purple and yellow-green stripes running through it.

The north-west Herefordshire uplands

Over the Herefordshire border one marked area of regional diversity is the vale of Wigmore, a former glacial lake that left deep deposits of morainic material which are surrounded in a horseshoe pattern by the eroded Bringewood anticline. At one stage the lake overflowed from the lowest part of the encircling hills to create a deeply-cut gorge, near the present village of Downton-on-the-Rock. After the ice receded and the glacial lake drained away, the river Teme used this outlet and it became integrated in the river's circuitous course. There are other striking examples of the effect of glaciation on the local topography in this area, including the gorge of the River Ludd between Sned Wood and Mere valley. Here gorges and

5 *The Severn Valley near Melverley in Shropshire. The River Severn meanders across a broad river terrace here. Extensive areas of ridge and furrow of medieval field systems is thrown into sharp relief by a light covering of snow*

dry valleys, created by short violent rushes of water at the margin of the ice fields, have dissected the foothill countryside into distinct blocks.

Difficult topography, generally poor soils and the bleakness of the area render the uplands of marginal agricultural value, and cultivation has traditionally been confined to the valley lowlands. Until the seventeenth century much of this area was included in the Forest of Mochtree.

The Shropshire hills

To the north-west of the Silurian uplands lie what are considered to be the true Shropshire hills. In this area a wide range of rocks create scenes of extraordinary variation where the relation of landscape to geographical structure is probably better displayed than in any other part of Britain. The general lie of the country here runs south-east to north-west. Caer Caradoc erupts steeply from the Stretton valley in a slope broken only by the occasional dark crag, but its eastern face is more irregular, with ribs of exposed rock extending up its flanks. Most of the hill is composed of Precambrian volcanic lavas and ashes. This long narrow hill is cut off by a great fault along its north-western side, a fact which accounts for the smooth face overlooking Church Stretton. On the same alignment there are other similar hills, Ragleth to the south-west and the Lawley Hill to the north-east.

Across the narrow faulted trough in which Church Stretton lies is the great bare mass of Long Mynd which, although rising higher than Caradoc, is less distinctive in its outlines. On the summit is a smooth-topped plateau that near its borders is deeply cut by narrow V-shaped valleys, of which Cardingmill valley is the best known. Like Caradoc, this plateau area is built up of Precambrian rocks, but because these rocks are less resistant and have been more heavily eroded, Long Mynd appears more rounded than its neighbours.

6 The Herefordshire landscape looking westwards from the Malverns

The country west of Long Mynd brings us to Wales and into upland landscapes characteristic of the principality; between Montgomery and Minsterley there are many irregular peaks and much bleak upland. This country was largely formed by Ordovician rocks of the Welsh type, rather more rugged than the east Shropshire variety, consisting chiefly of slates and shales, but also including beds of volcanic ash and lava. The harder beds now stand out as ridges running in a general north-easterly direction, emphasising the prevailing Caledonian 'grain' of the structures. The most pronounced ridge, which lies near the western border of the Long Mynd, is the Stiperstones, which was formed by hard, light-coloured quartzite, and stands out in bare, tor-like crags, the most dramatic being the imposing landmark known as the Devil's Chair. There are deposits of lead and silver in this area which were quarried both in antiquity and in the more recent past.

The Herefordshire plain

To the south of the Silurian upland there lies a far gentler landscape, the Hereford plain. These lowlands occupy something like 65 per cent of the ancient county of Herefordshire, and extend from the Shropshire border in the north to the Forest of Dean in the south, the Welsh border in the west to the foothills of the Malverns in the east. The region is set within a discontinuous frame of hills and is interrupted by the twin uplands of Dinmore and Wormsley, which divide the region into two main sub-regions, the plain of Hereford and the plain of Leominster. The plains are based almost exclusively upon Old Red Sandstone, which here consists of soft beds of red and grey marl. At intervals there are beds of more compact sandstone and cemented limestone. These have formed tabular hills such as the flat-topped plateaux with steep wooded scarp slopes at Wormsley and Dinmore, which rise spectacularly from the surrounding lowlands.

The geomorphological history of these hills emphasises the importance of glacial processes in the development of the Border landscape. At one time the isolated hills formed part of a continuous plateau surface, but glacial erosion has breached the harder beds and bitten deeply into the underlying marls. The results of this process can clearly be seen at Wormsley, a former upland which has been dissected to make three separate hill areas, Merryhill, Credenhill and the Nupton Hills. In the extreme south-east of the plain the absence of glacial drift has given the countryside a more mellow appearance, and accordingly has been traditionally a more prosperous area of arable farming. The charming town of Ross-on-Wye, with its sandstone buildings, provides a striking contrast to the other largely half-timbered Herefordshire market towns. Eastwards beyond the Wye lies the Forest of Dean, which in Herefordshire is represented by the still heavily wooded Penyard Hill.

Although generally speaking the flaky local sandstone does not make a particularly good building material it has been used extensively, particularly in churches and other public buildings. In this area many of the roofs were covered with a local fossil sandstone until Welsh slates became readily available during the nineteenth century. The remarkable Romanesque church at Kilpeck is built of the local sandstone, which becomes flaky and pliable as it weathers. Throughout most of Herefordshire timber has traditionally been the main material used in domestic buildings and accounts for the wealth of late and immediately post-medieval farms and manor houses to be found in this region.

The north-eastern Herefordshire uplands

The Herefordshire plain is surrounded by uplands. In the north-east is the Bromyard plateau (500-800ft), consisting principally of Dittonian sandstone which forms much of south-eastern Shropshire and north-west Worcestershire. The Herefordshire section is cut off from the main plateau by the River Teme, which here provides the basis of the ancient county boundary. The plateau is dissected by narrow valleys, draining to the River Frome. On the plateaux, soils tend to be shallow and poor, frequently carrying a moorland cover, but soils are deeper in those valley areas where streams have cut down into the underlying marls. The modern landscape owes its appearance partly to the large number of parks found here and partly to the fact that it remains one of the major fruit-growing centres in the Marches.

There is one geological curiosity that has made a small but impressive contribution to the Border landscape — the post-glacial calcareous tufa, or travertine, found in the Teme valley near Shelsley Walsh. This tufa is formed around the outlet of a spring whose waters are charged with a lime solution which leaves a spongy soft deposit, easily worked, but nonetheless fairly durable. It has been used in a number of churches in the county such as Bredwardine. This material was particularly popular during the Norman period and is extensively used in the fine Romanesque church St Michael, Moccas, where the isolated building stands remote within a landscaped park.

The Woolhope dome

To the south-east of Hereford lies the unusual and complex Woolhope dome, a remarkable Silurian outcrop. The core of this feature is made up of Llandovery flags, encircled by a ring of Wenlock limestones, and outside this there is a wide deposit of Ludlow rocks. These are fossil-rich rocks forming a complex scarp and vale topography. The dome, a major feature of the Herefordshire landscape, is very distinctive, consisting of alternating scarps and valleys. Settlement is sparse and the area has a heavy woodland cover intermixed with moorland. In antiquity the limestone beds were extensively quarried for building material.

The Malvern Hills

The oldest rocks in Herefordshire, those of Precambrian formation, are mostly deeply buried beneath later deposits, and are exposed only along a narrow tract in the extreme east of the county. Here they provide a striking natural boundary with the ancient county of Worcestershire in the form of the Malvern Hills. The water table appears as a regular spring line at about 600ft above sea level, corresponding to the limit of cultivation and of historic settlement.

The Malverns rise to just over 1200ft and their steep slopes are generally used only for rough grazing or woodland. There has been surprisingly little extensive quarrying of the igneous rock on the Herefordshire side of the border. The sharp crest of the Malverns' spine is marked by traces of former occupation and by an ancient boundary: the Shire Ditch, created in its present form as a hunting boundary in the Middle Ages, but almost certainly marking a much earlier tribal division.

South central Herefordshire uplands (Archenfield)

Moving in a clockwise direction around the hilly frame that encompasses Herefordshire we come to the south central hills. These consist of harder beds of the Old Red Sandstone. They extend from the Wye in the east to the Monnow valley in the west, and are drained to the south-east by several small tributaries of the Monnow. The hills rise from just under 100ft on the Wye to over 600ft overlooking the Monnow and to 1200ft on Garway Hill. This is both a geographically and culturally distinctive region, as it remained Celtic in character until the twelfth century, and the vast majority of place names are Welsh. Reputedly the Welsh and English names of the district, Erging and Archenfield, are derived from the Roman iron-working settlement of *Ariconium*, but as this site lies some distance away, to the east of Ross, there must be some doubt about this theory.

Because of the irregular terrain the area is characterised by a thin scatter of dispersed settlement and is largely devoid of nucleated villages. Today it carries a surprisingly thin woodland cover, except in the extreme west overlooking the Monnow and in the slower eastern meanders of the Wye, which have a high concentration of orchards on their banks.

The Black Mountain foothills

Some of the most impressive landscape in the whole of the Marches is to be found in the deeply dissected upland plateaux which border the Black Mountains. These occupy some 100 square miles of Old Red Sandstone extending into the adjoining pre-1974 Welsh counties of Brecon and Monmouth. The geological structure of this region is relatively simple: over much of the area the rocks are horizontal and, because of differing degrees of resistance, erosion has produced a tabular relief. The whole region is slightly tilted to the south-east, so that the highest hills occur on the northern and western fringes. Few summits rise above 1000ft, and the topography consists of a gently rolling plateau lying between 600 and 1000ft, deeply trenched by the narrow parallel valleys of the Olchon, Escley Brook, Upper Monnow, Dulas and Dore.

These five valleys dominate the human and economic geography of this corner of the Marches. The broadest and most fertile of them is the Golden Valley of the Dore River, whose name is an adaptation of the Celtic word *dur* meaning water. The present river is too small for the valley, the bottom of which is up to a mile wide in places; it is therefore probable that during the final glaciation ice extended down the valley as far as Vowchurch and on its retreat created a small temporary lake in the vicinity of Dorstone. This accounts for the flat marshy appearance of the area today. The presence of silty downwash from the adjacent slopes makes the Golden Valley live up to its name at least as far as its agricultural prosperity is concerned.

The valleys have naturally attracted settlement and communication in the region, giving it a north-north-west/south-south-east character; movement from east to west is strictly limited by their deeply ingrained courses. One of the consequences of this is that the upland areas have traditionally been very isolated. Even today, extensive spreads of woodland and rough stone grazing are typical; the density of population is still low and settlements are few and scattered.

The Forest of Dean

The Forest of Dean lies at an average height of about 650ft above sea level, sloping gradually downwards from north to south. The plateau drops away rapidly on all sides and this helps give the region its distinctive character. It consists of a number of different types of rock including Old Red Sandstone, which in places incorporates a quartz conglomerate that has often been used as a building material in the past; the Romans used it for making roads. The conglomerate gives rise to steep-sided hills along the plateau edge. On the inner margin of the outcrop of conglomerate there is a belt of carboniferous limestone containing pockets of haematite which were quarried for their iron content in antiquity, particularly in the area known as the Scowles.

In the middle of the Forest of Dean basin are coal measures, the seams varying in thickness from two to five feet. One of the sandstone beds, the Pennant, is particularly thick and resistant to erosion and underlies much of the high plateau country in the northern part of the forest centred on Ruardean Hill. The Pennant sandstone has been extensively quarried as a local building material. The area was designated as a special hunting area even before the Norman Conquest, and afterwards became one of the great Forests of medieval England, renowned for both its timber resources and its coal and ironstone mining, as well as its game reserves.

The Lower Wye valley

Southwards from Ross, the Wye has cut a course through the edge of the Forest of Dean plateau. In the slower section the river flows in a series of large meander loops, each loop having a steep river cliff on its outer side and a more gently sloping slip-off slope within the loop. Although this basic form is repeated many times, there are significant variations from one meander to the next, due in part to the fact that the river crosses many different types of rock, each of which gives rise to a characteristic valley form. At Welsh Bicknor, for instance, there is a long spur of shale with a gentle slope down to the flood plain, while at Symond's Yat the river cuts into the carboniferous limestone. These meanders are similar to those of the River Dee at Llangollen and are unusual in that such meanders are more characteristic of rivers winding across broad alluvial plains; they are not often associated with deep gorges. The Wye swings in big curves, some of them up to three miles wide, and in several, as in the bend at Symond's Yat, the river forms an almost complete loop.

These meanders are presumed to have started when the Wye flowed over a wide flood plain in an area of low relief. As the sea level fell, probably in several stages, the river was able to cut down its bed, but there was no time for valley widening and consequently its meanders became deeply entrenched.

Climate

Climatologically the Marches conform largely to the West Midland pattern, with an average precipitation of 27-30in a year. However, moving westwards precipitation increases markedly and on the summits of the Black Mountains and the Long Mynd it exceeds 55in. There is also a significant shortening in the length of the growing season in the western mountains, so much so that it is claimed that in the Black Mountains there are 11 months of winter and one month of bad weather.

This, then, is the canvas on which man has etched his works over the centuries. The Marches have much land which has been too steep or too wet for fertile agriculture for most of their history. Added to this, their remoteness has meant that they have never been heavily populated. Accordingly the region has changed very slowly and man's works once created have tended to survive longer here than in many other parts of Britain.

2 Early man in the Marches

Early man arrived in the Welsh Marches between half a million and a million years ago. Despite this enormous time span, beyond the ponderous prehistoric forts that dominate many Marcher hilltops the physical evidence of early prehistoric man is sparse, at least at first sight. The repeated glaciations which did so much to give the Borderland its final physical face removed most evidence of very early man from the landscape. It is true that some of the higher upland areas such as the Black Mountains, Caer Caradoc, the Long Mynd and the Long Mountain would have protruded above the glaciers, but the ice of the final glaciation covered much of the Borderland with a thick deposit; in the Herefordshire plain this was up to 600ft thick. Immense blankets of glacial moraine were then deposited over most of the areas which would earlier have been occupied by Lower and Middle Palaeolithic (Early and Middle Old Stone Age) man. Although a scattering of hand axes and flint cores have been found on hilly ground above 600ft, relatively little material of any significance has survived. Yet even if we were able to compile the complete archaeological record of the surviving material for this great span of prehistory, it is probable that there would be little of any substance within the modern landscape for us to look at: early man was essentially itinerant — a hunter-gatherer — moving across the countryside in small groups in constant pursuit of food.

The Old Stone Age (the Palaeolithic)

When humans first appeared on the scene in the Marches the geography of the region would have been very different to today; also, for many tens of thousands of years man's presence in the region was episodic. Throughout the Old Stone Age, man was knitted into the natural environment; he was a hunter-gatherer, who responded to the movement of herds of wild animals, which in turn reflected changing seasonal and climatic conditions. Man was a migrant and did not create permanent settlements, nor did he erect monuments either for the living or for the dead, except perhaps of a rudimentary and ephemeral kind. Man was in tune with his environment, functioning as an integrated part rather than as a manager, up until the last glaciation (12,000 BC). The first substantial traces of man in the Borderland date only from between about 10,000 and 8000 BC. Evidence from this period is derived from caves found in the carboniferous limestone deposits of southern Herefordshire. The most important of these is King Arthur's Cave, which overlooks the Wye landmark of Symond's Yat. The cave is located in a narrow valley between the Dowards leading to the Wye valley, from which there was presumably once a lake or a series of lakes in the Whitchurch/Goodrich area, before the

Wye had inscribed its present channel. King Arthur's Cave has two chambers with an entrance about 25ft wide and is spectacularly situated in woodland about 300ft above the River Wye. The cave was first excavated in 1871 by the Revd W.S. Symonds, who found the remains of numerous extinct animals, including mammoth, woolly rhinoceros, hyena, bison, great Irish deer and cave bear, lying beneath a thick layer of stalagmites. Flint tools found here show that it was occupied both in the Old and Middle Stone Ages. It would appear that to begin with the people lived inside the cave, but later, perhaps as the climate improved, the occupants moved to the mouth and ledge, where the ashes of their fires and the bones of the animals they hunted were found in deposits up to 6ft deep. The location of this cave is remarkably similar to the Old Stone Age caves found in the Cheddar Gorge. Such prominent landmarks and lookouts appear to have been attractive to the earliest settlers. Gorges and narrow valleys with caves would have been particularly important as they enabled the movement of herds of animals, such as wild horses, to be carefully monitored and impeded.

Close to King Arthur's Cave there is another cave, also named after an Arthurian character: Merlin. Excavations at Merlin's Cave by the Bristol University Spelaeological Society in 1924-7 located a possible Old Stone Age flint implement, but any stratification which once existed had been largely obliterated by later iron ore mining.

As the ice sheets receded the climate improved and more regular hunting and trading patterns developed. It is possible that after the middle of the eighth millennium BC, with the spread of hazel, pine and oak forests, Mesolithic man was more active in the Marches. Nevertheless, although finds have been made in upland Wales and the West Midlands, the relative absence of evidence from the Borderland is disappointing. The earliest flints found along the Clun-Clee ridgeway, a route which was much used for trading in the neolithic and Bronze Age, however, date from the Middle Stone Age (Mesolithic), suggesting an emerging pattern of communication. Scattered finds of the Middle Stone Age have also been found elsewhere in the region, but no substantial occupation sites have been located. It has been suggested by Dr Stanford, an archaeologist who studied early man in the Marches, that it may be useful to investigate around the edges of the old glacial lakes at places such as Wigmore, the middle valley of the Teme, along the Church Stretton Hills and in the valley of the middle Severn. Such locations would have been favourite places for hunting parties who would have taken wildfowl from the marshes to supplement their diet of venison and wild pig from the forest. In such locations it is possible that there would be deposits of animal and fish bones and shells as well as scatters of flint left behind from flint tool making. It is also possible that hearths and the remains of seasonal dwellings may have survived where conditions are favourable.

The New Stone Age (the neolithic)

The New Stone Age marked the appearance of settled farmers in Britain when agriculture began to replace a predominantly hunter-gatherer economy sometime after *c*.3500 BC. At this stage, apart from the highest hilltops, most of the region would have been covered by woodland with wet alder, carr and willow on the flood plains and in the river valleys, and broad leafed species, particularly lime, dominant on the higher drier ground. The sparse evidence available from the Marches indicates that there was patchy woodland clearance, sometimes of a relatively short-lived nature, in the later fourth millennium BC. At about the same time pioneer farming communities began to establish themselves, herding animals, especially cattle, and growing cereals, mostly wheat and barley. The first permanent settlements began to be established, along with an irregular network of fields and tracks, and funerary monuments. Pollen evidence from places such as Crose Mere, Baschurch posts and other sites in north Shropshire suggests that to begin with clearances were relatively small in scale; although there was an increase in birch and ash at the expense of lime, the total forest area was not significantly diminished. In other parts of Britain the process of settling down to a regime of permanent or semi-permanent agriculture was associated with the construction of substantial stone or, as they are generally known, megalithic monuments. In parts of the country it was necessary to clear large stones off the ground before cultivation could start. Stones would have been piled up into mounds or banks, and it would appear that some were used to build structures associated with burial or ritual practices. The most notable survivals from this period are the chambered tombs, or long barrows, consisting of one or more stone compartments which originally contained bodies accompanied by grave goods such as pots, stone tools and stone weapons. The chambers had a capping stone or stones and were often covered by an elongated earthen mound. In some instances the mound was surrounded by standing stones, but frequently these stones have disappeared as has the earthen mound, leaving just the exposed stone chambers.

There is a distinctive cluster of burial monuments distributed over the Mendips and the Cotswolds which spills over into south Wales and the Black Mountains, known as the Severn-Cotswold group of barrows. The most northerly members of this group overlap into Herefordshire, which appears to have formed the boundary of a cultural or political territory at one stage during the New Stone Age. The most dramatic surviving example of such a megalithic monument in Herefordshire is Arthur's Stone in Dorstone parish, which forms the focus for an important group of neolithic sites. This funerary monument has an irregular polygonal main chamber about 16ft long covered by an enormous capstone of local limestone and parts of at least two passages or chambers at the north end. There were several stages to the erection of the barrow, one of which included what appears to have been the construction of a false entrance. Such features were common to the Severn-Cotswold group and were thought to have been built in order to deceive tomb robbers, who ransacked such burial mounds for their grave goods. Other devices such as concealed side entrances were also adopted in order to protect the burial deposits. Such devices were often effective deterrents against both grave looters and early antiquarians, who started investigating such monuments from the seventeenth century onwards with reckless and normally destructive consequences.

At Arthur's Stone, there is a large blocking stone in the false entrance which is inscribed with some characteristic neolithic markings in the shape of small circular hollows known as 'cupmarks'. Originally the monument was probably covered by a long mound, but this has long since been eroded away and the interior of the tomb has been pillaged of its bones and grave goods. Close by at Cross Lodge Farm there is an intact long barrow which may incorporate another chambered tomb. In the same parish there is a standing stone with neolithic markings, and in the 1960s traces of a rare contemporary settlement site were excavated nearby. Almost certainly there were originally many more examples of long barrows in the southern Marches, but over the centuries they have been destroyed either to make more room for arable farming or for superstitious reasons. Such monuments were long regarded as the work of the Devil or evil spirits, particularly during the Middle Ages, when they often acquired supernatural names.

Numerous stray finds of neolithic flint and stone tools have been made, mainly in the southern parts of the Marches, but there have not been enough findings to build up a complete picture of the society of which they were part. Almost certainly much remains to be found and yet more painstaking fieldwork is needed. Eventually, when evidence hidden in peat bogs or lying on lonely upland wastes has been added to the findings already made, we may be able to paint a much fuller picture of life in the neolithic Marches, backed up by a more coherent narrative: as full as the story we have for the Cotswolds or for Wessex.

One of the problems of writing about the early prehistory of a region where stratified deposits are rare is that there are considerable problems involved in dating those few monuments which do survive. The division between the New Stone Age and the Bronze Age, when metal was first manufactured, is a convenience for those trying to present a continuous story. However, when this is applied to the frail early archaeology of the Marches it can be both frustrating and misleading, as there is no evidence of a clear break. Indeed the practice of erecting megalithic monuments which started during the New Stone Age continued well into the Bronze Age, and it is quite impossible to be certain into which chronological pigeon-hole some of the Marcher monuments should be placed. In the foothills of Corndon Hill in Chirbury parish (Shropshire) there are the significant remains of two stone circles sitting on dry islands in otherwise marshy ground — Hoarstone Circle and Mitchell's Fold. Mitchell's Fold consists of 15 stones arranged in a circle, the tallest reaching approximately 8ft. The Hoarstone circle is a little smaller, but originally consisted of 38 stones, most of which are now covered with peat. This area must have been a focus of local neolithic activity, and just across the Welsh border at Hyssington there is the site of an important axe factory based on a local outcrop of picrite, a rock much favoured by early tool manufacturers. The products of this and similar factories much further afield have been found along the length of the neolithic and Bronze Age trading route known as the Clun Clee Ridgeway.

This routeway extended across south Shropshire from the Kerry Hills in the west to the River Severn near Bewdley in the east. Numerous scatters left by neolithic and Bronze Age man have been found along its length in the form of flint and other stone implements and flakes. Dr L. Chitty, who over a lifetime studied the route in detail, believed that it became important as a result of the development of trade in perforated battle-axes and axe-hammers during the later neolithic and early Bronze Age. Concentrations of finds close to rivers indicate that established fording points already formed part of a regular trading system. Along these routes there are a number of places where unusually high concentrations of flint implements were found, and it has been reasonably suggested that such assemblages point to the presence of settlements or camp sites. For example, some

70 such sites have been found within a 12 mile radius of Clunbury — a density which is unparalleled elsewhere in the Marches. Along the north side of the trackway was the most productive locality for flints. George Luff, a schoolmaster from Clun, who began flint-hunting in 1877, recorded that flints were 'found in thousands' on the summit of Rock Hill, indicating a long period of settlement. He writes:

> The mass of implements upon Rock Hill are found imbedded in the subsoil
> beneath a growth of gorse, heather and coarse herbage. When the waste lands
> are brought into cultivation, and this growth is stocked up the plough turns up
> flints and 'little waggon wheels' (spindlewhorls) and after a shower of rain they
> may be seen glistening in the sun.

Regrettably, as yet, no accompanying evidence of contemporary buildings has been found in the region to complement the nineteenth-century schoolteacher's findings.

Neolithic dwellings are rare in Britain as a whole and the failure to locate them in the Marches is therefore hardly surprising. However, there is evidence from other structures which were associated with the route — some of them taking the form of embanked earth circles. Most of these monuments have been destroyed or severely mutilated, but their former presence has been recorded in a number of places. They include the Grey Stones near the Welsh Border in western Shropshire, Peny-y-Wern, near Clun, and near the summit of Titterstone Clee, where St John O'Neil excavated an 'Earth Circle' which had a wall of local dolerite (dhu-stone) blocks set in clay, about 3ft high and 60ft in diameter. Traces of such circles have been found elsewhere in the Border, normally at high altitude, and it seems possible that some of these sites represent the predecessors of Iron Age hillforts.

Other standing stones in the region appear to have been erected either during the neolithic or Bronze Age. Near to Trelleck in Gwent are Harold's Stones, three large standing stones set in a line, with cupmarks carved on them. Another isolated stone, known as the Queen's Stone, stands by the River Wye at Huntsham. This tall megalith (almost 14ft high) has sharply-cut parallel grooves incised on its sides, while yet another megalith at Michaelchurch Escley appears to be associated with a Bronze Age barrow cemetery. It is particularly noticeable that the majority of the surviving sites from this period lie in waste areas at a considerable height above sea level. Their survival has been due to the lack of intensive farming activity in such areas over the millennia; almost certainly other such sites and monuments would have been found in lowland areas as well, particularly along river valley terraces, but these have long been destroyed by farming and other activities.

Many megalithic monuments have folklore tales attached to them. According to one tradition, for instance, the name of Mitchell's Fold comes from 'fold', meaning a farmyard in Border usage, and Old English *mycel*, 'big', hence the big yard or big man's yard; and the story goes that a giant used to milk his cow here. An elaboration of this story is that the cow was a magnificent white animal known as the dun cow, which would willingly provide milk sufficient for all comers, as long as each person only brought one vessel to be filled. Eventually, however, a malicious witch milked the cow using a sieve and exhausted the apparently endless supply of milk. This resulted in starvation for the poor people who had relied upon the milk, so the witch was turned to stone and the other stones erected in a circle around her in order to keep her from escaping. Such stories, whose characters and events are often interchangeable, are attached to many early Marcher monuments. The Devil, or 'Grim', is often the principal character, others carry names associated with the Arthurian legend and others still are casually attributed to Caesar, Robin Hood or the British folk-hero Caradoc (or Caratacus), who defied the Roman armies in the Marches.

The surviving landscape evidence for the Bronze Age elsewhere is as incomplete as that of its forerunner, the neolithic period. Here and there we do find scattered surface hints of a culture period which lasted for more than 1000 years. Over recent decades, however, it has become increasingly clear that the evidence of standing monuments represents only one side of the picture. Just as in the neolithic period flint scatters hint at a much more significant presence than is demonstrated by the scarce distribution of long barrows, so in the Bronze Age the accumulating evidence from aerial photography indicates a much fuller landscape than that suggested by a glance at a plan of surviving surface features. The most important way of discovering buried or 'erased' sites and monuments in the landscape is through what are known as 'cropmarks'.

Cropmarks, parchmarks and soilmarks

Cropmarks are particularly important in prehistoric and Romano-British studies, but they can also be vital to the understanding of post-Roman landscapes. Cropmarks are features which are normally only visible from the air, in the form of differential markings in fields carrying a cereal crop. Generally these marks represent either areas where the crop is riper and thus usually more bleached than the rest of the crop, or where it is less ripe and therefore much greener. Such marks normally reflect the nature of the subsoil, principally its depth and richness and the amount of moisture present. Darker lines can indicate the presence of buried ditches where deeper root penetration has led to slow-ripening plants; conversely lighter lines will reflect wall foundations or roads, where resistance to growth has meant the plants are less luxuriant and will ripen earlier than the main crop. Deep-rooting plants tend to give a clearer picture than shallow-rooting ones. Although grain crops, particularly barley, give the best cropmarks, clover and sugar beet can also provide indications of buried features, and differential growth can even be distinguished in pea and bean fields. Archaeological markings in grass are generally only present early in the year, except in severe drought when dried-out areas or parchmarks may appear. Cropmarks result from ditched or buried features whose associated earthworks have been ploughed out. As such they represent an erased landscape, although analysis using the same groups of sites each year over a period of years has suggested that there are 10 to 14 days in a year, in mid to late July, when the marks are best seen as the crops are ripening. In good years, such as 1959, 1970, 1976 and 1984, as long a period as three weeks may be available, and some marks may even be visible throughout the whole growing period. The character of the subsoil is of great importance: generally the more porous it is the better

7   *The cropmarkings of a
    double enclosure at
    West Felton. Such
    enclosures normally
    represent Iron Age
    farmsteads which often
    continued to be
    occupied during the
    Roman period and are
    generally referred to as
    'native settlements'*

the chance of good cropmarks. Valley or plateau gravel, and Jurassic and carboniferous limestone produce good cropmarks, but sand and sandstone are normally less revealing. Sites on clay rarely show up well, and even on valley gravels surface patches of clay will effectively mask traces of earlier occupation. All these factors will affect the nature and value of the cropmark features. Only a proportion of the buried features in the ground will show up as cropmarks. Often the most important part of the site can be revealed only by excavation or geophysical survey. For this reason any group of cropmarks can be taken only as an indication of part of what is buried below — in fact, as a clue to the hidden evidence. In the Marches local drift geological conditions have often given rise to natural cropmarks such as frost cracks or silted streambeds, and these can sometimes be confused with man-made features.

Since it is often difficult to interpret the date of crop marks, descriptions of sites are normally based on the shapes of features. Archaeologists therefore tend to speak of 'ring ditches' and 'rectangular enclosures' rather than 'Bronze Age barrows' and 'Romano-British farmsteads', though a detailed knowledge of a region can lead one to anticipate the regular occurrence of certain types and forms of site. Occasionally it may be possible to discern a relative chronology of features showing up as cropmarks. For instance, it is sometimes possible to identify later tracks, buildings or enclosures sitting on top of earlier field systems. More frequently, however, excavation or survey is required to determine the relationship between overlapping cropmarks.

In recent years many earthwork sites in the Marches have been ploughed out, giving rise to soilmarks. Soilmarks appear after an archaeological earthwork site has been ploughed for the first time, but over the years the marks normally become blurred and disappear as the material from the earthwork is scattered over the field. In some conditions, the soilmarks remain fresh for a considerable time. Soilmarks show up wherever the fill of a ditch is a different colour from that of the surrounding soil; however, buildings, banks and ridges will gradually merge with the rest of the field, although perhaps remain discernable in the form of crop markings. Deep ploughing will hasten the process. Examining a soilmark occupation site on the ground will often reveal pottery and other artefacts as well as burnt material from hearths, but over the years these too will be dispersed.

Aerial photography has led to the recognition that there is far more evidence of man in the Marches from the neolithic period onwards than was previously thought and that settlement was not largely restricted to upland areas. Large segments of Britain which in the past have been written off as archaeological deserts are now seen as having carried considerable Bronze Age, Iron Age and Romano-British populations. The Severn valley above the Ironbridge gorge is proving to be particularly rich in archaeological cropmarks, but many of the smaller river valley terraces are also producing exciting evidence of early settlement. The work of collecting, plotting and analysing this evidence in the Marches is still in progress. Nonetheless, the extent to which man occupied and managed parts of the Marcher landscape from at least the Bronze Age onwards is already in need of considerable re-evaluation.

The Bronze Age

Everywhere in Britain during the Bronze Age the long barrow gave way to the round barrow as the principal funerary monument, and the low conical burial mounds found, for instance, along the line of the ancient track known as the Portway, which follows the spine of the Long Mynd, are the most characteristic monuments of the Bronze Age in the Marches. Such mounds tend to be found (or to survive best) on high ground, which has led some observers to suggest that they were constructed during a warmer period when the population could have grown crops and lived at higher altitudes than was possible subsequently. The identification of circular cropmarks, known as ring ditches, of Bronze Age burial mound dimensions in the lowlands suggests that this is an oversimplification and that Bronze Age settlements and cemeteries are to be found both on higher ground and in the valleys. A particular problem which is associated with the interpretation of circular burial mounds is that although they commonly date from the Bronze Age, they appear to have been used from time to time from the neolithic age to the Saxon period. This often makes the dating of such features virtually impossible without excavation. The probable siting of an Anglo-Saxon circular mound is suggested in the place name of Wolferlow, in north-east Herefordshire, which means 'Wulfhere's burial mound' and possibly Ludlow, which means 'Lluda's burial mound'.

At Bromfield a number of such mounds now occupy part of Ludlow racecourse and golf club, and were neatly landscaped during the nineteenth century when each one had a tree planted at its centre, thereby probably damaging the monuments' contents irrevocably. Excavations in one of them known as the Butt Tump revealed the remains of

8 *Plan showing the continuity of occupation to the north-west of Ludlow*

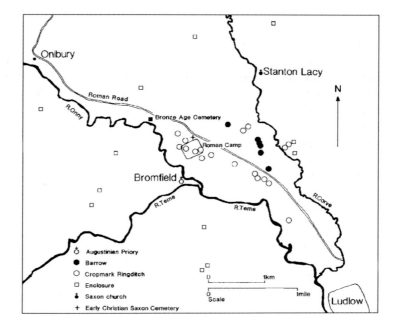

a teenage child buried with a bronze knife. Four other barrows on the racecourse have been flattened since they were dug in 1884. One of these contained a second burial urn and the contemporary description of the excavation is very interesting, although the techniques used would appal modern archaeologists:

> We now come to the fifth and last of the barrows opened at this time (there being another left for future exploration at a distance of about 300 yards from it), which turned out to be one of a most interesting character. It is somewhat larger in diameter than the 'Butt Tump', but not so deep, being only eight feet to the ground level. The work of exploration commenced, as in every other case, by cutting a trench from above. At a depth of two feet only from the top of the mound, to the astonishment of all engaged in the work, an urn containing a quantity of burnt bones was met with. Unfortunately, in consequence of its having been come upon so unexpectedly, it got broken into many pieces by the spade of a workman. The urn, which is of rather crude and ill-burnt pottery, is nevertheless of elegant design, with some attempt at ornamentation round the upper part.
>
> Having carefully removed the urn with all the pieces that could be found, the excavations were continued, when at a depth of about seven feet, a quantity of small flattish stones were come upon, which, as the work proceeded, proved to be the top stones of a cist. This appears to have been constructed in the following manner: the ground having been scooped out to the depth of a few inches in an oval form, head and foot stones composed of flat slabs of sandstone, about fifteen inches square, were placed edgewise at either end, and faced north and south. Other similar stones, but of smaller size, and also placed

31

edgewise, completed the oval. The interior of this oval space was filled in with small stones, the under layer of which, and consequently those placed next to the body and in direct contact with it, upon being turned over, were found to have small portions of bone adhering to them, and there was distinct evidence upon all of their having been subjected to excessive heat.

On all sides were observed large quantities of wood ashes, which proclaimed the fact that the crematory process had been carried out in the most complete manner. The inside measurement of the cist, between the head and foot stones, was three feet eight inches. It would seem, therefore, that the body, supposing it to have been that of an adult or fully grown person, must have been placed in a cramped position, in accordance with the prevailing custom of those early times.

There are still five upstanding barrows surviving, as well as evidence of 14 other destroyed barrows in the form of ring ditch cropmarks nearby. For a short stretch the A49 close to Ludlow follows their alignment and at the point at which the modern road swings westwards to cross the River Onny at Bromfield, they continue northwards suggesting a fording place some half a mile to the north of the present crossing. Excavations close by have revealed an extensive Bronze Age cemetery with over 130 burials dating from between 1800 and 900 BC. In the words of the excavator, Dr Stanford, 'Their contents revealed a complexity of burial routine, the significance of which still escapes our understanding.' However, there is significant evidence of continuity of use of the burial ground and of the marking of graves with small heaps of earth — miniature barrows perhaps?

The burials at Bromfield form part of an area of intensive occupation extending over a considerable period of time, with evidence dating from the neolithic through to the Anglo-Saxon period. It is a unique complex in the region not least because it has produced the only genuine evidence of early Christian Anglo-Saxon burials in the region. The Bromfield-Stanton Lacy-Ludlow triangle is one of considerable archaeological and historical interest. The concentration of occupation here is sufficient to mark it as a special area of 'preferred' settlement where, over the centuries and in radically different economic, social and climatic conditions, it was attractive enough to be used continuously as a settlement and perhaps as a religious centre. The presence of a Roman road and marching camp also indicate Romano-British interest in the area. The building of a substantial Saxon church at Stanton Lacy, followed by the post-Norman Conquest development of Ludlow as one of the foremost Marcher towns, highlights the continuing significance of the area.

The Bromfield concentration lies at the confluence of two south Shropshire rivers, the Teme and the Corve, and it has been shown that such river junctions were particularly important in prehistory. The symbolic significance of such locations was perhaps supplemented by more practical considerations, not least the attraction of the lighter alluvial valley soils and the possibility of transporting goods by water. A similarly positioned Bronze Age settlement and cemetery has been found to the south of Shrewsbury at Weeping Cross, sited close to the River Severn and the Rea Brook. As with so much early prehistory in the Borderland our understanding is at an early stage, but aerial photography is helping us build up a much more substantial picture of Bronze Age occupation and activity in the region.

During the middle and late Bronze Age the area of land under cultivation in the Marches appears to have increased. The survival of 'Celtic Fields', small regular earthwork enclosures, found on the sides of Caer Caradoc Hill near Church Stretton, point to the extent to which the higher land was being used at this time. Sometime after 1000 BC such areas of upland cultivation appear to have been abandoned, perhaps as a result of climatic deterioration. Cultivation continued in lowland areas, although at about this time many settlements and farmsteads appear to have been enclosed, possibly indicating a move towards more concentrated pastoralism. The development of the salt trade from Worcestershire and Cheshire at this stage is evidenced by the identification of briquetage salt containers from a number of sites in the region, and may be indicative of pastoral farmers requiring salt for meat preservation.

The pre-Roman Iron Age

The final phase of British prehistory is traditionally known as the Iron Age. The most outstanding monuments in the landscape from this period in the Marches are undoubtedly those massive defended enclosures, demarcated by turf-covered ramparts and ditches, the hillforts. Indeed, they form the most impressive monuments in the region of any period and are rivalled in their impact only by the medieval castles. In the parts of western Herefordshire and Shropshire virtually every hilltop is capped with one of these massive earthwork fortifications. Indeed Shropshire's uplands have one of the densest concentrations of hillforts of anywhere in Britain.

Most of the Border hillforts are to be found to the west of the Dee-Severn line, although there are some notable exceptions to the east of this boundary. We know from Roman sources the names of the tribes that occupied the region at the time of the conquest and there are marked differences in the distribution and size of their forts. In the north, to the west of the Dee estuary, was the territory of the Deceangli tribe, where there are relatively few hillforts, although some of those that do exist are of a considerable size. In particular, there is a line of forts commanding gaps on the eastern side of the vale of Clwyd, which includes Foel Fenlli (29 acres), Moel Hiraddug (36 acres) and Penycloddiau (64 acres). Among this group there is also the much smaller Moel Y Gaer, one of relatively few in the region that has been subject to excavation.

To the south, based on the fertile middle Severn valley, lay the territory of the Cornovii, in which there are many hillforts of varying dimensions. These include the massive multi-valate fort at Old Oswestry, which enclosed only about 20 acres, and which has up to seven ramparts, and Titterstone Clee, which was one of the most formidable hillforts in Britain until it was mutilated by quarrying. Further south were the Decangi, whose territory occupied the Herefordshire basin. Here the hillforts were larger, armed with strong ramparts, and more evenly spread. The central position of Credenhill Camp, enclosing over 70 acres, suggests that it could well have been their tribal capital. At the

9 *The Iron Age hillfort on Titterstone Clee is one of the largest in Britain, its single stone rampart enclosing an area of about 70 acres. An encroaching modern stone quarry can be seen on the right*

south-western end of the Marches, in the Dean-Trelleck uplands, were the Silures, whose territory also extended over much of southern Wales. The chief characteristic of the hillforts in this area is the comparatively small area they enclosed (rarely more than four acres), as well as the existence of several ramparts.

It used to be thought that the Iron Age hillforts were all built in the century or two before the arrival of the Romans, as a result of internal quarrels between neighbouring tribes, and that they were strengthened in response to the threat of the Romans. It was also thought that they only had one function, that is they really were forts and as such enjoyed only a brief existence. Investigation over the past 40 years, however, has demonstrated that the Border hillforts had a much longer lifespan. Ffridd Faldwyn, for instance, which sits above the modern town of Montgomery, has produced evidence of neolithic occupation, as have a number of other Border hillforts. Indeed, wherever excavation has taken place the evidence points to an early origin for the forts. At the Breidden, Powys, for instance, the earliest feature is a double palisade dated to 975 BC, while at Moel Y Gaer the earliest structures have been dated to 820 BC and excavations at Dinorben in Clwyd have produced evidence from as early as 1170 BC. This is not to say that all the Border forts have such early origins — Croft Ambrey, for instance, appears to have begun life only about 550 BC — but the idea that hillforts arrived on the scene only in the two centuries immediately preceding the Roman conquest has now been truly discarded. Furthermore, there is considerable evidence to suggest that a number of forts had already been abandoned or were in decline well before the arrival of the Romans, indicating perhaps changing political conditions and social disruption or fragmentation during the later Iron Age.

Not only have ideas about the dating of hillforts changed but the interpretation of their function has also altered. Initially their obviously bellicose appearance and location in remote strategic positions led to the belief that they had an exclusively military use,

10 Cropmarkings of prehistoric field boundaries near to Llandysilio (Four Crosses) in the Vyrnwy valley, a little way to the west of Offa's Dyke. The boundaries are demarcated by lines of closely set pits, known as pit alignments. The regular modern field is a product of nineteenth-century parliamentary enclosure. At the top centre there is a circular marking known as a ring ditch, probably representing a ploughed-out Bronze Age burial mound

perhaps being occupied only during the periods of unrest. Thus they were given the name 'fort' which itself tended to perpetuate the belief that they were essentially military in character. Evidence of forts away from the Marches shows that some of them had specialist areas for craftsmen, and that very widely varying activities were carried out within the confines of the defences. Excavations at Moel Y Gaer and Croft Ambrey have clearly demonstrated that these forts were not some form of prehistoric barracks, but that they contained many domestic dwellings which in some instances had been rebuilt on several occasions over the centuries. The identification of buildings regularly aligned along roadways within the forts also shows that they could have been organised in the same way as later villages or towns. In some hillforts there were special areas for keeping cattle or sheep and there were also storage pits for grain. These, together with the identification of corn-grinding querns, show that the hillforts probably served to store and redistribute agricultural produce.

It is clear, therefore, that the Marcher hillforts performed a range of functions which almost certainly changed over the years. It is quite true that some of the higher more remote forts might have acted largely as defended lookout-posts, which probably were only occupied in times of unrest or on a seasonal basis. However, the majority of those forts lying at between 500 and 1500ft seem to have offered a range of services to the surrounding countryside in the same way that market towns did in the Middle Ages and after. The largest and most prominent forts may also have performed political and administrative functions as well as acting as tithe and tax-collecting centres for their region or territory. It is even possible that they were able to monopolise regional trade in certain commodities and thus extract profitable tolls.

Naturally enough today our eye is taken by the massive fortifications, which have often survived because of their inaccessibility and the difficulty of levelling them. Until recently archaeological excavation too has tended to concentrate on hillfort defences and their gateways, which were investigated to provide a chronology for sites. As a result, elaborate histories of hillforts have been constructed often on the basis of very small excavated samples. Recent research has confirmed that it is necessary to investigate the interiors of the forts if we are really to understand them fully. The fort boundaries, which were often originally in the form of earth banks revetted with stone walls and the associated ditches, performed functions other than that of pure defence, although undoubtedly at times this was of the utmost importance. They could well have acted in the same way as medieval town walls, proclaiming the presence of an important settlement and providing a symbol of urban 'status' and privilege. Moreover, they would have provided the means by which goods and produce entering and leaving the fort could be monitored and taxed.

When we examine hillforts we are looking at the top of the Iron Age settlement hierarchy. What is often missing is the great spread of lesser settlements, which must have occupied large areas of the countryside, but which over the centuries have been absorbed back into the ground. In recent years aerial photography has added a new dimension to our understanding of the Iron Age. Cropmarkings have demonstrated that numerous prehistoric villages and farmsteads, together with their associated fields and trackways, lie buried beneath the soil of the Borderlands. Such Iron Age evidence is particularly common on the lighter soils of the terraces of the major river systems and on glacial sands and gravels, but has also been identified in other areas. It is clear that considerable parts of the lowland Border region were managed and farmed in the centuries preceding the time of the Romans. What is more, unlike the hillforts, many of these settlements appear to have survived virtually unaltered into the Romano-British period. The vast majority of lowland settlements have been located in the valleys of the Severn, the Wye and the Teme. In those areas the most common Iron Age feature is the simple cropmark enclosure. In Shropshire, for instance, several hundred of these have been located in the Severn Valley. The majority of sites are rectangular, marked out by a single ditch enclosing, typically, about an acre. Interior features are rarely visible, but gaps or entrances in the enclosure ditch can frequently be seen. In other cases the enclosures are surrounded by a double ditch while some also have attached compounds. In certain rare cases there is a complicated pattern of ditches which seems to mirror the elaborate hillfort pattern. More often, however, in this part of Britain enclosures tend to be found in isolation, although occasionally there is a complex of cropmarkings that suggests either repeated rebuilding or possibly the existence of a more complicated village structure.

Although evidence of field systems is less common in lowland contexts they have been found in close relationship to settlement enclosures. The earliest field systems appear to consist of small, irregular fields which were very closely knit together. Sometimes these were within a larger, well-defined enclosure, as at Muckleton and Shawbury Heath, while other systems show fields divided by pit alignments and ditches, for example near Stanton Upon Hine Heath. Here the pit alignments run as parallel lines, perhaps delineating a trackway, with ditches running laterally off this to divide the land into small fields. Often these small fields are overlaid with a pattern of parallel ditches forming roughly rectangular fields; this 'brick wall' type of pattern was occasionally interspersed with trackways. Excavations of a site at Four Crosses, Powys, has shown features, including pit alignments, that date back to the late Bronze Age. If the same holds true of other areas in the Marches then perhaps there were several phases of field creation with the more regular fields dating from the late Iron Age or Romano-British periods. In the case of Shawbury, there are two settlement sites which border a Roman road, both showing field systems of the 'brick wall' type on aerial photographs.

The pattern of Iron Age cropmarkings in the Marches is far less complicated than that found in, for instance, the upper Thames valley. The comparative simplicity of this pattern might suggest that many of the farmsteads were contemporaneous, associated with a period of colonisation similar to that which took place during the early Middle Ages. Alternatively there could have been a major agrarian reorganisation, perhaps associated with an expansionary phase of the hillforts. For instance, the evidence from pollen analysis suggests that there was intensive woodland clearance during the Iron Age in the Welsh Borderland region. To begin with there was a large-scale clearance of broad-leaved trees, followed a little later by alder and willow woods on the lower flood plains. Palaeo-environmental data from a group of sites in the Severn basin have shown that this woodland clearance *c.*500 BC brought about extensive erosion and an increase in the accumulation of flood-lain alluvium. Much work remains to be done on the identification and investigation of these traces of early settlement and agriculture, but we should not forget when viewing the splendours of the hillforts that there is a submerged Bronze and Iron Age landscape beneath our feet.

Sites to visit

Arthur's Stone, Dorstone, Herefordshire SO 318 431

The ancient monument known as Arthur's Stone is situated at 1000ft above sea level on Merbach Hill at the head of the Golden Valley. The monument lies in the large parish of Dorstone, and until the mid-nineteenth century was the gathering place for village celebrations. Arthur's Stone consists of an elongated polygonal chamber built of sandstone with its long axis north-north-west to south-south-east, approached by a passage to the north-north-west of it which is set on an east-west axis. Between the passage and chamber, and bridging over the different orientations of the two parts of the monument, is a smaller antechamber or passage consisting of two great stones. The main chamber is roofed over by one large capstone (now broken in two) and consists of nine low wallstones. To the south of the chamber are two isolated stones set in the ground whose relationship to the chamber is not clear. It is difficult to reconstruct the monument with confidence as the varied alignments of surviving stones indicate that there were several phases of construction. There are the distinct remains of the earthen barrow around the chamber, but they are not clear enough to reconstruct the shape of the original mound either, although records from an investigation in 1881 suggest an oval mound, 60ft long and 30ft wide.

Dorstone village is itself of considerable interest. It lies 400ft below Arthur's Stone, and has a medieval castle at one end and a medieval church at the other. In between is a triangular

11 The massive earthworks of Caer Caradoc hillfort a few miles to the south of Clun in Shropshire. The fort is named after the legendary British hero Caratacus, whose last stand against the Romans was made somewhere in the Welsh Marches

market place, typical of many dormant medieval Marcher boroughs. However, it has no market hall, only a market cross. It has the appearance of a planned castle-village of which there are large numbers in the western Marches. Dorstone was attacked and severely damaged by Owen Glendower in 1404, but before that Richard de Brito, one of the assassins of Thomas Becket, came here and founded a chapel in the church, probably after returning from completing his penance in the Holy Land. Dorstone was also for a time the terminus of the Golden Valley Railway, which opened from Pontrilas in 1881 before it was extended to Hay. The line finally closed in 1957 leaving behind Dorstone as one of the several forlorn abandoned railway stations of western Herefordshire.

Caer Caradoc (Gaer ditches), Clun, Shropshire SO 477 953

In the uplands of southern Shropshire lies the densest concentration of hillforts in the region. Although it only encloses an area of three acres, Caer Caradoc, a few miles to the south of Clun, is at the centre of this cluster. It is one of the finest hillforts in the region, with commanding views in all directions. On the south-east side is a single rampart, ditch and counterscarp; on both sides there are extensive and deep internal quarry ditches which are thought to have been hut platforms. Such internal quarries linked to the construction of the ramparts are a frequent feature of Marcher hillforts and can be clearly identified on aerial photographs. The entrances at the east and west are inturned and the western one may have had attached guard chambers. Outside the easily accessible west entrance is an additional defence in the form of a bank and ditch which lie across the direct approach, sitting in the position of a medieval castle barbican. Opposite, on the northern side of the entrance, the outer bank rises up higher than elsewhere, as though to complement the hornwork, forming a platform from which missiles could be hurled. Rabbits have dug into the banks and here and there have revealed sections of the solid stone walls which originally made up the exterior face of the fortification and today serve as a reminder of the energy and resources that went into the building of these abandoned early 'towns'.

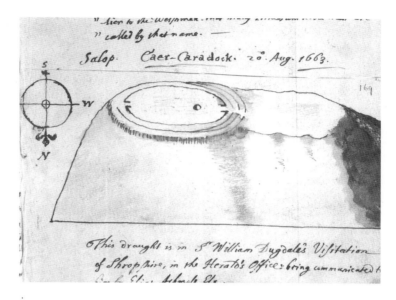

12 An early sketch of Caer Caradoc hillfort by the eighteenth-century antiquary William Stukeley

We know little of the history of Caer Caradoc apart from its association with the legendary British tribal leader Caratacus, whose name is attached to two other Border hillforts where he was believed to have made his final stand against the Romans. Caratacus was a Belgic prince based in the south-east of England. Soon after the initial phase of Roman conquest in AD 43-8 Caratacus established himself as a leader of the Welsh tribes against Rome and from Wales he carried out raids into Roman-held territory. At this stage the Roman frontier which had been established by Aulus Plautius ran between the Humber and the lower Severn. Ostorius Scapula moved his army westwards towards the Severn to search out and bring Caratacus (who in the meantime had moved from southern to central Wales) to battle. Caratacus's last stand was in AD 50, when the Roman legions were forced to make a frontal assault. Tacitus describes the geography of the site of Caratacus's last stand as follows:

> He chose a place for the battle where the entrances and exits were to our disadvantage, but favourable to his own troops. On one side there was a precipitously steep gradient, and where there were gentler approach routes he piled up stones to form a kind of embankment. There was also a river of uncertain depth flowing past and here bands of fighters were stationed to provide defences.

Although the Romans won the battle the British tribesmen melted away into the woods. Caratacus escaped and fled to the Brigantes of northern Britain, but he was eventually captured and sent back to Rome where the Emperor Claudius spared his life. The brief topographical descriptions provided by Tacitus are insufficient to locate the site of Caratacus's last stand with any precision — indeed the description would fit any one of 30 or 40 border hillforts. Three of these carry Caratacus's name (in the form of Caradoc), but there is no compelling evidence to substantiate any of these locations. Nevertheless one feels that if such an event did take place, nowhere could have provided a more appropriate setting for such a heroic scene than the remote and beautiful site of Caer Caradoc.

Herefordshire Beacon (British camp) and Midsummer Hill Camp, Malvern Hills, Colwall, Herefordshire SO 760 399 and SO 760 375

The Herefordshire Beacon is one of the finest examples of a contour fort in Britain, with its ramparts and ditches clinging to the distinctive slopes of the Malvern Hills. The highest point of the hill is crowned by a medieval castle mound known as the Citadal, which has been dated to the twelfth century. Around the base of this mound was the earliest Iron Age fort on the site, an enclosure of about 10 acres with entrances at the north-east and south-west. The little fort was enlarged to over 30 acres through the construction of the massive ramparts and ditch with counterscarp that surround the site today. Much of the material for the main defence came from a quarry which can be clearly identified in the form of an irregular ditch around most of the southern part of the fort. Of the four entrances, that at the north has been damaged by the modern footpath, but the southern gateway is approached by what might be an Iron Age zig-zag pathway. Under the right circumstances, in low light or under a thin covering of snow, traces of terracing and hut circles can be identified within the fort and it has been estimated that the total population of the fort at its height would have been between 1500 and 2000 people. A little to the south-east of the fort is Clutter's Cave. The cave has produced no conclusive prehistoric evidence although it is tempting to think that there should be some. Shire Ditch, which runs from the southern tip of the fort, may have been constructed as a hunting or county boundary in the thirteenth century although it probably represents the rebuilding of an earlier territorial boundary.

Some way to the south of the Herefordshire Beacon lies Midsummer Hill Camp, which consists of two hilltops enclosed by a bank and ditch incorporating an area of about 40 acres. This fort is an irregular shape with a long narrow spur jutting out to the south and an oval area to the north-west. Its rampart is stone-faced and there are traces of shallow internal quarry ditches. At the north-west is an entrance which was originally inturned and there is another entrance at the south-west. Excavation of the latter has shown that it was rebuilt on several occasions, with guard chambers made of both wood and stone. Hollows in the interior suggest there were about 250 huts: those which have been excavated appear to have been rectangular in shape. The buildings seem to have been laid out in a regular plan with streets between them. Radiocarbon dating suggests that occupation of the fort began about 400 BC and possibly ended when it was burnt down by Ostorius Scapula in his attack on the Decangi in AD 48. There is a low rectangular mound on the eastern side of the fort which is probably a pillow mound, that is an artificial rabbit warren dating from medieval times.

Croft Ambrey, Croft, Herefordshire SO 444668

Excavations on another Herefordshire site, Croft Ambrey, have graphically illustrated the story of that site. The excavator, Dr Stanford, has shown that there was a sequence of wooden buildings there which were repeatedly rebuilt. His excavations also show some 20 successive gateposts set up before they were finally dug out at the time of the Roman conquest. Croft Ambrey appears to have been disarmed and abandoned in AD 50, when Ostorius Scapula pursued his campaign in the Marches against Caratacus. Even after the site was abandoned it was probably used as a sanctuary, and Stanford concludes that the British population 'survived and returned to worship outside their ancient stronghold'.

The fort at Croft Ambrey occupies a long narrow hill, with a very abrupt scarp on the north, and gentler, though still steep, slopes on the other sides. In about 550 BC, a small rampart and ditch were built on the summit of the hill, to protect an enclosure of about seven acres. The interior was closely set with small 'four-post' buildings regularly spaced along streets. This house pattern continued with little change throughout the six centuries of the hillfort's life. The gateway in this phase was a simple double portal, formed by three large posts, which was rebuilt several times. No pottery, and very few finds of any kind, survive from the occupation of this earlier fort.

About 390 BC a new and massive rampart was built, following a line mostly outside the old one. Although large, the rampart was of simple design, with a single bank and ditch, and on the crest there was a timber palisade. This rampart style remained unaltered for almost three centuries. There were, however, changes in the design of the gateways during that time: the gate passage was lengthened and a pair of rectangular guardrooms provided. Sandstone, brought from the foot of the hill, was used for the lower courses of walling. This phase lasted until about 260 BC, when the guardrooms were abandoned. In the last phase the gateway arrangements were similar, except that a bridge was added across the passage in front of the gate. To this period also can be attributed the second bank and ditch formed outside the main bank. There were no further alterations, and the effective occupation of the hillfort ended with the arrival of the Romans in AD 48.

Outside the main enclosure there is an annexe of about 15 acres. No evidence of intensive occupation has been found inside, but the annexe does contain a remarkable sacred site, which in its earlier phases consisted of a levelled terrace cut into the hillside. The religious ceremonies, whatever form they took, left much charcoal, ash and burned bone, and many fragments of broken pottery, the latest dating from about 300 BC.

The occupants of the first enclosure lived in small rectangular huts. Some similar buildings were used as storehouses or granaries — we know this because carbonised grain has been found there. The buildings were regularly set out in streets and they had been repeatedly rebuilt on the same site, sometimes as many as six times. This barrack-like settlement differs so radically from the haphazard round-house pattern usually to be found in this country that Dr Stanford concluded that the Croft Ambrey settlers must have come from outside Britain, although Croft Ambrey itself was probably the work of descendants of the original invaders. However, this interpretation has proved to be controversial.

Another interesting result of Stanford's research is the evidence for the development of an extensive trade system. In the early stages there is hardly any pottery, but later on pottery becomes plentiful, originating from potters' workshops in the Malvern Hills region, 18 miles away. The discovery of a large proportion of potsherds, which were repaired using iron rivets, suggests that even these supplies arrived infrequently.

Mitchell's Fold, Chirbury, Shropshire SO 304 983

This stone circle stands on level ground on the ancient ridgeway which follows the axis of Stapeley Hill. The position is an exposed one with very extensive views both to east and west over the Severn valley and the Welsh hills. A hard stone called picrite is found here and was exploited in the early Bronze Age for the manufacture of axe hammers.

The 14 stones remaining give the circle a diameter somewhere between 85 and 90ft.

Possibly there are only 13 stones since some of the low pieces in the eastern sector may be natural, and much of the site is buried and overgrown. The stones are irregularly spaced: each sector has wide gaps in it, suggesting that many stones have been moved. Four stones or stumps which form a group on the east side are separated by distances varying between some 4 and 8ft, which makes it difficult to estimate the original number of stones in the circle, although some think it may be as many as 30. Of the stones now standing, the tallest is 6ft high, but all the others are much shorter than this (up to 3ft), and some are only stumps. The circle does not appear to have changed much since 1754, when the antiquarian William Stukeley made a drawing of it showing 14 stones in exactly the same positions as they are today.

Old stories of Mitchell's Fold abound. According to one a nearby tenant farmer removed one of the stones from Mitchell's Fold intending to use it as a step for a cowshed, but was so alarmed by a violent thunderstorm in the night that appeared to him as a threat that he returned it the next day. About 80 yards to the south-east is a much-weathered cubical block which stands on a small cairn. This is the so-called 'altar'. A second cairn, much ruined, lies just north-west of this.

Mitchell's Fold has been known by a variety of names in the past: Stukeley calls it Midgel's Fold, or the Druid's Temple, before relating the story of the dun cow which provided an endless supply of milk. An alternative ending to the legend has been provided by some folklore historians. According to this tradition, after the witch had milked the cow dry it went to Warwickshire where it turned into the Wild Dun Cow which was killed by Guy, Earl of Warwick, on Dun's More Heath between Coventry and Rugby. There is a variation of this story associated with the Cow Stone or the Dead Cow Stone which lies on the west side of the ridgeway close to Mitchell's Fold.

There are a number of other sites with related folklore stories, many of which lie a little to the west in Wales. Among these are the Speckled Cow's Crib in Powys and the Hag's Milking Fold, also in Powys. The legend of the Dun Cow at Mitchell's Fold appears to have been current by the later Middle Ages. There are numerous hotels, inns and public houses bearing the name Dun Cow in Shropshire, Warwickshire and County Durham. Not far from Mitchell's Fold, at Middleton, in Chirbury parish, in a chapel which was consecrated on Christmas Day 1842, there is a carved capital illustrating the folklore of Mitchell's Fold. The sculptor incorporated into his design a sequence of three events: firstly the village folk queuing to obtain their pails or jugs filled with milk, secondly the witch milking the cow into her sieve, and thirdly the construction of the stone circle.

However quaint such legends may seem to us today, Mitchell's Fold in its remote and wild part of the Marches still possesses an eerie atmosphere, particularly in the depths of winter.

Old Oswestry (Yr Hen Ddinas), Selatynn, Shropshire SO 296310

Iron Age forts were a feature of the lowland Marcher landscape as well as the hills. Old Oswestry fort crowned the summit of a low clay glacial hill on the western edge of the Shropshire plain. With its multiple ramparts it ranks among the largest of the forts within the territory of the Cornovii and rivals the Wrekin in its claim to be the focus of power in their Iron Age territory. Since it is a site under the guardianship of English Heritage it deserves to be better known.

13 Old Oswestry hillfort occupying a relatively low-lying position, but with defences presenting a formidable obstacle to attack. The purpose of the hollows on the right-hand side of the photograph has yet to be identified. The suburbs of modern Oswestry spread out along the railway line towards the foot of the fort

It was covered by trees until the beginning of the twentieth century, which may explain why it received relatively little attention up until quite recently. The site, which lies on a minor road about a mile to the north-east of the modern town of Oswestry, was described by the famous Border archaeologist Sir Cyril Fox as 'the outstanding work of early Iron Age type in the Marches of Wales'. It covers some 40 acres and appears to have undergone many vicissitudes. Work by Barrie Jones and others in the area has shown that the stronghold was surrounded by a significant number of native farming settlements. Such farmsteads must have been producing an agricultural surplus sufficient to support such a massive hillfort and its inhabitants. Old Oswestry was excavated by Professor Varley in

1939, but unfortunately there is no final report on his findings. The earliest settlement, of timber-built round-houses, was unfortified. Subsequently it was deserted for some time, and the remains became covered with turf. Next, the hilltop was enclosed by a rampart about 10ft thick, with a stone revetment on both sides and an accompanying ditch, plus a second rampart and ditch. The ditches and their associated ramparts were some 30ft apart, possibly to allow for the instability of the hillslopes, which are built of glacial gravel. The dwellings built of stone during this phase were also round.

In the next phase the innermost bank was enlarged, partly burying one of the huts, and two more similarly spaced banks and ditches were built; at the same time the entrance was inturned.

The final stage of the evolution of the defences at Old Oswestry saw the construction of a pair of very large banks around the base of the hill, enclosing and partly burying the earlier works. These ramparts were also constructed using unstable glacial material, but were reinforced with layers of clay, and boulders were used to form the outer edges. The internal dwellings were still round in shape, but one at least had two internal rooms, and they were massively built with thick stone walls reinforced with upright posts.

At the western entrance there are a series of deep hollows, or concave annexes, which are preceded by a pair of outer banks. Despite their striking appearance it is not at all clear what function they served. They cannot have been cattle enclosures, as some observers have suggested, for they have no entrances. In very wet conditions they do hold water and it is possible that they were used as cisterns, but if so they are unique in their size and situation. It may be that they were designed solely to protect and define the very long entrance passage, and that the spaces within served no practical purpose, but were not worth the labour involved in refilling them. However, until they are investigated further either by the trowel or geophysically their function will remain a mystery.

During the Roman period the fort appears to have been deserted, though a few fragments of Roman pottery have been found in the ditch silting. However, Old Oswestry has long been proposed as one of those sites where occupation was resumed at the end of the Roman era. The traditional name of the place was Caer Ogyrfan, the 'fort of Gogyrfan' (named after Gogyrfan the father of Guinevere). For a while it was believed that there was evidence for Dark Age use in the form of some crude pottery which was interpreted by the excavator, Varley, as Anglo-Saxon. However, in view of the revised interpretation of the pottery as Iron Age oven linings, one must now regretfully put on hold the romantic vision of King Arthur riding through the ruins of the great west entrance to visit his future in-laws. No firm evidence for reoccupation exists although in view of the important historical role played by Oswestry in the emergence of Anglo-Saxon domination in this part of England it would seem probable from purely circumstantial evidence that the site was resettled. Added to this, in the eighth century the fort was incorporated into the line of a linear earthwork known as Wat's Dyke, which can be traced both in earthwork and cropmark form to the north of Old Oswestry.

3 The Romans in the Welsh Marches

14 The Wrekin in Shropshire, capped by an Iron Age hillfort, which was probably the tribal headquarters of the Cornovii, before the arrival of the Roman army

Although Roman rule in Britain lasted for almost four centuries, relatively little above-ground evidence survives from this period in the Welsh Marches. However, although standing Roman buildings and Roman earthworks are uncommon, there is a great deal of evidence hidden below the ground. Apart from the archaeological record, evidence of the Romans is to be found hidden in place names, the most obvious being Chester. Chester derives from the Old English word *caester*, which was the Saxon adaptation of the Latin *castra*, meaning fort; *caester* was regularly and somewhat indiscriminately applied by the incoming Saxons to settlements which they believed to have had Romano-British associations. Other Roman settlements to incorporate the '*cester*' suffix in the region are Worcester, Wroxeter and Kenchester. Indications of Roman occupation also come in the street patterns of some towns and villages, in the alignment of modern roads which follow their Roman predecessors, and occasionally in the form of isolated stretches of standing masonry, as at Caerleon and Wroxeter.

Roman Britain begins with the conquest by Emperor Claudius in AD 43. This event marks the beginning of written history, when we know the names of the principal comm-

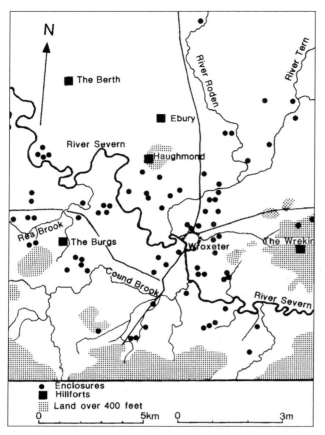

15 Prehistoric and Romano-British 'native' settlement in the middle Severn valley

anders involved in the conquest of the country and of the tribes they fought. We even know the names of some of the native leaders, as well as the dates of main rebellions. In the Marches the Roman general Quintus Veranius stormed the chief hillfort of the Cornovii tribe on the Wrekin in AD 47.

Caratacus stands out as a beacon of defiance against the Roman army and according to Tacitus was successful in many battles. Caratacus appears to have been supported by a *comitatus*, that is a retinue of free warriors drawn from different tribes. One of the most important battles of the conquest, which became known as the 'last stand of Caratacus', took place in or close to the Marches in AD 51 (see chapter 2). The circumstances and location of the battle are described by Tacitus in some detail:

The Romans now moved against the Silures, whose natural spirit was reinforced by their faith in the prowess of Caratacus, whose many battles against the Romans . . . had raised him to a position of pre-eminence amongst the other British chieftains. Since his strength lay not in military superiority but in the tactical advantages to be gained from knowing difficult terrain, he transferred the scene of the conflict to the territory of the Ordovice. He recruited from those who dreaded the establishment of the Roman peace and staked his fate on one last confrontation. He chose a place for the battle where the entrances and exits were to our disadvantage but favourable to his own troops. On one side there was a precipitously steep gradient, and where there were gentler approach routes he piled up stones to form a kind of embankment. There was also a river of uncertain depth flowing past and here hands of fighters were stationed to provide defence.

Antiquarians of past generations, in their attempts to identify this famous site, have often been more inspired by local patriotism than a close study of the words of Tacitus, and there are several hills which bear the name Caer Caradoc — none of which precisely fit the description given by the historian. From Tacitus' description we know the site must be in Ordovician territory and by a river with a difficult crossing. This implies a sizeable river and the most likely one is the Severn. Earlier antiquarians have always chosen a hillfort, but only a rampart of stones is mentioned as defending the steep slope and this at one point only; the rest of the hill rose sheer. So the site could be one of a number of hills close to the Severn in its upper stretches, possibly in the narrow valley below Caersws. The most likely hills would be those above Newtown, since this is where the old east-west trackway, the route that would probably have been followed by the Roman army, meets the River Severn.

Tacitus goes on to describe how the Roman commander Ostorius Scapula led his troops to victory, forcing the British to retreat into the Welsh mountains, and succeeded in capturing Caratacus and his family. As a result of this resistance, however, Caratacus's fame spread beyond Britain and he was acclaimed as far as Italy. According to Tacitus, Caratacus was subsequently taken to Rome, where, after he was displayed before the Emperor Claudius and having made an eloquent speech, Caratacus and his family were given the freedom to live out their lives in Rome. How much of the Caratacus story is historical fact and how much legend is impossible to say; it is clear, however, that his story captured the popular imagination both of the Romans, the British and later on of the English. His position as a legendary folk hero closely linked to the Welsh Marches is therefore an important and enduring one.

Roman forts

For a few decades in the middle of the first century AD the Marches formed the western boundary of the Roman Empire. There was a network of large legionary forts at Chester, Wroxeter and Caerwent as well as a series of smaller military forts and marching posts elsewhere, many of the latter short-lived. The fort at Caerwent (Venta Silurum) was refortified with a substantial stone wall in the middle years of the third century AD, providing us with the most substantial surviving military structure in the Borderland. The process of subduing the British continued after Caratacus had been defeated.

The fortress at Wroxeter, which would have held an entire legion of 5000 men, was probably constructed in the mid-50s by the XIV Gemina legion, which had previously been based at Mancetter in Warwickshire. In about AD 66 the fourteenth legion was sent to the eastern empire to Armenia, to help in its conquest. It was replace by the *legio* XX Valeria Victrix. The twentieth legion participated in the final conquest of Wales; Wroxeter then became the base for the advance up the west coast and into Scotland led by Agricola. Eventually in AD 90 the twentieth legion moved to its new base at Chester (*Deva*) where it was to remain for the next 250 years. The site of the demolished fortress was taken over by the local tribe as their capital and the new town is given the name *Viriconium Cornoviorum*. A number of other forts have been found within a five-mile radius of

Wroxeter. These include a campaign fortress at Eaton Constantine, four miles to the south, a small early fort of the AD 60s just to the south of Wroxeter village, and at least three forts immediately to the north of Wroxeter, in the vicinity of Attingham Park. All of these are now only visible in the form of cropmarks.

Throughout the remainder of the Roman occupation of Britain Chester and Caerleon formed the cornerstones of the Roman defensive system in the west. They controlled movements out of Wales along the northern and southern coastal plains and were also sited close to tidal water, which helped in the maritime supply of the necessary stores required for their own garrisons and those of the outlying auxiliary forts.

Elsewhere a network of forts was set up to cover Wales, the eastern boundary of which ran along the Welsh Marches at places such as Usk, Abergavenny and Jaylane, which lies just to the west of Leintwardine. Subsequently a more permanent fort was established at Leintwardine indicating that all was not necessarily peaceful in the Marches after the body of the army had moved on. Eventually, towards the end of the Roman period, attention switched to the northern Marches where defences were refortified against potential attacks from across the Irish Sea and from northern Britain. The historical record is, however, for the most part as silent on these developments as it is about the civilian conditions that prevailed throughout the Roman Marches.

At Chester, the playing-card shape of the Roman fort is still etched out and can readily be identified in the town plan. Streets such as Bridge Street, Eastgate Street and Hall Street follow lines originally marked out as part of the internal communication pattern of the Roman fort. The Chester fortress called *Deva* after the Celtic name for the Dee, which meant 'goddess', lay on the north bank of the river where it flowed around the end of a low sandstone plateau. It was a site well located to serve both north Wales and north-western England. The lines of the eastern and northern walls of the fortress were later reused for the medieval walls, parts of which survive. Additionally a section of the Roman quay survives below the medieval wall some 600ft away from the fortress, although the line of the Roman river-course is now completely silted up. The earliest activity at Chester appears to have been the building of turf and timber defences which were built in the late AD 70s. Early in the second century AD a stone wall was added to the front of the rampart and stone gate-towers were built. The plan of this stone fortress carefully followed that of its wooden predecessor. Excavations within this fort have so far revealed second-century barracks, granaries and workshops as well as a substantial *principia* (headquarters building). Additionally there was an intramural bath building with a *palaestra* (covered exercise hall). Outside to the east of the fortress was an amphitheatre originally built in wood and later reconstructed in stone.

Unlike the majority of lowland military sites Chester does not appear to have attracted a substantial civilian population. However, just to the south along Watling Street at Heronbridge, there was a small manufacturing settlement with stores and workshops and tile and pottery producing centres nearby. The other major fortress, *Isca*, at Caerleon, was also named after the river on which it stood, located on a spur of higher ground in the valley of the tidal Usk. The defences, enclosing some 70 acres, were originally constructed of clay, turf and timber in the 70s, but by the end of the first century the conversion of the fortress to stone was well underway. A stone wall was inserted in front of the rampart, and

16 *The small town of Leintwardine occupies the site of a Roman fort. The layout of the fort is reflected in the overall shape of the settlement. The road (called Watling Street) to the right of the church of St Mary Magdalene follows the line of the eastern ditch of the Roman fort, although the church itself lies over the eastern fort wall, which is reflected by a sharp drop in height between the chancel and nave (see 22)*

within the fort there were barracks and the other usual military buildings. To the west there was an amphitheatre, substantial remains of which survive today. The amphitheatre seems to have lain within a walled annexe that accommodated a parade ground and bath buildings, part of which lies beneath the medieval castle bailey. Outside the annexe walls there was a civilian settlement which contained the *mansio* (official guesthouse), which dates from the mid-second century. Inscriptions mentioning Diana and the Mythriad have been found, presumably from temples dedicated to these deities in the vicinity.

An unusual survival of the Roman period can be seen at Leintwardine in northern Herefordshire where the village high street mirrors the *via principalis* (principal road) of a Roman fort and later civilian settlement and where traces of ditches and ramparts can still be identified around the village. The fort at Leintwardine village was built sometime after the nearby fort at Bucton had been demolished in the first century AD. It was constructed on rising ground to the north of the River Teme and there was a small annexe containing a bathhouse between the fort and the river. It would appear Leintwardine functioned as a supply depot for the central Marches, held perhaps by a single unit of about 500 men.

The chancel of Leintwardine parish church which sits on the eastern line of the defences is significantly higher than the nave, because it was built over the defensive rampart. At Leintwardine the Roman road known as Watling Street West crosses the River Teme, and this crossing formed the focus for a number of military and civilian settlements. Close to Leintwardine is another unusual Roman survival in the Iron Age hillfort at Brandon Camp, where cropmarks of an apparently Roman military nature have been identified within the boundaries of the hillfort ramparts, alongside the more usual Iron Age ring ditches and enclosures. The Roman reuse for military purposes of

17 In the centre of the photograph are the cropmarks of a first-century Roman fort lying on the eastern bank of the River Severn near Wroxeter. Such forts were built of turf and timber, but conformed to the regular 'playing-card' shape of later stone-built forts

prehistoric hillforts is not unknown, the best example being the Roman fort which lies within the massive hillforts at Hambledown Hill and at Hod Hill, Dorset, but such examples from Marcher hillforts are rare.

There appears to have been a fort, similar to that at Leintwardine, at Forden Gaer, near Montgomery, where there was one of the most important Roman stations in mid Wales. This lay close to the traditional political watershed, later to be marked by Offa's Dyke, on a ford at the point where the River Severn turns due west to run into central Wales. The fort, which is about 7 acres in size, is still identifiable on the ground through earthworks marking the former defences, but it is best seen from the air from which its conventional playing-card shape can be clearly appreciated. Forden Gaer was probably founded during the early stages of the Roman attack on Wales, but the main period of military activity here was somewhat later when the defences were rebuilt on a substantial scale sometime after AD 150. The fort appears to have been abandoned by the 230s.

Roman towns

Most of the Roman Marcher towns had military origins and changed to a civilian role only as the theatre of conflict moved decisively northwards and westwards. Apart from Wroxeter, the towns were relatively small, serving as administrative, judicial and commercial centres for a local rural population. Again with the exception of Wroxeter, the Roman towns of the Borderland did not survive long into the post-Roman period. With the eventual collapse of Roman administration sometime in the fifth century, the urban tradition appears to have died out completely. The advanced level of Roman technology had meant that Romano-British towns did not require hilltop sites. They could be located in lowland areas and defended, if need be, by massive man-made walls and ditches. But this situation did not last very long after Roman control had ceased, and when urban life began to revive three or four centuries later in the mid-Saxon era, sites were chosen with completely different criteria in mind.

One of the enigmas of the Roman period in the Borderland is the size and apparent affluence of the Roman town at Wroxeter (*Viroconium Cornoviorum*). It was a substantial town with the fourth largest circuit of town walls in the whole of Roman Britain, enclosing an area of about 180 acres. However, unlike towns of similar size, it does not seem to have had the subsidiary network of villas which operated around places such as Cirencester (*Corinium*) or St Albans (*Verulamium*). Indeed evidence of Roman villas is rare in this part of the Borderland, and although there may be many sites yet to be discovered, the Romanised rural infrastructure hardly appears to have been strong enough to support a town of the size and apparent prosperity of Wroxeter. Instead of the normal pattern of villa estates, the area around the city was dotted with native British farmsteads, survivals from the Iron Age, where the lifestyle appears to have changed little following the Roman conquest. The most obvious change for the British was in their adoption of mass-produced Roman pottery and utensils, as opposed to the locally-made products they had previously used. It is therefore clear that we are dealing with a pattern of settlement and a Romano-British agricultural regime that was somewhat different from that operating in southern and central England, and possibly one in which the vestiges of military control remained stronger than in the rest of the Civil Zone of Roman Britain.

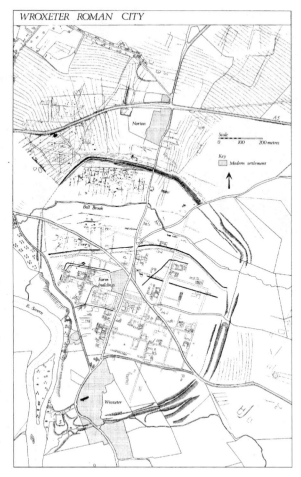

18 *A plan of Roman* Viriconium *based largely on aerial photographic evidence. The street layout and the foundations of a considerable number of buildings are visible within the town's defences. The defended area covered approximately 180 acres.* White and Barker

Wroxeter was a city built on a flat glacial plateau overlooking the Severn. It was originally established as a military base from which the conquest of Wales could take place, but was developed as a civil town after the western command was transferred to Chester in about AD 78. The town became the capital of the British tribe, the Cornovii, whose original headquarters appears to have been in the hillfort on top of the nearby Wrekin.

An inscription from over the entrance to the forum was erected about AD 130 in honour of the Emperor Hadrian by the *Civitas Cornoviorum*. When the forum gateway collapsed the inscription was smashed into fragments, but it has been restored and is housed in Rowley's

19 *Brandon Camp, an Iron Age hillfort to the south of Leintwardine. In addition to the prehistoric cropmarks visible inside the fort, there are some faint rectilinear markings which appear to represent Roman military buildings. This suggests the fort, which lies in an area of intense Roman military activity, was garrisoned probably during the early phases of the occupation*

House Museum in Shrewsbury; there is also a replica on display in the site museum. The visible buildings at Wroxeter represent part of a large bathhouse complex from the middle of the town, with the famous upstanding masonry known as the Old Work forming the gateway between the baths and the exercise area. It is one of the few substantial pieces of civilian Roman building that has survived in Britain, because in most towns where there was later medieval occupation the walls have been dismantled and the stone reused elsewhere. The Old Work has the appearance of the skeleton of a great brooding primeval beast, and although now it is seen completely out of its original context, it gives us some idea of the size and scale of the original Roman city. In the area away from the baths the main lines of the street plan and associated buildings of the city have been identified from parchmarks on aerial photographs, or by geophysical survey.

There is a long history of digging at Wroxeter which can be shown to go back to Saxon times; for example, a ninth-century bronze Anglo-Saxon strap tag was found in a robbing trench on the baths' basilica site. The earliest recorded digging here, though, was in 1292 when four men were brought to court for having 'dug by night at Wroccestre in search of treasure', but it was reported that they found nothing. The Roman city has provided a ready source of worked stone over the centuries for farmers and road builders. The great civil engineer Thomas Telford noted that the site of the city was distinguished by 'a blacker or richer soil or mold than the adjacent fields and the stone foundations of ancient buildings at no great depth under the surface of the ground are manifest in long continued drought, so that when the occupiers of the land need any stone for building they mark the scorched parts and after the harvest dig out what serves their purpose'. This is one of the earliest references to the phenomenon of parchmarks, features which are widely used by archaeologists to identify stony sites from the air. Among his many other claims to fame Telford was one of the first people to have undertaken archaeological excavations at Wroxeter; he claimed to be the first to identify the baths here. After some small pillars and a paved floor had been found, Telford 'caused the place to be cleared to a considerable extent and thus brought to light a set of Roman baths'. Although excavations have recorded a considerable volume of information about the Roman city and its economy many questions remain. The larger quantity of cattle bone found in contexts from the first to fifth centuries suggest that the cattle trade may have formed the basis of the city's economy and, rather like Oswestry in the Middle Ages, funnelled the trade between the highland and lowland region.

It used to be thought on the basis of rather slender archaeological evidence that Wroxeter suffered a violent end, possibly at the hands of unruly mercenaries. However, extensive excavations have demonstrated that Wroxeter did not share the same fate as many other Romano-British cities, and life appears to have gone on with relatively little change into the late fifth century. When the Roman buildings collapsed or were dismantled, substantial structures were built on top of the rubble. At the heart of this reconstruction on the site of the baths' basilica was a mansion over one 100ft long and almost 50ft wide. It is not known for whom this house was built, perhaps one of the 'tyrants' described by the sixth-century monk chronicler Gildas or perhaps Wroxeter's bishop. Nevertheless by the middle of the seventh century *Viroconium* appears to have been finally abandoned and left to generations of stone robbers who used the crumbling buildings as a convenient quarry. The present parish church of the small hamlet of Wroxeter contains substantial amounts of reused Roman masonry as well as part of a late eighth-century cross built into the south wall. The pillars flanking the gateway to the churchyard are appropriately and poignantly formed by Roman pillars. When urban life revived in Shropshire in the Saxon period a naturally-defended loop in the Severn at Shrewsbury some five miles to the north-west of Wroxeter was eventually chosen in preference to the flat Severn terrace site as the centre of commerce.

In Herefordshire, the Roman town of *Magnis* at Kenchester presents something of an enigma. It lies on a gravel terrace in the Wye valley a few miles to the west of Hereford, just below the extensive Iron Age fort at Credenhill. Nothing survives above ground but the unusual hexagonal shape of the defences. These are a little like that of a distorted kite in plan, and they can still be traced in field boundaries enclosing an area of about 22 acres. The pattern of roadways and internal divisions has been identified from cropmarkings. The eighteenth-century antiquary William Stukeley, visiting the site in 1721, identified its gateway and recorded that Kenchester

> was a palays of Offas, as sum say . . . Peaces of the walles and turrets, yet appere prope fundamenta and more should have appeared if the people of the town and other therabout had not in tymes paste pulled down muche and myked out the best for these buildings. Of late one Mr Brainton buylding a place at Stretton a myle from Kenchester dyd fetch much tayled stone there towards his buildings.

Subsequently there have been a number of excavations which have shown that the massive town defences, which are over 6ft thick, were rebuilt on at least three occasions between AD 150 and 350 and that within the walls there are many substantial buildings

20 A photograph of the Old Work and bathhouse at Wroxeter, taken early last century. A considerable amount of excavation and restoration has taken place since then, but the picture captures the atmosphere of an abandoned Roman city, the fourth largest in Roman Britain

including some with mosaic pavements. Among the 'excavators' were a 'party of gentlemen' from Hereford, who dug here in the 1840s with Dean Merewether, an early excavator of the great prehistoric tumulus at Silbury Hill in Wiltshire. When Professor Richard Atkinson was excavating the heart of the hill in the 1960s, he came across an urn which had been deposited by the Dean to mark his earlier abortive search for a 'golden horseman' at the core of the great mound. The precise nature and function of the settlement at Kenchester is still not entirely clear: it seems to fall into the category of a small town although some authorities have suggested that it was little more than an extended village. The presence of bastions added to the defences would, however, put it in the very rare category of a fortified village. It is possible that the town has substantial extramural suburbs and that it was a far larger settlement than the walled area suggests. There is, however, no evidence to indicate that Kenchester was ever a regional capital and it is commonly assumed that the whole of Herefordshire was governed from Cirencester as part of the administrative canton of the *Dobunni*. In the post-Roman period it was abandoned and its successor was at Hereford on a crossing of the River Wye some six miles to the east. The font in the nearby church is of reused Roman masonry and farm buildings in the vicinity use stones from *Magnis*. The place name, however, was incorporated into the Saxon tribal name of the Magonsaetan who occupied much of Herefordshire and southern Shropshire in the post-Roman period.

A number of other small-sized towns appear to have existed at places such as Whitchurch (*Mediolanum*) in Shropshire and *Ariconium* close to Ross-on-Wye in Herefordshire. At *Mediolanum* a military fort was build in the first century AD on the road running from *Viroconium* to the legionary base at Chester. Later a small civil settlement grew up here. The modern high street follows the line of the original Roman road and the basic street plan reflects that of the Roman town. At *Ariconium* extensive evidence of iron working has been found and it has been suggested that the Roman complex here may have extended over as much as 250 acres, comprising a posting station, villa estate and industrial site. *Ariconium* was included in a Roman road gazetteer, the *Antonine Itinerary*, and the survival of its name for the district of Erging or Archenfield which lies to the west of the Wye shows that it was a settlement of some significance. Early Roman material has been

21 Aerial view of the Roman town of Kenchester. Much of the interior road system shows up in the form of parchmarks and the 'kite' shape of the town defences is demarcated by the modern field boundaries

located here and it is possible that it was occupied in the pre-Roman Iron Age. The persistence of a dialect word *scowles*, a Celtic term to describe the muddled overgrown holes and hillocks of ancient iron-ore workings, suggests a very long history of industry in the region. Not far away at Whitchurch another industrial site of Roman iron processing was uncovered in the 1950s. Excavation here has revealed a number of iron workings dating from the fifteenth and sixteenth centuries as well as the Roman period. It is clear that the Romans had considerable interest in the mineral resources of the Borderland. Five pigs of lead inscribed with the name of the Emperor Hadrian have been found near the Stiperstones and a hoard of 30 Roman *denarii* was discovered in a copper mine on Llanymynech Hill.

One of the most interesting of the Roman industrial sites in the Marches is at Linley Hall, where the West Onny river emerges from the hill country between the Stiperstones and Corndon Hill. The Roman interest in this district is undoubtedly because of the lead mentioned above. The Linley Hall site has an area of some 12 acres and the complex earthworks here appear to cover a major Roman industrial plant associated with lead working and possibly silver mining as well. Elsewhere extensive mining in the eighteenth and nineteenth centuries at Shelve and Snailbeach have removed or obscured all evidence of Roman occupation. It has also been suggested that industrial remains found at a group of three Roman marching camps at Brompton may have been connected with silver working.

It is difficult to assess just how deeply Romanised the Welsh Borderland became. Apart from the towns, evidence of mineral working and a scatter of villas there is relatively little that is distinctively Roman. Villas such as that at Whitley Grange, Yarchester, Crickton and Lea Cross are rare, and several of these have more of the characteristics of Roman farmsteads than villas found in southern Britain. There are, however, undoubtedly a number of others awaiting discovery. Far more common are the 'native' Romano-British settlement sites,

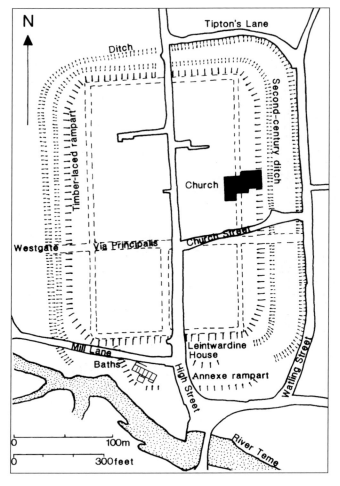

22 Plan of Leintwardine showing the relationship of the Roman fort to the modern settlement

which have been located by aerial photography largely on river, sand and gravel terraces. Although few of these have yet been excavated they appear to represent the continuation of Iron Age settlements into the Roman period. So far little is known about the make-up of such settlements, but they do represent the predecessors of later Saxon and medieval villages.

Roman roads

Part of the Roman road system has been preserved in the pattern of modern communications. The eventual movement of the political and commercial centre from *Viroconium* to Shrewsbury in the post-Roman period, however, brought a subtle adaptation of the original network. Watling Street, which linked Wroxeter with Redhill (*Uxacona*), Pentridge (*Pennocrucium*) and eventually London, has been preserved in the line of the A5. A minor detour from the Roman road at Overley Hill forms part of Telford's improvements to the London/Holyhead road early in the nineteenth century. The ancient road alignment is nevertheless preserved in parish boundaries. West of Shrewsbury the Roman road joining *Viroconium* to the massive fort at *Lavobrinta* (Forden Gaer) is preserved as a secondary road only as far as Westbury. The Roman road then proceeded westwards along Long Mountain, the line now being marked for two miles by Westbury parish boundary; the modern road, however, follows the River Ray southwards implying that during the Roman period the floor of the marshy Ray valley was not used for access into central Wales. Along the Roman road travelled the consignments of minerals which the Romans extracted from the central Welsh hills as soon as they had established themselves at Wroxeter. The road from *Viroconium* to *Mediolanum* is only preserved in short stretches as a modern road (A49), but it can be identified from field boundaries and

23 A Roman road in the region of Eardisley, Herefordshire, which still plays an important role in shaping the modern landscape, as it is followed by modern tracks and field boundaries

cropmarks. The road running southwards from *Viroconium* to Leintwardine is easily identifiable on the ground running southwards through the always important Church Stretton gap. There is also a remarkable stretch of Roman road between Craven Arms and Leintwardine which stands out very clearly in aerial photographs, and which also goes under the name of Watling Street.

In eastern Shropshire the line of the road running from *Pennocrucium* to *Mediolanum* can be traced in the modern road pattern. A stretch of this road which crosses the flood plain of the River Tern to the south of Market Drayton has been known as the Longford since at least the thirteenth century. The name Pave or Pavement Lane, found in Woodcut parish near Newport and elsewhere in the Marches, may also refer back to former Roman roads. There are also a considerable number of villages in the Marches which incorporate the name Stretton (Old English, *straet-ton* — literally, street village), indicating settlement by or along a Roman road. The preservation of Roman roads both as parish boundaries and as incorporated into later road systems indicates that there was a substantial degree of survival of the Roman communication pattern into the Saxon period.

24 The forum inscription from Wroxeter. Excavations at Wroxeter in the 1920s produced one of the largest and finest inscriptions from Roman Britain, recording the erection of the building by the Civitas Cornoviorum (the Cornovii tribe) under the Emperor Hadrian in AD 130. The original is in the Rowley's House Museum, Shrewsbury, but there is a copy in the little museum on the site at Wroxeter

Places to visit

Wroxeter (Viroconium), Shropshire SO 566 086

Wroxeter lies five miles to the south-east of Shrewsbury. The most obvious Roman feature is the Old Work which has miraculously survived generations of stone-robbers and over 1800 years of Marcher weather. In 1788 Thomas Telford built a turnpike road, linking Shrewsbury to Ironbridge, across the Roman town, at about the same time that the Old Work became a romantic landmark for artists and writers. In the twentieth century A.E. Houseman, Wilfred Owen and Mary Webb were all inspired to write poems about Wroxeter. It was originally part of the south wall of a large aisled building which occupied the area between the site museum and the wall: this was an exercise hall (*palaestra*) for the baths. About AD 350 the structure collapsed and in the building rubble several timber structures, some of them very large, have been identified by excavation. Philip Barker, the excavator, conclusively demonstrated that the buildings were occupied into the fifth and sixth centuries. The rest of the site belongs to the public baths, which has been exposed since the middle of the nineteenth century, meaning that the associated stratified data is missing and that a detailed history of its development cannot be recovered. The *piscina*, or swimming bath, however, was excavated in the 1960s. It was constructed AD 120-50 to a standard design found throughout the western Roman Empire.

The bathhouse was entered through the double doors leading from the exercise area which partially filled the present gap in the middle of the Old Work. On the underside of this gap can be seen the two rounded impressions left by the relieving arches, now disappeared, which lay above the lintels of the two doors. The bath complex itself consists of the normal range of rooms including the *fridgidarium* (cold plunge baths), *tepidarium* (moist heat) and *caldarium* (hot). On either side of the latter are recesses for hot baths, where there are small tile columns known as *pilae*, which enabled warm air to circulate below the floor. The small swimming bath, *piscina*, has an apse at each end, an unusual

25 The gateway of the churchyard of St Andrew's, Wroxeter, with its appropriate use of Roman columns. The church, which lies within the defences of the former Roman city, incorporates a considerable amount of reused Roman masonry in its walls

feature of Roman baths. Indeed the Wroxeter *piscina* is the only visible example of a Roman *piscina* in Britain apart from the great bath at Bath. The excavated evidence suggests that in fact the Wroxeter *piscina* may never have been completed. Adjacent to the present road there are the foundations of a market hall and two square rooms which have been interpreted as taverns.

On the other side of the road from the bathhouse complex is a long line of column stumps which formed part of the portico of the eastern side of the forum. The whole of the latter was excavated in the 1920s, but only this part has been left exposed, providing an impressive but tantalising hint of the former splendour of civic Wroxeter. The remainder of the site is presently under farmland and represents one of the most important archaeological reservoirs anywhere in Britain. The opportunity it represents for fully understanding the nature of a large Romano-British town has yet to be completely grasped. In addition to an interpretation centre on the site at Wroxeter, much excavated material from the Roman town is on display in Rowley's House Museum in Shrewsbury.

It is not surprising that the Romans paused once they reached the River Severn at Wroxeter: just a few kilometres to the west are the lowering hills of the Welsh massif, a region which although conquered by the Romans was never intensively occupied. Today it is an evocative site in its isolation but for the Romans it would have been the most westerly edge of the civilised world, rather like *Volubilis* in Morocco which represented the last serious outpost of civilisation before the Atlas mountains and the Sahara desert.

The other monument which must be visited at Wroxeter is the now redundant church of St Andrew. The church was founded in the second half of the eighth century, built with large stones taken from the Roman city. A ninth-century carved cross which originally stood in the churchyard was later taken down and incorporated into the south wall of the church. The pillars of the churchyard are also made up of reused Roman pillars. One wonders just what lies below the floor of St Andrew's, sited as the church is within the heart of the former Roman city. In recent years the work of the Wroxeter Hinterland Project has done much to uncover the Roman infrastructure in the region around Virconium.

26 Roman head from Kenchester

Caerleon (Isca), Gwent ST 340 907

Caerleon, which means the 'city of the legion', was the home of the second Augustan legion and is situated four miles to the north-east of Newport. It is sited on raised ground by the tidal estuary of the River Usk, which would have made it safe from flooding, while making is accessible to seagoing vessels. The fortress was established by Frontinus in AD 74/5 after the conquest of Wales. There was reconstruction in the third century, but before the beginning of the fourth century the fortress was no longer garrisoned, part of the legion having been transferred to Richborough in Kent. Regular excavations since 1926 have provided many details of the layout of the 70-acre fortress, but only one small portion in the west corner is visible today. Discoveries in the area around the fortress have demonstrated that there was a considerable extramural settlement here, with cemeteries on the far side of the river and substantial docks on the river, which flowed closer to the fort than it does today.

The interior of the fortress was occupied by rows of barrack blocks, originally 64 in all, arranged in pairs facing each other. The parish church of Caerleon overlies part of the headquarters and thus roughly marks the central point of the Roman fortification.

The outstanding Roman monument at Caerleon, however, is the amphitheatre which was excavated by Sir Mortimer Wheeler in 1926-7. It is still the only completely excavated Roman amphitheatre in Britain. It was constructed in AD 80 and appears to have been primarily used for military exercises and displays, although no doubt blood sports and gladiatorial combats were staged here too. There were various modifications in the middle of the second and at the beginning of the third centuries until it was finally abandoned when the garrison left. Long before Wheeler's excavation the amphitheatre was known locally as King Arthur's Round Table. Geoffrey of Monmouth in his *History of the Kings of Britain* (1136) linked the Arthurian legend with Roman Caerleon, much of which must have still been standing to a considerable height in the early Middle Ages when he was writing. Next to the little museum which was originally founded by the Caerleon Antiquarians in 1850 is the parish church dedicated to a sixth-century saint, Cattwg (Cattock) of Llancarfan.

Chester (Deva), Cheshire

Unlike Wroxeter Roman *Deva* has largely been built over. With the outstanding exceptions of the north wall and the amphitheatre, its surviving remains are in the form of isolated fragments scattered throughout the modern city. The first major fortress was built here around AD 76-8. The initial garrison, as shown by tombstones, was the second Adiutrix

27 Excavations in progress at the amphitheatre at Caerleon in the late 1920s. The work was directed by Sir Mortimer Wheeler, then director of the National Museum of Wales

legion. This legion was replaced in AD 87 or later by the twentieth Valeria Victrix, which then remained at Chester throughout the Roman occupation. The rebuilding of the fortress in stone started at the beginning of the second century, firstly with the defences and the internal buildings. The defences were again rebuilt on a larger scale during the early fourth century. The final withdrawal of the garrison occurred about 380. To the north of the east gate is a fine portion of Roman fortress wall. King Charles Tower stands on the Roman north-east corner and from here to the north gate runs an amazing section of well-preserved Roman wall standing to a height of 15ft and missing only its wall-walk.

Elsewhere in the town can be traced the remains of the Roman street pattern as well as a considerable range of other fragmentary Roman building, including the *sacellum*, where the legionary standards were kept, the *principia*, and the bathhouse. However, the most interesting monument in Roman Chester is the amphitheatre, which is now open to the public. Only the north half is visible, the remainder lying buried under a convent. Excavations have shown that the original timber amphitheatre was replaced at the end of the first century by a stone one. Adjoining the entrance on the left was a small room which was used as a shrine to Nemesis, the goddess of fate. The arena floor shows traces of repair in about AD 300 after a long period of disuse. There are two other extramural monuments of intrinsic interest: part of the Roman quay wall, situated on the racecourse opposite the end of Black Friars, and a much-weathered figure of Minerva in the public garden called Edgars Field, to the south of the river. The Grosvenor Museum in Grosvenor Street contains one of the finest displays of Roman military material and sculpture to be found anywhere in Britain.

Caerwent (Venta Silurum), Gwent ST 469 905

One of the most impressive sites in the whole of Roman Britain, Caerwent was the market town of the Silures tribe. It covered only 44 acres, but had all the usual buildings, forum, basilica, temple and baths, expected of a tribal capital.

Caerwent was a frontier town founded at the end of the first century which may have originated as a yet unlocated fort; however despite its apparently military layout the site displays most of the characteristics of a Romano-British town. The main street, which is in fact part of the road from Gloucester to Caerleon, crosses the settlement between opposite gates. In the middle of the town the forum and basilica were the dominant features, yet because of the relatively small size of the town these structures are modest in size compared to those at Wroxeter. Other public buildings included a bathhouse complex to the south of the forum and a temple to the east. There was another sub-circular temple just outside the eastern wall of the town. A large building just inside the town's southern gate is believed to be a *mansio*, the official guesthouse and inn, and consists of some 20 rooms arranged around three sides of a courtyard. To the north of the forum there is the base of a structure which may have been an amphitheatre. In addition to the public buildings there were a number of large courtyard houses which were furnished with mosaic floors and fitted out with a high level of plumbing; perhaps these were occupied by former tribal leaders. The remaining areas of the town appear to have been occupied by shopkeepers and craftsmen.

The defences at Caerwent, which form by far the most spectacular surviving remnant of Roman occupation here, started in the form of an earthen rampart erected sometime after AD 130, possibly in reaction to increasing local unrest following the removal of many troops from south Wales. In the second half of the third century a massive stone wall was inserted at the front of the rampart. This was 10ft wide at the base and stood over 16ft high in places. Later on, sometime after AD 350, a series of bastions, probably intended for housing catapults, was added as a precaution during deteriorating political conditions.

The greater part of the Roman town now lies under fields and orchards. However, there is still much to be seen: in addition to the massive Roman walls, there are the foundations of a number of the houses and there are also the remains of a Romano-Celtic temple. In the church porch are two Roman inscribed stones, one of which records Paulinus who, having commanded the second Augustan legion at Caerleon, went on to become the governor of two Roman provinces in Gaul, Narbonne and Lyon. The parish church is dedicated to St Stephen and St Tathan; the latter was a fifth-century Irish missionary. It therefore seems probable that an earlier church here was dedicated to the Irish saint, who reputedly founded a monastic school at Caerwent. In the south-east corner of the Roman town is a mound, believed to be a Norman motte which utilised the surviving Roman walls as part of its defences. It was probably one of the castles built by William Fitz Osbern, Earl of Hereford, during the initial stages of the Norman Conquest of Wales in about 1070.

4 The Dark Ages

The Roman legacy

The centuries following the end of the Roman administration in Britain are conventionally known as the Dark Ages. They form one of the most fascinating yet tantalising periods in Borderland history. They are fascinating because it was during this time that the subtle balance between English and Welsh culture developed; it was also when many places acquired the Anglo-Saxon names by which we now know them. They are tantalising because of the absence of very much firm evidence, either documentary or archaeological, with which to build up a clear picture of what happened at the end of Romano-Britain even though investigations at the Romano-British town of Wroxeter have clearly demonstrated continuous occupation on parts of that site through until the seventh century. Therefore any historical account of the period must remain sketchy and tentative. Legends from the early part of this period are common, involving larger-than-life figures such as Ambrosius Aurelianus, King Arthur and a collection of early British saints.

It is clear that the Romanisation of the Borderland had been very patchy, with villas and Roman settlements concentrated in the areas around the major towns, notably in the Wye valley around Kenchester and the Severn valley around Wroxeter. Elsewhere, particularly in the hilly areas, there is little evidence of Roman activity and occupation apart from mining, and it seems probable that throughout the Roman era the inhabitants of much of the region lived a life very similar to that of their Iron Age forebears.

For example, it appears that Latin made little progress as a vernacular language and that native British (or Celtic) was still spoken by the vast majority of people in the Borderland in the fifth century AD. Roman place name survivals in the Marches are surprisingly rare. Only the names of major settlements appear to have survived, and even then they are in a modified form. Roman *Magnis* (Kenchester) appears to survive in the tribal name of the Magonsaetan and possibly in the place name, Maunde. However the largest Roman settlement of them all, *Viroconium*, has influenced the form of several local place names, including Wroxeter, Wrockwardine and the Wrekin, which the place name historian Margaret Gelling considers may have carried the Romano-British name *Viriconio* even before it was applied to the town. As British was the principal spoken language of Roman Britain, most of the place names in the Roman Marches would also have been British. The issue is confused as in this context 'British' is synonymous with Welsh. Hence British place name elements are similar to later Welsh place name elements. This is reflected in the fact that many places such as Shrewsbury (*Amwithig*), Wenlock (*LlanMeilen*), and Leominster (*Llanllieni*) carried both English and Welsh (British) place names well into the Middle Ages. Such place name usage does suggest that the

British language did survive for several centuries over quite considerable areas. However, it does not explain the relative paucity of pre-English names in parts of the region. There are far fewer of these in Shropshire than there are in Herefordshire or even Worcestershire. In Herefordshire there are many names which appear to date from Roman or pre-Roman times, as well as many early medieval Welsh names, indicating continuity of British or even pre-Roman speech, such as Treville, Kilpeck, Hentland and in the Archenfield area of South Herefordshire. It is true that there are numerous Welsh minor names in western Shropshire, but these probably represent the return of Welsh speech in the post-conquest period. The absence of pagan Saxon sites from the Marches suggests, along with the archaeological evidence from Wroxeter, that British life for the most part continued uninterrupted into the sixth and seventh centuries, indeed until the establishment of the Saxon kingdom of Mercia, when there must have been both a significant influx of English speakers and a radical and apparently rapid change in place names from British to Anglo-Saxon.

28 Crucifixion carved on panel from St Beuno and St Peter's church, Llanveynoe. Although it is probably ninth- or tenth-century, some authorities suggest that it may be Dark Age in origin

Early Christianity

One legacy that may have survived the end of Roman Britain in the Marches was Christianity. Romano-British Christianity was essentially urbanised, and the main focus of the Christian church in the Marches in the late Roman period was most likely to have been Wroxeter and Caerleon, which probably had their own bishops. The collapse of the Roman cities may not, however, have resulted in the complete disappearance of Christianity. One clue to the survival of British Christianity is in the place name Eccles, which comes from the early Welsh *egles* — church. The presence of this place name element implies that the introduction of Christianity preceded the adoption of the Anglo-Saxon language in places where it is found. Eccleston, near Chester, and Eccleshall, in Staffordshire, both incorporate the distinctive *eccles* element, and both lie within the former territory of the Cornovii. Further south, in Herefordshire, are Eccleswall and Eccles Green, whose names may also represent communities of British Christians who survived the general breakdown of Roman life in the Marches. The question of post-Roman Christian continuity, however, remains unresolved and is made all the more difficult to unravel by the arrival of the new wave of Saxon Christianity in the sixth and seventh centuries which must have largely subsumed the relics of Roman Christianity.

Christianity was stimulated not from its traditional sources in post-Roman Continental Europe, contact with which had been more or less severed by the advance of the pagan Anglo-Saxons in eastern England. Instead it came from the Celtic west and from the Mediterranean. From the mid-fifth century onwards contact between the Celtic west and the Mediterranean world was re-established in trade routes along which spiritual ideas appear to have travelled as freely as commercial traffic. Christianity expressed itself through monasticism and led to the so-called 'Age of the Saints', which marked the golden age of Celtic piety and devotion in the south-west, in Wales, and to a lesser degree in the Marches.

Church dedications provide valuable hints about the degree of British survival in the face of pressure and influences from outside Britain. It is true that

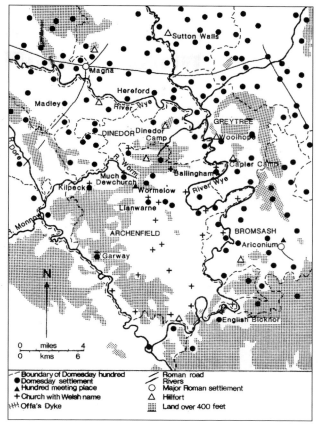

29 *Archenfield and central Herefordshire, showing the survival of Welsh church dedications*

during the early Middle Ages, many churches, belonging to Celtic saints, were re-dedicated to fashionable Norman saints; however there was often considerable opposition to this process and the proposed Norman saints' names were frequently rejected locally. A compromise was often made by re-dedicating the church to the Virgin or to St Michael and All Angels. This sometimes resulted in the renaming of the village as well, and so on the Herefordshire/Monmouth border there are a large number of Llanfihangels and Michaelchurches, as well as a dozen or more Llanfairs (dedicated to the Virgin): there are at least 150 such dedications altogether in Wales and the Border counties and there are also clues to be found in earlier dedications. The most notable of these is Dubricius or Dyfrig, who died in the early sixth century, and who was one of the earliest and most important saints of south Wales. Reputedly he was born at Madley, near Hereford, the son of Pepin, king of Erging (Archenfield). He went on to found churches at *Ariconium*, Hentland, Whitchurch, Madley and Moccas. As with all such early saints little is known of his life but Geoffrey of Monmouth would have us believe that Dubricius crowned Arthur king of Britain at Caerwent. He is also said to have consecrated Bishop Sampson, the chief saint of Brittany. Dedications to other

Celtic saints include those to Dewy (or David) at Dewchurch and Kilpeck, and St Beuno at Llanveynoe, where there is an early Christian memorial stone. Sellack, near Ross, was anciently known as *Llan Sulluc*, called after St Tysylio who was born at Pengwern and passed through Herefordshire on his way to south Wales and then on to Brittany.

Following in the wake of Anglo-Saxon political success and conversion to Christianity, we find church dedications to early Saxon saints, many of whom would have replaced existing Celtic dedications and many of whom in their turn also disappeared after the Norman Conquest. While the majority of surviving Celtic dedications are found in Herefordshire and the southern Marches, most of the early Saxon dedications came from Shropshire and the northern Marches. St Mildburge (d. *c*.AD 715) at Much Wenlock, whose shrine became an early pilgrimage centre, and St Oswald (d. 642) at Oswestry are particularly important early Saxon saints in this region. It has been suggested that the place name Cressage (Old English, Christ's Oak) was a reference to a prominent tree at which the gospel was preached. Such preaching places were common during the mid-Saxon period and often provided the location for later parish churches. Significantly perhaps the ancient church at Cressage was dedicated to the Celtic Saint Sampson. Appropriately enough, another early dedication is found at Wroxeter, where the church is named after St Andrew, one of the most popular saints with early Christian Anglo-Saxons. Close by, on the River Severn, is a unique dedication to St Eata (d. 686), a companion of St Aidan and Bishop of Hexham. The place name of Atcham means 'Lands in a river-bend belonging to the followers of Eata'. Excavations carried out a short distance from the church of St Eata uncovered part of a settlement site dating to the first half of the eighth century, possibly providing a direct link with the saint. In Hereford there were also dedications to St Owen, a sixth-century Breton saint, who came to England with St Cadfan, and St Guthlac, a late seventh-century Mercian hermit saint.

Among the slightly later Marcher saints of this period was Alkmund (d. *c*.800), who was originally entombed at Lilleshall, which became an important cult centre before his body was translated to Derby. At Aymestry, close to Wigmore, the parish church has a double dedication to St Alkmund and St John Baptist. This may represent an original Saxon dedication with later Norman dedication to St John superimposed on it, or it could represent the vestiges of two churches lying adjacent to each other on the site. One of the most important of the Border saints was Aethelbert, King of the East Angles. He was venerated as a martyr because of his murder by King Offa of Mercia. The story is that Aethelbert was visiting Offa's daughter, Aelfthryth, at Sutton Walls with a view to marriage when he was assassinated there on 20 May 794. His body was placed in the River Lugg at Marden and later translated to Hereford, where the cathedral is dedicated to him. During the Middle Ages, Hereford became a pilgrimage centre, reputedly second in popularity only to Canterbury in England.

Sub-Roman survival

Let us now turn our attention to the political story of the Marches during the post-Roman era. During the last part of the fourth century it appears that conditions in the region were deteriorating fast and that most of the troops were being redeployed in Britain in response to attacks, principally from the north, from the Picts and the Irish. Under the Emperor

30 The ruined church of St John the Baptist at Llanwarne in Archenfield, Herefordshire. The inscribed lintel over the south doorway here is mid-Saxon in form and appears to continue a tradition of early Celtic Christian inscriptions

Theodosius (379-95), posts were given to district officers known as *praefecti*, on the understanding that they ruled their districts as petty kings and passed their titles and responsibilities on to their heirs. It is probable that Maximus, who had been an officer serving under Theodosius the Great, subsequently established such an organisation in Wales using either Irish settlers or the native Celtic tribes as an army. Various attacks from outside England seem to have been repulsed by General Flavius Stilicho during the last years of the fourth century. Stilicho was a colourful personality, a Vandal by birth, but married to Theodosius' niece, Serena. The court poet Claudian reports that Stilicho and his troops were taken away from Britain in about 402. Claudian implies in some lines he wrote that the removal of Stilicho's legion, which had curbed 'the savage Irish and [read] the marks tattooed on the bodies of dying Picts', was responsible for allowing these barbarians into the region.

During the confused events of the following years, we hear of the rise of Vortigern, which is not a personal name, but a title such as 'the high chief'. There are various stories and legends concerning Vortigern's attempt to maintain the kingdom; and according to one tradition, Vortigern's son, Brittu, became the ruler of the kingdom of Powys, a territory which incorporated both north Wales and much of the northern central Marches. It is believed that the name Powys is derived from *pagenses* — 'the people of the countryside'. This appears to have been a period of relative stability in the Marches and there are strong indications that the town of *Viriconium*, at least, still continued to be occupied. Evidence for this comes from excavations in the town, which have shown

31 The parish church of St Eata at Atcham, just upstream from Wroxeter. St Eata was a seventh-century saint and churches dedicated to him are singularly rare. Although parts of the building were constructed during the Middle Ages, the large blocks of stone used in the nave were originally from the Roman town

substantial post-Roman buildings sited on the top of collapsed Roman buildings and evidence of attempts to prop up and restore existing buildings. Considerable efforts had been made to strip the tile-linings off the city's drains, perhaps in order to repair the roofs of surviving buildings, at a time when the sources of traditional Romano-British building materials had dried up.

One of the intriguing aspects of Borderland archaeology during this period is the virtual absence of metal and ceramic artefacts, pottery, and coins, all of which ceased to be produced. Utensils appear to have been made from friable materials such as wood, leather and basketry, which normally leave little tangible evidence for the modern archaeologist to study. One exception to this was found, however, at Wroxeter in 1967, a much-used stone with the following funerary inscription:

CUNORIX

MACUS MA

QUI COLINE

This has been interpreted as 'The mighty king Cunorix, son of the Holly'; it is believed that Cunorix was an Irish not British chieftain. The tombstone has been dated to the latter part of the fifth century, and by inference it is suggested that he was a mercenary commander employed by the local citizens for protection. Such mercenaries were known as *feoderati*, which simply means 'allied'. The employment of these mercenaries shows that organised military life at Wroxeter survived into the sixth century. This is perhaps not surprising in view of other clear evidence of the survival of town life there into the seventh century.

Early Anglo-Saxons in the Marches

The story of the Anglo-Saxon takeover of the Welsh borderland is problematic. We do not know the real scale of Saxon folk penetration in the Marches, and linguistic and place name evidence suggests that as late as the ninth century the true Saxon element in the population was relatively small. Conventionally, the initial conquest and occupation of the area later known as Mercia is attributed to the kings of Wessex in the late sixth century. The early Mercians were an obscure people, politically dependent on the northern kingdom of Deira. A crucial battle was fought at Chester in 614, when the Saxon Aethelferth defeated the combined forces of Gwynedd and Powys. Some centuries later, Bede records the victory of the pagans over the Christians thus:

> The warlike king of the English, Aethelfrid . . . having raised a mighty army, made a very great slaughter of that perfidious nation [the British] at the City of Legions [Chester]…Being about to give battle, he observed their priests . . . Most of them were of the monastery of Bangor [on Dee] . . . Many . . . resorted among others to pray at the aforesaid battle…to defend them against the swords of the barbarians. King Aethelfrid being informed . . . said, 'If then they cry to their God against us, in truth, though they do not bear arms, yet they fight against us, because they oppose us by their prayers.' He therefore commanded them to be attacked first, and then destroyed with the rest of the impious army, not without considerable loss of his own forces.

It is generally accepted that this battle opened the route to north Wales for the Saxons, which was taken by Aethelferth's successor, Edwin. It has also been suggested that it was at this stage, with an English army on the doorstep, that Wroxeter was finally abandoned as the political capital of the Cornovii (or even of Powys) and a better protected site chosen.

In AD 628 the Mercians, led by a pagan king, Penda, broke into the region of the lower Severn and later, together with the Welsh, defeated Oswald at the battle of Maserfelt (AD 641); Maserfelt is better known as Oswestry (from St Oswald's tree). Oswald, a Christian, was later canonised, and the Norman town founded subsequently was named after him. The resulting Saxon kingdom of the Magonsaetan embraced both Shropshire south of the Severn and the plain of Herefordshire. The boundaries of this territory are still preserved in the diocese of Hereford. Bishops of Worcester were frequently styled Bishops of the Hwicce (a tribal name), and by analogy it has been suggested that the Bishops of Hereford could originally have been regarded as the Bishops of the Magonsaete. The northern part of Shropshire formed part of the kingdom of the Wreocensaetan.

32 The largely Norman church of St Michael at Moccas. This is the probable site of an early Celtic monastery founded by St Dubricius in the sixth century. The church is largely built of tufa or travertine, a sponge-like rock formed by water running over calcareous rock deposits, of which there is a good source close to Moccas Court

The transfer of economic and political power from Wroxeter to Shrewsbury which was the eventual consequence of these events may not have been a straightforward process. One account relates that Cynddylan, an early seventh-century British hero, who was said to have lived in a great hall at Pengwern (Hall of the Welsh) — a white town by the Alder woods. A number of ninth-century poems, notably the *Cann Llywarch Hen*, mourn the death of Cynddylan and his family. According to the poem, Pengwern is in ruins, the well-known lands by the Tren (River Tern) are empty and all Powys grieves; only Cynddylan's sister, Heledd, survives to weep:

> My brothers were slain at one stroke,
> Cynan, Cynddylan, Cynwraith,
> Defending Tren, ravaged town . . .
> White town between Tren and Trafal,
> More common was blood on the field's face
> Than ploughing of fallow . . .
> The hall of Cynddylan, dark is the roof,
> Since the Saxon cut down
> Powys's Cynddylan and Aelfan . . .
> It's not Ffreuer's death I mourn for tonight
> But myself, sick and feeble,

My brothers and my land I lament . . .
Heledd the hawk I am called.
O God ! to whom are given
My brothers' steeds and their lands ?

The poem contains topographical references to places and features such as the River Severn, the Wrekin, Ercall, and Baschurch; it appears from the poem that the Kingdom of Powys then included the later county of Shropshire, a claim which was later re-stated by the medieval Welsh historian Giraldus Cambrensis.

Various attempts have been made to identify the site of Pengwern, as the intermediate centre between Wroxeter and Shrewsbury. Suggestions have included Wroxeter and Shrewsbury themselves, as well as the hillfort at Bury Walls, which lies at Bayston Hill immediately to the south of Shrewsbury. The most likely candidate, however, is the Berth by Baschurch, a fortified glacial hillock surrounded by a rampart and inturned entrance linked by causeways across an area of marsh close to where it is recorded that Cynddylan was buried. The site of the Berth is an evocative one today, silent and eerie, well suited as the home of one of the last British heroes. It is also worth noting that other hillforts in the region, such as the Breidden, also appear to have been reoccupied at this time.

If such a hiatus in the history of settlement did occur, it would explain why Shrewsbury did not acquire a cathedral and the county of Shropshire became divided between the dioceses of Hereford and Lichfield. For if Shrewsbury had been in existence as an important political centre in the seventh century at the time the diocesan map was created, it seems unlikely that it would not have administered ecclesiastical control over the Wreocensaetan territory and had its own bishop.

Penda himself was killed at a battle near Leeds in 654. He was succeeded by his son Peada, who was baptised and founded a monastery at Lichfield. Another of Penda's sons was Merewalh, who is recorded as 'king of the Magonsaete'. Among his possessions was the land on which a convent was founded at Much Wenlock in 618. Merewalh's daughter Mildburge eventually became Abbess of this convent. A medieval version of the life of St Mildburge relates how her father was baptised in 650. These decades in the middle and later part of the seventh century were critical ones in the history of the Marches. They saw the establishment of Anglo-Saxon political control over much of the region, control that was often unstable and which looked eastwards rather than westwards for support. In 660 the document known as the 'Tribal Hidage' recorded that the boundaries of Mercia extended to the Severn. These decades also saw the large-scale conversion of the new Saxon rulers to Christianity, and after the Synod of Whitby, in 663, the Celtic Church bowed to the power of Rome and St Peter.

Despite the establishment of Anglo-Saxon political control by the seventh century, the process of Anglicisation in the Border appears to have been slow and there remain questions about the nature and extent of the settlement by the English in the Marches. The absence of pagan Saxon cemeteries confirms that any actual English settlement which did occur in the region was Christian in character, placing it firmly in the seventh century or later. Even though the majority of villages carry English place names, there is no archaeological evidence to support the idea of a substantial English folk movement into the region during either the seventh or the eighth century. English control was established through the towns and the church over a predominantly native British population and only gradually did Anglo-Saxon place names and language replace their British predecessors. Normally the arrival of such a small ruling class does not bring about a wholesale change in place names. In the Marches, however, such a change does seem to have occurred, and Saxon names are by far the most numerous. Margaret Gelling, the place name historian, has argued that this might have resulted from the thoroughness with which the Mercian rulers administered the area to the east of Offa's Dyke. She has also pointed out the extraordinary degree of repetition of some place names incorporating the element 'ton'. For example, Shropshire has ten Astons (East Town), eight Westons (West Town), seven Nortons (North Town) and eight Suttons (South Town). These names could have originated in the speech of Mercian administrators, who might have been in the habit of talking about the East or West Township of a large estate. Such terms could gradually have come to be perceived as place names, and they came to replace the earlier British names of these places.

Dr Wendy Davies has demonstrated that there was considerable variation in the scale of the Celtic survival of culture and language. To confuse matters, in parts of the Borderland Welsh customs and language were reintroduced from time to time. It is therefore perhaps surprising that relatively few British place names survive. Amongst these, however, are Ercall, Hodnet (*hoddnant* — peaceful valley), Lizard (*llysgarth* — hall by the hill), and Prees (*prys* — brushwood); but Celtic names for hills and rivers such as Bredon, Neen, Dulas, Lugg, and Meole are far more common. Severn is a Celtic name and the river is alternatively known by the Welsh name *Hafren*, where the S has been replaced by an H. There are other indications of British survival — the place name element *walh*, for example, was a term used by the Saxons for the Celts and in western Shropshire there are nine Waltons and four Walcots. During the later Saxon period, though, the element *wal* appears to have been applied to settlements of serfs, who were not necessarily British.

Important evidence for Celtic survival has also been provided by a study of the dialect peculiar to the Border shires. This shows that up to the eighteenth century, a linguistic frontier between English and Welsh ran well to the east of the political frontier, from a point between Oswestry and Ellesmere through Upton Magna, two miles to the east of Shrewsbury, and then along the Severn to Bewdley. West of this line it appears that the inhabitants were the descendants of Welsh speakers and that the English of the region was traditionally a Welsh English.

There were other strong legacies on the English side of the border. Some of these might have been reintroduced during one of the eastward Welsh movements, or they could originally have been British. For instance, throughout the Middle Ages in the western parts of Herefordshire and Shropshire, the Gwaeli Bond, a system of Welsh communal ownership, survived; also, many western Shropshire manors had a number of Welsh inhabitants, known as the Walchera, throughout the Middle Ages. Welsh dues continued to be paid in parts of the Borderland — *trethnedion*, a tribute of oxen, was practiced in the Clun region, and a special Welsh court was held at Clun throughout the Middle Ages. Welsh dues also survived at Oswestry until the seventeenth century.

In south-west Herefordshire the area of Archenfield, known as 'Herefordshire in Wales', formed part of the Welsh diocese of St David's in the nineteenth century. The River Wye formed the eastern boundary of Archenfield, and the nature of the place names found in the Domesday survey on both sides of the river underline the pronounced differences in cultural history on either side of this boundary. On the eastern bank are Saxon names such as Brockhampton, Fawley, Brompton Abbots and English Bicknor, while on the western bank we find British names such as Kilforge, Tryseck, Llanfrothen, Craddock, Daffaluke and Ganarew. Even today, over half the field and farm names in Archenfield are Welsh. Quite apart from the obvious Welsh characteristics of Archenfield, there are a number of legends especially associated with the district. One of these was recounted by the early Welsh historian Nennius as follows:

> In the district of Ergyng there is a tomb near the well which is called the Eye of Amr: and the name of the man who is buried in the tump was Amr. He was the son of Arthur the knight and he [the knight] slew him [the son] and buried him there. And men come to measure the tump. It sometimes measures in length seven feet, sometimes fifteen feet, sometimes twelve feet, and sometimes nine feet. Whatever measure you may make it at one time, you will not again find the same measurement. And I myself have proved this.

The brook called Amyr is believed by some to be known as Gamber, and the eye, or source of the brook, is the round pool a few yards north of the buildings of the farmhouse known as Gamber Head. From this pool the Gamber has its origin, and it is the boundary for half a mile between the parishes of Much Birch and Much Dewchurch. The tumulus in which Amyr the son of Arthur was buried was traditionally believed to be a place called Wormelow Tump, of which nothing now remains beyond the name.

Over the centuries English names percolated westwards across the border into Wales, and periodically Welsh names moved eastwards. For instance, many Welsh names were introduced into Herefordshire in the sixteenth century after the break-up of the Marcher lordships and the large influx of Welshmen into England that followed the Act of Union (1536). The complexity of the situation is illustrated in the thirteenth century by some examples from the Monnow valley. The settlement known as Michaelchurch (itself a Normanised Welsh name) by the sixteenth century had become Llanfihangel-eskley; but it was then retranslated into English by eighteenth-century antiquarians and is now known as Michaelchurch again. Lower down the valley, Silas Taylor reported in the seventeenth century that the Welsh Clodock 'hath lately taken the name Longtown'. Yet even at this time some English names were being crowded out by the Welsh: Foscombe and Burycombe, which were found in Longtown in 1540, are no longer there; and today considerably more than half the farm names in this area are Welsh. A few miles lower down the river, it was only at the end of the seventeenth century that the Welsh Pontrilas completely replaced the English Heliston. The process of gradual reconquest of territory by the Welsh language can be traced in the former county of Flintshire, where such typically English Domesday names as Preston, Westbury, Merton and Bishopstree have become the modern Prestatyn, Gwespyr, Mertyn and Bistre.

Places to visit

Baschurch and the Berth, Shropshire SJ 429 238

Baschurch is a village some eight miles to the north of Shrewsbury. All Saint's Church is a much-restored building of medieval and later date. The church is built of local Red Sandstone and contains no obvious pre-Norman Conquest features. This is obviously a successor of a minster church, which had responsibility for an extensive estate possibly from pre-Saxon times onwards. Baschurch was the site of a failed attempt at a town plantation by the Abbot of Shrewsbury in the early thirteenth century. A few hundred yards to the east of the old village he laid out a new settlement in a simple T-shape. The area is still called Newtown although the borough failed, and a number of enclosures representing decayed burgage plots can still be traced on the ground. Its Dark Age associations are with the hero of the legendary Welsh poems, Cynddylan, and Baschurch is where he is reputedly buried. A mile and a half to the north of Baschurch, not far from Western Lullingfields, lies the Berth, a lowland hillfort which it is believed is the site of Pengwern, a stronghold which appears to have been the centre of British power between the collapse of *Viroconium* and the rise of Shrewsbury. The site consists of two glacial hillocks, one about three times larger than the other, linked by causeways to each other and to the mainland. Although the earthwork fortifications are relatively simple, the prominence of the two mounds rising from surrounding marshland makes them appear particularly imposing, giving them an appearance not unlike the classic Dark Age sites of Glastonbury and South Cadbury in Somerset. As early as 1825 the historians Owen and Blakeway proposed that the Berth was the site to which Cynddylan, the prince of Powys, fled after his capital of Pengwern was destroyed by the Saxons. Others have subsequently suggested that the Berth was Pengwern itself. Cynddylan is known only from a series of poems known as *The Eulogy on Cynddylan* in which Cynddylan's sister Heledd, in a series of dramatic monologues, laments his death and the destruction of his homeland. It is generally believed that the poems were written in the early ninth century but were recalling events two centuries earlier. The reference to 'Eglwyseu Bassa' in one of the poems cannot very well be to anywhere else but Baschurch, but the actual site of Pengwern is more difficult to determine.

Moccas, Herefordshire SO 357 433

Today Moccas consists of a fine country house, a park and a largely Norman church, which sits by itself close to the River Wye. Although the church is of intrinsic interest as a Norman foundation built in an unusual material — travertine or tufa — it is Dark Age Moccas which is particularly important.

The name Moccas is derived from the Welsh *moch* (plural of *mochyn*, meaning pig) and *ros* (moor). It was a low-lying area originally surrounded by water and is therefore characteristic of many early Christian sites. St Dubricius, or Dyfrig, the son of King Pepin of Archenfield and a predecessor of St David, founded a religious school at Hentland near Ross, and from there, accompanied by his disciples, he moved to Moccas. One legend among many says that St Dubricius left Hentland at the bidding of an angel who told him to found a monastery at a place where he would find a white sow with her piglets.

He found the place further up the River Wye 'well wooded and abounding in fish which he called Moccas [or the moor of the pigs]'. Although he founded other monasteries, he lived chiefly at Moccas and is said to have died on Bardsey Island about AD 550. Among the stories told about him was one that he owned land in Caerleon and also that he crowned King Arthur there. These legendary links with the Roman town indicate his close connection with Romano-British Christianity. It is said that pestilence laid waste to Moccas about AD 600 and that the last known abbot of Moccas was Bishop Comereg in about 590. After him Moccas Abbey slipped into obscurity and was recorded in later charters simply as a church.

By the time of Domesday Book Moccas was owned jointly by St Guthlac's Priory, Hereford, and Nigel the Physician. By the reign of Edward I the manor of Moccas had long been in the hands of the de Frene family. A royal license was granted to Hugh de Frene to fortify his manor house here and it is possible that this license referred to the castle, which has all but disappeared, on the edge of a deer park.

The present church of St Michael and All Angels is an almost perfect example of a Norman village church and was built of travertine, probably obtained close by at Depple Wood. Moccas is perhaps best known today for its fine deer park (now privately owned) so lovingly described in his diaries by Kilvert, who was for a while rector of the adjacent parish of Bredwardine in the nineteenth century.

Saturday, 22 April 1876
After they had left William and I walked up to the top of Moccas Park, whence we had a glorious view of the Golden Valley shining in the evening sunlight with the white houses of Dorstone scattered about the green hillsides 'like a handful of pearls in a cup of emerald' and the noble spire of Peterchurch rising from out the heart of the beautiful rich valley which was closed below by the Sugar Loaf and the Skyrrid blue above Abergavenny. We came tumbling and plunging down the steep hillside of Moccas Park, slipping, tearing and sliding through oak and birch and fallow wood of which there seemed to be underfoot an accumulation of several feet, the gathering ruin and decay probably of centuries. As we came down the lower slopes of the wooded hillside into the glades of the park the herds of deer were moving under the brown oaks and the brilliant green hawthorns, and we came upon the tallest largest stateliest ash I ever saw and what seemed at first in the dusk to be a great ruined grey tower, but which proved to be the vast ruin of the king oak of Moccas Park, hollow and broken but still alive and vigorous in parts and actually pushing out new shoots and branches. That tree may be 2000 years old. It measures roughly 33ft round by arm stretching.

I fear those grey old men of Moccas, those grey, gnarled, low-browed, knock-kneed, bowed, bent, huge, strange, long-armed, deformed hunchbacked misshapen oak men that stand waiting and watching century after century, biding God's time with both feet in the grave and yet tiring down and seeing out generation after generation, with such tales to tell, as when they whisper them to each other in the midsummer nights, make the silver birches weep and the poplars and aspens shiver, and the long ears of the hares and rabbits stand on end. No human hand set those oaks. They are 'the trees which the Lord hath planted'. They look as if they had been at the beginning and making of the world, and they will probably see its end.

Oswestry, Shropshire

The place name Oswestry means St Oswald's tree, and *Croes Oswald* is the Welsh translation. The field where the Roman Catholic church now stands is believed to be the site of the battle of Maserfelt in AD 642, when the pagan king Penda of Mercia defeated and killed Oswald, the Christian King of Northumbria. The site was named after the defeated king. The town developed close to the castle which was built by Rainald, Sheriff of Shropshire in about 1086. The motte of the Norman castle survives as a large tree covered mound in the town centre. The nucleus of the Norman town lay within a large bailey, and by 1276 22 burgage plots had been laid out there. The castle site has been made into a public park which offers fine views from the top. King Oswald's Well is fed by a spring which, according to legend, sprang from the spot where an eagle dropped one of Oswald's limbs after the battle of Maserfelt.

Oswestry, although a Norman foundation planted with English settlers, eventually became thoroughly Welsh, and a proportion of the townspeople were and still are bilingual. Many place names and street names within the town are Welsh or have their Welsh equivalents. There were also important links between Welsh bards and Oswestry, indicating the presence of a flourishing Welsh culture. In the fifteenth century Gutor Glyn was made a freeman of the borough for his *cwydd* (poem) in praise of Oswestry, and other Welsh bards came to sing the town's praises as well. Religious life in the town, too, had a strong Welsh element and Welsh services were held in St Oswald's parish church up until 1814.

The town was a frequent bone of contention between the Normans and the Welsh tribes. King John burnt it down in 1215 and 18 years later Llewellyn of Wales did the same. Owen Glendower sacked the town and almost demolished the church in 1400. There were also three accidental but disastrous fires between 1542 and 1567. The result of all this destruction and pillage is that the buildings of Oswestry are largely a product of the nineteenth century. But evidence of earlier structures remains: in the Norman foundations of the tower of St Oswald's church; in the original buildings of the Grammar School dating from 1407 and now divided into three cottages; and in the early seventeenth-century Llwyd Mansion in the centre of the town, a well-preserved black and white building bearing, curiously, on its wall the double-headed eagle of the Holy Roman Empire. This coat of arms was reputedly granted to a member of the Llwyd family, owners of the mansion, for distinguished service during the Crusades.

Oswestry's other claim to fame is that it was once one of the country's major railway centres. The first line arrived here in 1848 and by 1866 the town had become the headquarters of the Cumbrian Railways, with extensive locomotive and carriage works.

5 Offa and after — the late Saxon Marches

The establishment of political dominance by the Saxon Kingdom of Mercia in the seventh century appears to have been followed by the westward movement of the Anglo-Saxon language and place names. Just how much English folk movement and settlement there was in the Borderlands remains a matter of speculation. Undoubtedly Mercian and Briton mingled over the years, and the long, subtle and unrecorded takeover of Celtic lands by the Saxons is remembered in the seventh-century poem of Llywarch Hen where he recalls:

> Mae Wyn, when I was of thy age
> No one trod on my mantle,
> No one without bloodshed ploughed my land.

Later in the same poem there are some lines which may refer to a small band of Mercians who took over land in the Golden Valley: 'A gift has been stolen from me, from the valley of Mafwrn.'

We have already seen that the distribution of English and Welsh place names on the modern map was not the result of one simple process of English settlement, but it is possible that groups of place names with '-ton' endings, such as those found well to the west of Offa's Dyke in the Radnor basin, may reflect an early phase of Anglo-Saxon colonisation. Similarly, a group of English settlements in the Severn corridor, between the Welsh border and Montgomery, appear to have been cut off from their Anglo-Saxon base with the establishment of Offa's Dyke later in the century. After 700, Mercia's expansion into the Welsh Borderland proceeded more rapidly, and during the eighth century Mercia became the most powerful of all the Anglo-Saxon kingdoms in England. Aethelbad of Mercia was recognised as overlord of England south of the Humber, and later in the century Offa of Mercia was recognised by the Emperor Charlemagne as one of the princes of Europe. And so, for the time being Mercia was in the ascendancy.

The Mercian dyke systems

Whatever the scale of British survival, by the middle years of the eighth century Anglo-Saxon political control had been established throughout the Marches. On the western boundary this control was expressed physically in one of the Border's most famous and intriguing archaeological monuments, Offa's Dyke. The Dyke is the most extensive linear earthwork in

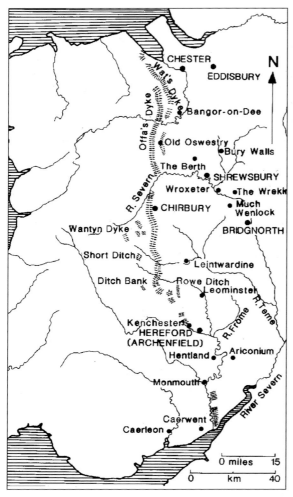

33 The Mercian dyke systems in the Welsh Marches

Britain and is named after Offa, King of Mercia (757-96). In the ninth century Bishop Asser described Offa as the king who 'ordered the construction of a large rampart the whole way from sea to sea between Britain and Mercia'. This frontier with the Welsh, comprising a combination of rivers and artificial banks and ditches, ran for over 100 miles, from the mouth of the Wye to the estuary of the Dee. There are a number of other shorter stretches of dyke which run more or less in parallel with Offa's Dyke and are believed to be roughly contemporary with it. Indeed if we take all the Marcher linear earthworks of this period, they measure just under 150 miles in length. The Dyke runs in and out of England still following part of Shropshire's border with Wales to the west of Chirk. Earthworks of this magnitude have traditionally attracted legend and superstition, often associated with supernatural forces, and a popular Marcher story is that Offa's Dyke was ploughed by the Devil in a single night.

The Dyke follows the western margin of the Welsh massif tracing roughly the geographical line along which one might have expected the Mercian advance to have halted. In the south the Dyke crosses the Hereford basin and reaches the Severn estuary by following the course of the River Wye, implying that the district of Archenfield to the west of the Wye was recognised then as being under Welsh control. In broad terms the present boundary between England and Wales follows the Dyke, but today national boundary and Dyke are only occasionally coincidental. The greatest discrepancy is in north Wales, where Offa's Dyke runs to the west of the present political boundary, and in the south, where the Dyke cuts through the western part of Herefordshire and therefore lies to the east of today's boundary line. In its central section the Dyke and the border do not diverge to any great extent, but only along very limited stretches do they coincide exactly.

One interpretation is that the Dyke reflected a negotiated boundary between the Mercians and the Welsh, built perhaps to control trade between the Border peoples. Over the centuries

Offa's Dyke has been used as if it were a natural topographical feature in the same way that an escarpment or a stream defines later parish and field boundaries. However, relatively few parish boundaries (only approximately 13 per cent) follow the line of the Dyke, and it could be argued that most of these boundaries were created after the Dyke had been built. As the proportion should have been considerably higher, we are left with the intriguing possibility that some parish boundaries in this part of the world were founded earlier than the eighth century, originating perhaps as the bounds of large tribal or family territorial units.

Offa's Dyke may have been the culmination of several attempts to define the border by the creation of linear earthworks. Some four miles to the east of Offa's Dyke in northern Shropshire and Cheshire runs Wat's Dyke. Wat's Dyke appears to have been an earlier attempt to define the border, and may be the work of an earlier Mercian ruler, King Aethelbald (716-57). Further south, the Rowe Ditch crosses the flood plain of the River Arrow near Pembridge, some three miles to the east of the Dyke. Sir Cyril Fox interpreted this work as a barrier across the cleared valley land, closing the gap between a forested area to the south and the hills to the north. To the west of Offa's Dyke there are a number of very short linear earthworks known as the Short Dykes. David Hill, who as co-director of The Offa's Dyke Project has studied the Dyke system intensively over the past 30 years, is of the opinion that all these works are more or less contemporary with Offa. Furthermore, he believes that Fox's interpretation of both the northern and southern sections of Offa's Dyke is incorrect. He argues that in the north Offa's Dyke stopped well short of the Irish Sea, being overlapped by Wat's Dyke for the final stretch, which reached the coast at Basingwerk, not Prestatyn as Fox believed. However, a recently obtained C_{14} date from Wat's Dyke gives a latest date of about AD 600, and if this is correct it would place the Dyke two centuries before Offa, in the late or sub-Roman period.

Hill also believes that the Dyke did not continue as far south as the Severn estuary, but others argue that the River Wye was used as the boundary over this southern stretch.

Hill and others have argued that two surviving documents, the Tribal Hidage and the Burghal Hidage, show that the country was already assessed in taxable units (*hides*), which were theoretically linked to the productive capacity of the land. They further speculate that each hide was responsible for supplying a certain quota of workers to build, repair and perhaps garrison the Dyke if required. Although Sir Cyril Fox considered it to be 'the product of one mind and one generation of men', Offa's Dyke was almost certainly constructed by different groups of workers, perhaps working at different times. The building of such linear earthworks by groups of men linked or tied to different geographical locations may well have its origins in prehistory. The Dark Age Dykes perhaps echo the building processes of the Iron Age linear boundaries in southern England and also the great hillforts. These may well have been erected and later repaired by the inhabitants of a region in return for their protection in times of trouble. Evidence for the building of fortified *burhs* (defended towns) in response to Viking attacks in the late Saxon period suggests that they were erected and repaired in a similar manner. Individual sections of the defences seem to have been the responsibility of different communities lying within the hinterland and under the protection of the *burh*.

34 *The Wye bridge at Hereford with the cathedral in the background. The crossing here was the focal point for a fortified settlement (burh) in the mid-Saxon period*

Anglo-Saxon towns

The process of town creation in the Marches was not a smooth one. During the later Iron Age some of the great hillforts of the Marches appear to have been developing urban functions; however, the Romans effectively stopped the development of these proto-towns and replaced them with their own urban centres. Thus, although hillfort occupation of a sort continued in some cases throughout the Roman period and afterwards, except in isolated cases and for brief periods the forts appear to have ceased to operate as regional or even local centres. The fundamental disruption which followed the collapse of the Romano-British way of life and the political upheavals associated with the Anglicisation of the border did not create favourable conditions for the immediate rebirth of towns. Nonetheless the establishment of an ecclesiastical framework involving the creation of diocesan and monastic centres, perhaps linked to evolving political centres, did help bring places such as Hereford, Leominster and Much Wenlock into prominence and in the case of Hereford certainly aided its development as an important regional centre. The relatively peaceful conditions of the mid-eighth century appear to have acted as a stimulus to urbanisation in the Marches, and it is from this period that the first authentic documented references to Hereford appear. However, it is another 200 years before the other principal Marcher shire capital, Shrewsbury, appears as an important centre.

It seems to have been the threat from another wave of invaders from the north, the Vikings, that spurred the development of town life in the Marches. There were two main phases of Scandinavian settlement in England. The first was between 866-80, when, despite successful resistance from the Kingdom of Wessex under Alfred, the Danes defeated the Saxons and settled in the eastern part of Mercia, all East Anglia and all but the northernmost part of Northumbria. The second was in the early years of the tenth century when Scandinavians, chiefly Norwegians, along with some Irish, began the occupation of the country on the west side of the Pennines from the Wirral peninsular to the Solway. Alfred was able to hold his own and place a limit on the Scandinavian-held area through a treaty with the Dane Guthrum in 886. This treaty formally recognised the northern domination by the Scandinavians in the area covered by the Danelaw. However, early in the tenth century the joint campaign of Edward the Elder and his sister Aethelfleda, the Lady of the Mercians, began to reduce the area under the Danelaw by means of military campaigns and progressive occupation. In due course the whole of the

35 *Aerial view of Shrewsbury showing the siting of the early town within the loop of the River Severn. The Anglo-Saxon town probably lay in the area just above the railway station, which unusually was built partly over the river*

country as far north as the Mersey and the Humber, including the Welsh Marches, came under the rule of Wessex kings.

The Scandinavian advances appear to have resulted in the creation of fortified centres known as *burhs*. It is not surprising that during the late Saxon period the terms 'town' and 'fortress' were synonymous. The need for an integrated system of defence against the Scandinavians was met by a rapid growth of defended centres in Wessex, accompanied by largely successful attempts to foster urban life. At the beginning of the ninth century a number of former sites which still had their Roman walls were refortified and a century later, during the reconquest of the Danelaw, the Roman defences of Chester were also restored. The process of urban fortification, however, extended beyond former Roman towns, bringing into existence a brand new generation of towns, many of which were to become the shire capitals of the Middle Ages. The choice of places for fortification seems to have been determined largely by the communication system that had evolved during the post-Roman period. For example, particular attention was paid to river crossings, where bridgehead fortifications were built on the opposite bank from the main settlement in order to maintain control of vital fording points.

The archaeological and topographical evidence for these centres has been widely studied. The most important surviving written evidence is contained in a document known as the Burghal Hidage, which in its present form belongs to the reign of Edward the Elder, but which probably recapitulates practices dating from the time of his father, Alfred, sometime before 892. Defence had traditionally been the responsibility of local magnates (*ealdormen*) who led locally raised armies known as the *fyrd*. By the early tenth century the defence of Wessex was organised on new principles laid down by the Burghal Hidage, this involved the building and manning of a widespread system of new local fortresses designed to restrict the movement of Scandinavian armies. The Burghal Hidage lists some 32 places as fortified centres, but it is concerned only with southern England. The distribution of these *burhs* was such that no place in Wessex was more than 25 miles from a fortified centre of refuge and resistance. The Mercian Register, which forms part of the Anglo-Saxon Chronicle, records how the building of a number of other fortresses was carried out alongside the campaign of reconquest of the Danelaw begun in 910 by Edward the Elder and his sister Aethelfleda:

Edward built 10 and Aethelfleda built 11 forts. A number of these were located in the Welsh Marches, although not all the sites have yet been definitely identified.

Along the Severn the main bridging points at Gloucester, Worcester, Bridgnorth and Shrewsbury were guarded by *burhs*. In 895 a Danish army broke out from a blockaded camp near London, perhaps seeking to link up with the Welsh, and built a *geweorc*, or palisaded camp, at a place which the Anglo-Saxon Chronicle calls *Cwatbrg* (Quatbridge). They reputedly spent the winter there (later accounts call the place Bridge, which is the early name for Bridgnorth). In the Middle Ages there is a reference to the 'Heathen's ditch' some way to the south of Bridgnorth at the foot of the spur on which Quatford church now stands — the term 'heathen' was one commonly applied to the Danes, who at this stage were still pagan. The Danes were again at Quatbridge in 910, after raiding areas to the west of the River Severn, and accordingly it is recorded that in 912 Aethelfleda built a *burh* at *Bricge*. The precise location of Aethelfleda's *burh* at Bridgnorth remains something of a mystery. There are at least three possible locations. Shropshire's great nineteenth-century antiquarian, the Reverend E.W. Eyton, argued that it was sited on Panpudding Hill, a fortified hillock which lies to the south-west of the present town. Florence of Worcester, writing in the twelfth century, was very precise about the size of the burh: it was, he said, on the western bank of the Severn at a place called Bridge. Later Florence stated that the Norman Robert de Bellême refortified Bridgnorth in the early twelfth century. Topographically, too, the present castle site seems to be the most probable candidate, as a number of other Saxon promontory *burhs* occupy very similar types of location. However, Bridgnorth was not recorded in Domesday Book, although there was a *burgus* at Quatford which was said to yield nothing. Quatford therefore has to be viewed as the third candidate, but excavations here have failed to provide any corroborative evidence and therefore the question of the location of the late Saxon fortification must remain open. What is certain is that later after the Norman Conquest, a highly successful borough developed at Bridgnorth close to the Norman castle.

The precise location of the Saxon defences at Shrewsbury is also uncertain, although they almost certainly occupied the highest part of the town. The town was in existence as early as 901, when it was recorded in a charter of Aethelred and Aethelfleda. Coins were issued from Shrewsbury mint by Aethelstan (929-39) and his successors right up until the Norman Conquest, so the town must have been fortified, as from the tenth century onwards mints were only allowed to operate in defended places, known as either *ports* or *burhs*. In terms of the number of moneyers found in Saxon mint towns, Shrewsbury ranks fourteenth in England, compared to Hereford, which was twenty-fourth. Shrewsbury was one of the most important mint towns and provides a textbook example of a river-defended site. The Severn meanders around a sandstone outcrop creating an almost complete natural moated circle, with a narrow gap on the eastern side. The logical location for the defended settlement would have been on the highest part of the town overlooking the eastern gap and it is from this area, particularly in the vicinity of St Mary's church, that mid and late Saxon material has been uncovered. It has been suggested that the Saxon *burh* roughly corresponded with the ancient parish of St Alkmund and that the High Street, Pride Hill and St Mary's Street defined the limits of the *burh*. Whatever the precise location of the Saxon town, however, by the time Domesday survey was compiled (1086) Shrewsbury was sufficiently important to possess five churches. Its large population in the late Saxon period is reflected by the fact that when Roger de Montgomery added the outer bailey of his castle between 1074 and 1086, some 51 houses had to be destroyed. In 914 Aethelfleda built another *burh* at Eddisbury, presumably reoccupying the hillfort there, and in 915 another at *Cyricbyrig*, believed to Chirbury, just a few miles to the east of Montgomery. This is a promising site with an undated earthwork enclosure close to Offa's Dyke and Montgomery, but as yet no evidence of Saxon occupation has been found here.

Places to visit

Hereford, Herefordshire

The *burh* which has left the greatest imprint on a modern townscape in the Marches is at Hereford, the centre of a bishopric since the late seventh century. A cross erected about 740 was said to commemorate three earlier bishops of the diocese, along with Milfrith, king of the Magonsaetan. There are also traditions of an earlier Celtic church here. The church of St Guthlac, on a site later enclosed by castle earthworks, was probably founded

36 Vertical view of Hereford, showing the lines of the Saxon and later medieval defences. The core of the ancient town is occupied by the cathedral and the remains of the Norman castle

in the first half of the eighth century. Conflicts with the Welsh in the region were recorded after the kingdom of the Magonsaete was incorporated into Mercia. These included a battle at Hereford early in the reign of King Offa in 760. Excavations have revealed a sequence of city defences, the very earliest of which belong to the mid-eighth century. This early town, which was almost square, lying either side of an east-west high street and enclosing an area of about 40 acres, was approximately the same size as the Roman Kenchester (*Magnis*) which Hereford succeeded.

The early rampart was subsequently enlarged and provided with a substantial timber revetment, possibly in the early tenth century at the time that other *burh* defences were being constructed in England. We know that Hereford had the status of a *burh* in 914, when it is recorded that the Danes were raiding Archenfield. In 1055 the city was besieged by the northern Welsh under Gruffydd ap Llewellyn and it was probably following this attack that the ramparts were provided with a stone face. Gradually the town's defences were extended to accommodate the growing population until they reached their maximum extent of some 120 acres during the later part of the twelfth century. Substantial traces of this line of defences can still be identified on the ground today incorporated within the modern town plan.

The Saxon town lay round St Aethelbert's cathedral and the crossing of the River Wye. The grid of streets in the vicinity of the cathedral dates from this period and the modern inner ringroad precisely follows the line of the Saxon and medieval defences. The ramparts of the Saxon town are clearly marked in the streets around the cathedral. In the north, an earthen bank and timber palisade ran along Bthyndthewall Lane (now Packers Lane) to meet St Owens Street, and continued to the river at the castle ford. The western defences ran from Little Packers Lane by way of Eign Gate to the river at the Wye Bridge. An outlying ditch, thrown up on the south side of the river (possibly in the ninth century), was later named the Row Ditch; such bridgehead fortifications were an important element in Saxon river-crossing defences. A small section of this Saxon rampart is exposed to view on the corner of Mill Street, behind a modern building block. The shape of the *burh* was later distorted by the insertion of a great Norman castle on the eastern side and by the growth of the cathedral precinct in the centre. The latter gradually pushed the bridging point further westwards until today the major Wye crossing is actually outside the area of the ancient city defences. The gradual expansion of the cathedral precinct and its associated buildings not only nudged the Wye crossing westwards, but effectively took over much of the interior of the early Saxon town. Accordingly, when a new area to the north of the early town was enclosed within the defended area in the early Middle Ages, a broad new market area had to be laid out running east to west which was at total variance with the traditional north-south axis of the town. Subsequently this large market area has itself been all but infilled by encroachments. These developments explain the apparently confused layout of the street pattern in Hereford. The main reason for this pattern of expansion is that in late Saxon towns little provision for trade and commerce was made within the defended areas: these functions tended to be carried out around churches or in narrow streets. It was not until after the Norman Conquest that broad open streets and market areas were deliberately made an integral part of town plans as commerce and trade became the prime factors in urban development.

During the first half of the eleventh century, Edward the Confessor appointed his nephew, the Norman Ralph, the son of the Count of Vexin, Earl of Hereford, in succession to Swein Godwinson. Ralph almost certainly had a castle built at Hereford — one of the first in the country — and established a Norman garrison here well before the Norman Conquest. After Ralph's defeat in 1055 by a combined army of Welsh and disaffected English, the city was sacked and burned and he was replaced by Harold Godwinson (later King Harold), who refortified the settlement and made it his base for raids against the Welsh.

Domesday Book account makes it clear that Hereford already had many of the special characteristics of a Saxon shire town by 1086. The lordship was divided between the king, bishop and earl: the customs of the 103 king's *burgages* (merchants' houses and plots) and the 27 owing allegiance to the earl are listed in unusual detail, and these descriptions resemble those for the other prominent military Welsh Border outpost, Shrewsbury. There were six royal moneyers and six smiths who made the king's iron (presumably obtained from the nearby Forest of Dean) into horseshoes. There were women brewers within and without the city, and there was regular trading of salt with Droitwich, where the church of St Guthlac appears to have possessed nine *burgages*. The trading character of the city is confirmed by the description of the bishop's share, recorded, significantly, under the heading 'Hereford port or market', a name already used on a number of earlier occasions in the Anglo-Saxon Chronicle. All in all, the picture is that of a thriving late Saxon shire town.

Offa's Dyke

Offa's Dyke provides a tangible relic of the conflict between the newly established English and the Welsh. The Dyke is now much overgrown and in places crosses some of the loneliest countryside in England. It is an evocative monument whose full story has yet to be told. The Dyke runs mostly north to south across the grain of the countryside, rarely following a straight line and tending to follow a switchback course that constantly changes direction. The engineers who constructed the Dyke made use of west-facing slopes wherever possible, even if this meant taking the boundary eastwards. In the north the Dyke is almost always accompanied by a western ditch, frequently accompanied by a counterscarp; but in the south there is less ditch, and over short stretches an eastern ditch can be found. At its most pronounced the top of the bank is almost 20ft above the bottom of the ditch, and originally was in the region of 24ft above it, with the ditch averaging 6ft in depth. In places it has been heavily ploughed and sometimes completely removed. The most complete section of the whole Dyke is in south-west Shropshire in the Clun Forest, where the Dyke runs through some of the Border's wildest countryside.

Largely through the efforts of the late Mr Frank Noble, in the early 1970s the Offa's Dyke Path was created. The path provides the walker with an unrivalled opportunity to admire both the earthwork and the magnificent countryside through which it passes. The Offa's Dyke Path runs from Prestatyn to Chepstow, about 140 miles in all, providing some of the most varied and exciting walking of any of Britain's long-distance footpaths. Particularly recommended are the lengths over the Black Mountains, across the Radnor and Clun Forests, and through the countryside between Llanymynech and the Clwydian range. A set of strip maps, route notes and other valuable information can be obtained from the Offa's Dyke Association, West Street, Knighton, Powys, where there is a visitor's information centre.

Bridgnorth, Shropshire

Bridgnorth sits on a ridge of old Red Sandstone overlooking the River Severn. It consists of two parts, High Town on the west bank of the river, and Low Town on the east. These are linked by a cliff railway, the steepest and shortest inclined railway in the country, and by a bridge from which the town derives its name (Old English, *bricge*). The present bridge was built in 1822; earlier bridges would have used the islands, or bylets, which lie in the River Severn here. Only one of these islands survives, to the south of the bridge; but a late sixteenth-century map marks two, the 'great billet' and the 'weures billet'.

As mentioned already, the origins of the town are unclear. As early as AD 896 there was a bridge over the Severn at *Cwatbryg* (Quatbridge) and a *burh* was created on the river bank in 912 by Aethelfleda. The site of Aethelfleada's *burh* is not known. Possibly, it is the earthwork known as Panpudding Hill, but Dr John Mason and others have argued that

37 *The promontory site at Bridgnorth overlooking the River Severn may be the site of a Saxon burh. The ruins of the medieval castle and Telford's eighteenth-century church of St Mary lie on the left-hand side and the medieval church of St Leonard on the right, located rather unusually at the edge of the medieval town*

the *burh* stood on the site of the present castle. It is not known how long the bridge at Quatford continued to operate, but the use of the place name Bridgnorth to describe a second town upstream suggests that it was not completely forgotten in the thirteenth century. The establishment of this second town followed the transfer of the military site from Quatford in 1101, when the twelfth-century Shropshire-born writer Ordericus Vitalis records that the rebel earl Robert de Bellême abandoned Quatford and transferred his castle, church (St Mary's) and borough to Bridgnorth. The new town lay originally within the large Anglo-Saxon parish of Morville. The castle's medieval chapel of St Mary's was parochially dependent on the minster church at Morville.

Bridgnorth Castle, the remains of which now form the centrepiece of the town park, was originally built by Robert de Bellême and was later fortified by Henry II, who granted the town its first charter in 1157. The new borough was probably laid out in the traditional manner during the later twelfth century, with a broad highstreet and a series of streets, and burgage plots, running off at right-angles. During this period a second medieval church was built (St Leonard's). Following Welsh disturbances the new town was surrounded by a turf rampart and ditch between 1216 and 1223. Some 40 years later, the stockade was partially replaced by a stone wall. Although Bridgnorth, along with Shrewsbury, was in the front line of defence against the Welsh in the eleventh and early twelfth centuries, the defences were left to decay with the coming of more settled times in the late thirteenth century. By the early sixteenth century the castle was said to be 'totally to ruine' and it was recorded that townspeople were building themselves houses in the bailey.

By the time of Leland, Henry VIII's antiquary, the town walls were all in decay. Their remains can still to be seen at the west end of Lisley Street and the Half Moon Battery off Pound Street, however. Of the five original town gates, only the North Gate, much remodelled in 1910, still stands. Whitburn Gate survived until 1761 and the Hungry Gate until 1821.

The area enclosed by the town walls was inadequate to accommodate the late medieval expansion and new suburbs grew up outside the North Gate, in New Town and Littleburg, now known as Pound Street. A suburb also grew up at Low Town across the river. Although Leland dismissed it as 'a pretty long street of mean buildings', on early maps it appears to be as large as High Town, Bridgnorth.

Medieval Bridgnorth was an important route centre: the road from Chester to Bristol crossed the River Severn here and the river itself was of major importance in the development of the town. Along with Bristol, Gloucester, Tewkesbury and Shrewsbury, Bridgnorth is one of five ports on the River Severn to be marked on Gough's 1360 map of Britain.

During the Middle Ages the textile industry was important and so too were tanning and brewing. In 1540 Leland recorded that the town 'standeth by cloth, and that now decayed, the town sorely decayed'. Indeed by this time the textile industry was virtually extinct. Later the town turned with only modest success to cap- and hat-making. Today there is little evidence of early cloth working, except the names Tainter Wall and Tainter Hill at the west end of Lisley Street; here freshly woven cloth was 'tented' or stretched out to dry. The carpet industry did not arrive until the end of the eighteenth century, when Joseph MacMichael established the first carpet factory in Lisley Street.

Because of destruction during the Civil War (much of High Town was burnt down), little remains of the buildings of medieval or Tudor Bridgnorth. At the bottom of the Cartway, which was the only way up from the river to High Town until the building of the New Road, stands the fine Bishop Percy's House (1580), one of the few surviving half-timbered buildings in the town. An appeal to Parliament was made for aid, the fire having consumed 'almost the whole subsistence of the Corporation, consisting of very faire and ancient buildings, to the value of ninety thousand pounds'. The new town hall was completed in 1652 on a new site in the middle of the High Street, where it still stands today with the traffic flowing through it.

The real reconstruction, however, did not come until the eighteenth century, when Bridgnorth emerged as a gracious and pleasant town with some fine Georgian terraces. In 1763, Bridgnorth was described as a 'place of great trade, both by land and water'. In Low Town new residences were built in Mill Street and St John's Street; the Post Office (c.1700) is a good example of this phase. In High Town, Anthony Weaver attempted to improve the inhabited area within the ancient limits of the castle. The ultimate sequel to these improvements came with the rebuilding of the fourteenth-century church of St Mary's, earlier described by Leland as a 'rude thing'. A new church in white freestone in the classical style was built by Telford at the end of East Castle Street in the late eighteenth century on a different alignment. This church was designed to blend with the spacious streets and buildings of this part of the town, which displays considerable elegance. During the nineteenth century a number of large fashionable residences were built around the edge of Castle Park.

As Bridgnorth lay only a few miles downstream from Coalbrookdale and the coalfield there, there were links with the iron industry in the town. From 1760 the Coalbrookdale Company leased the Town Mills as a forge and Thomas Cranage, the ironworker, was employed there as 'master Hammer-man' in 1766. On the east bank of the river behind Mill Street are the remains of John Hazeldine's once-famous foundry. Crude iron was stored at Bridgnorth before being shipped downstream to Stourbridge. This trade was mainly controlled by the Knight family who had furnaces at Charlcote about eight miles from Bridgnorth and at distant Bringewood near Ludlow. Until the coming of the railway in the 1850s, Bridgnorth remained a major river port. During the eighteenth and nineteenth centuries, coal from the pits at Broseley and agricultural produce from the surrounding countryside were the main cargoes. The river warden's house, built in the late eighteenth century, can still be seen with an area of old wharves in front of it. Other surviving signs of the once-flourishing river trade include the flights of landing steps at the Old Quay, which originally included Skinner's Load, Friar's Load and Foster's Load. On a map of 1739 there are three dockyards on the Severn, and in about 1800 it was recorded that the river at Bridgnorth presented a 'constant moving picture of boats and barges'. The coming of the railway did not bring any immediate advantages to the town. Indeed, the first consequence was to kill the river trade; the last barge to use Bridgnorth came down the Severn in 1895. Symbolically this barge, which was carrying firebricks, sank after hitting one of the bridge piers.

Chirbury, Shropshire. SO 262 986

In AD 915 Aethelflaeda, Lady of the Mercians, constructed a '*burh*' or fortified enclosure at a place called *Cyricbyrig*. This is believed to be the village of Chirbury, one and a half miles east of Offa's Dyke at the head of the Rea and Camlad valleys. Both these provide direct and easy access to the Upper Severn valley and thereby the heart of Wales. No doubt this strategic location dictated the siting of the '*burh*' here, presumably to deter Viking incursions into the Upper Severn Valley. A rectangular earthwork butting onto the road at the top right of the photograph has been suggested as the site of this '*burh*', but excavations here in 1958 proved inconclusive, providing no evidence to date or to explain the defences. A closer study of the core of the village, however, shows it to be laid out on a rectilinear plan, perhaps reflecting the original form and location of the '*burh*'. The large and impressive church of St Michael was an Anglo-Saxon minster church, and mother-church for a huge parish throughout the Middle Ages. Its foundation must date back at least to the beginning of the tenth century, as the existence of a church at this time is clearly indicated in the place name *Cyricbyrig* which means 'church fort'. Around 1200 the church became a priory for Augustinian canons, being rebuilt to serve the needs of both priory and parish. Unfortunately, only a tiny fragment of the monastic range of the Priory survives today.

6 Castle and borough in the Marches

The Normans in the Marches

It is difficult to overestimate the impact of the Normans on the Welsh Border landscape, both in the short and the long term. The Normans came as conquering feudal lords to a region which in 1066 had very few towns and a scattered rural population. They stamped their mark very firmly in the form of castles, towns, villages and churches. Before they arrived in the late Saxon period the Borderland had been politically unsettled, local border skirmishes were common, and on a larger scale the region was coveted by both the Anglo-Saxons and the Welsh. Despite the continued existence of Offa's Dyke as a tangible western boundary and the recent formation of the Mercian shires during the early eleventh century, there was no finite border between the Saxons and the Welsh. The historian Round sums up the position at the time of the compilation of Domesday Book 20 years after the Norman Conquest:

> There is no fixed western Anglo-Saxon boundary, only a border which was ever shifting with the ebb and flow of conquest . . . What Harold recovered with his light infantry, what William Fitz Osbern [Earl of Hereford] and his male horsemen can hold at lances' point — that at the moment of the great survey was all part of Herefordshire . . . No more and no less.

Until the early 1060s the Welsh held the initiative, with the English on the defensive, largely because of the emergence of two energetic Welsh leaders. Gruffydd ap Rhydderch of Deheubarth found the rich pickings of Gloucestershire and Herefordshire an irresistible temptation until his death in 1055, and he was followed by Gruffydd ap Llewellyn of Gwynedd. Wales was briefly, if uneasily, unified under the latter. Gruffydd raided into England as far as Chester and Leominster, until his death at the hands of Harold Godwinson and his half-brother Tostig in 1063. Partly in response to this situation Edward the Confessor, who had been brought up in Normandy, had introduced a number of Norman lords into positions of power in the Borderland in the 1050s. One of these Norman lords, called Osbern, established the lordship of Ewyas Harold in the Black Mountains, where he built one of the first castles in England. Another Norman lord appears to have built a castle at Richards Castle, a little to the south of Ludlow, and, as already discussed, Edward the Confessor's nephew Ralph built himself a castle at Hereford. The Anglo-Saxon Chronicle recorded in September 1051 that 'The foreigners had built a castle in Herefordshire in Earl Sweyne's territory and inflicted all injuries and insults they could upon the King's men in that region.' These early Norman lords were clearly very unpopular and they were eventually

38 Plan of Norman England showing areas under special control including the Welsh Marcher Palatinates

ousted as the Godwinson faction prevailed. This early Norman incursion into Herefordshire, however, represented only a modest foretaste compared to what was to come with their total domination of the Borderland after 1066.

It is not difficult to understand why the Normans acquired a strong taste for this region — Normandy itself had started life as a Marcher duchy. There were geographical as well as political similarities: gently undulating country with plenty of natural stone and timber for buildings, and a frontier zone with potentially rich pickings, in this case beyond the Welsh border. Additionally Wales was a hilly, misty, Celtic country, reminiscent of Normandy's coveted neighbour, Brittany. A kingdom tailor-made for the Normans, it is perhaps not surprising that they were so attracted to it, and that in their ambitions and their feuding they left behind such a deep impression on the landscape.

However, the apparent similarities between Wales and Brittany were to be dangerously deceptive. Brittany is a region which in many ways has more in common with Cornwall than with Wales. The Breton landscape of weathered granite rarely reaches above 1000ft, so in comparison with Welsh mountain terrain its geography is gentle. Brittany had been a far more prosperous and integrated region in Roman Gaul than Wales had ever been in Roman Britain, and despite the legendary Celtic links between the two peoples, the Bretons shared more of a cultural and a political heritage with the rest of France than did the Welsh with Anglo-Saxon England.

The Norman Conquest of 1066 represented more of a watershed in the Welsh Borderland than perhaps anywhere else in Britain. Whereas the complete conquest of England was achieved within 20 years, the conquest of Wales took over 100 years after the Battle of Hastings, and even then it was far from over. The Marches formed the base from which this conquest was achieved. The risings which occurred between 1068 and 1070 first alerted William the Conqueror to the political and military problems of the Welsh. Although the mountainous geography of Wales made it a difficult country to control, the divided and relatively weak nature of the independent princedoms in 1070 meant that at first the

Normans had little difficulty in defeating or intimidating the Welsh. The main problem, however, was in maintaining political control after the initial Norman military victories, and there was a series of significant Marcher revolts in 1075, 1088 and 1100. Following a rebellion by Welsh princes in alliance with a Herefordshire thegn known as Eadric the Wild, King William devised a scheme by which the Marches were administered as semi-autonomous earldoms based on the Saxon towns of Chester, Shrewsbury and Hereford. Within this framework the land was divided between Marcher lords — in all some 153 separate lordships were created, functioning almost as little kingdoms, which, technically at least, did not revert to their mother counties until the Act of Union (1536). The units chosen for the lordships appear to have been pre-Norman, and coincided with the *commotes*, the social and territorial cells of the Welsh kingdoms. Within each lordship one or more castles were built, and these castles formed the nuclei on which the border boroughs were subsequently created. In this respect the Marcher lordships were similar to the castleries of Normandy, where they formed the basic unit of administration. The only other places in England where a similar organisational structure was introduced by the Normans was in Sussex, divided into rapes, and the Palatinate of Durham.

The parts of Wales conquered by the Normans came to be known collectively as 'The Welsh Marches' (*Marchia Wallia*) to distinguish them from the unconquered parts, which were known collectively either as 'Wales' (*Wallia*) or 'Wales proper' (*pura Wallia*). The distinction between Wales and the Marches was not simply geographical; it was also legal and constitutional. 'Wales proper' lived under what was then conventionally called 'the law of Howel', i.e. the indigenous Welsh law; 'the March of Wales' on the other hand lived under what were called 'the customs of the March', according to which the Norman Marcher barons were granted a large degree of autonomy, while the rest of England was strictly under royal control.

There was, therefore, a real distinction between Normanised England and the Normanised March of Wales. The lords of the Welsh March were allowed to exercise extensive judicial powers in return for bringing the Marches and Wales under Norman control. These lords had jurisdiction over all civil and criminal cases, high and low, with the exception of crimes of high treason. They established their own courts to try these offences and executed sentences and collected fines. They possessed all of the royal perquisites — salvage, treasure-trove, plunder and royal fish. They could impose forests and Forest Law, establish boroughs, and grant extensive charters of liberties. They also had unique rights of unlicensed castle-building and of declaring and waging what was called 'private war'. The Marcher lord was thus established in the position of a petty king, exercising both royal and lordship rights. In this respect, a lord of the March of Wales differed from a lord of an estate in England, for the latter enjoyed none of these royal privileges, and held his lordship as a direct grant from the king. The Marcher lord took responsibility for the defence of his own lordship, and though he regarded the king as his sovereign, the king had little right to interfere in the lordship except on the lord's death, when he might conduct an inquiry about the legal heir and arrange for the succession. He could not, however, normally interfere with this succession, which usually passed from eldest son to eldest son by the custom known as primogeniture. In the absence of male heirs, the lordship was divided equally among the daughters. If, however, the lord abandoned his territory, or if he were found guilty of treason or another serious felony, the king could then confiscate the estates.

The three great Norman Border territories based on Chester, Shrewsbury and Hereford were defended by a network of castles both internally and, where possible, westwards into Wales. Hugh d'Avranches (made Earl of Chester in 1070) was based in the north with a forward defence under his cousin Robert against the Welsh at the newly established borough of Rhuddlan. In the centre Roger de Montgomery, Earl of Shrewsbury, built an outpost on the Welsh side of Offa's Dyke in the region of Montgomery. In the south William Fitz Osbern, Earl of Hereford, defended the Wye basin with castles at Wigmore, Clifford and Ewyas Harold, and, following an invasion of Gwent, established the Lordship of Striguil around Chepstow. By the time the Earl of Hereford returned to Normandy in 1070, he had pacified his section of the Border and had completed the organisation of the Marches from Ludlow to Chepstow. William Fitz Osbern was killed in Flanders the following year leaving as his legacy a chain of Norman strong points on the Welsh border, as well as a number of infant boroughs which he had created in order to centralise Norman political control. The franchises and laws of his boroughs, such as Hereford, were based on the laws of Breteuil in Normandy and these later also served as a model for a considerable number of newly created towns in other parts of England and Wales. William Fitz Osbern was a powerful and ruthless man, typical of the eleventh-century Norman Marcher barons. Ordericus Vitalis described them thus:

> Puffed up with pride they gave no heed to the reasonable complaints of his [the king's] English subjects and disdained to wave them in the balance of equity. They shielded their men at arms who most outrageously robbed the people and ravished the women and those only incurred their wrath who were driven by these grievous fronts to be allowed in their remonstrances.

Time places a shield between us and the worst excesses of the early Norman Marcher lords, but even after nine centuries they are not men to romanticise.

By 1086 the Normans held Caerleon and the line of the River Usk and in 1093, following the defeat of Rhys ap Tedwr, they extended their control over south Wales, with the establishment of the lordships of Brecon and Glamorgan. The sequence of military events was in many ways reminiscent of the Roman conquest of Wales. Roger de Montgomery, the Earl of Shrewsbury, attacked Wales along the Severn valley to gain control of a number of Welsh lordships, thus imposing Norman control on the waist of Wales, while from Oswestry the Normans pressed north-westwards into Welsh lands beyond Offa's Dyke and in the far north moved quickly along the coastal plains to establish castles at Deganwy, Conway and Caernarvon.

Castles of the Conquest

The castle was the first and most important physical manifestation of the Norman Conquest. Throughout the Borderland castles were built both of stone and of earth and

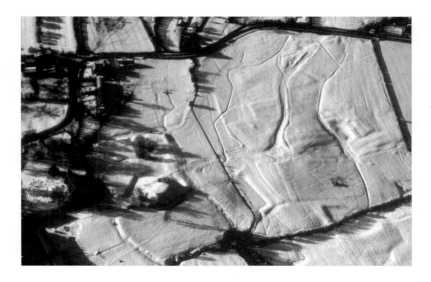

39 Aerial view of medieval earthworks at Lingen, Herefordshire. There is a distinctive flat-topped motte and bailey castle below St Michael's church, and a large area of settlement earthworks indicating that the village has migrated from here to its present location south of the church

timber to proclaim the new Norman dominance. Castles were clearly one of the reasons for the rapid Norman success in subduing the countryside: they were constructed in virtually every town and in many villages and hamlets and acted as strategic centres from which Norman political control was exercised and military dominance clearly demonstrated. Ordericus Vitalis believed that it was the castle which enabled the Normans to establish themselves in England:

> The fortifications called castles by the Normans were scarcely known in the English provinces, and so the English — in spite of their courage and love of fighting — could put up only weak resistance to their enemies.

Contemporary chroniclers sometimes imply that the castle was a secret weapon which gave the Normans an unfair advantage, and in 1137, during the civil war between Stephen and Matilda, the compiler of the Anglo-Saxon Chronicle was sufficiently moved to complain:

> They [the Normans] sorely burdened the unhappy people of the country with forced labour on the castles. And when the castles were made they filled them with devils and wicked men.

The castles were not merely defensive strongholds but also provided bases for active operations. The Norman cavalry used castles to respond swiftly and decisively to any uprising and to dominate the surrounding countryside, as well as for making sorties

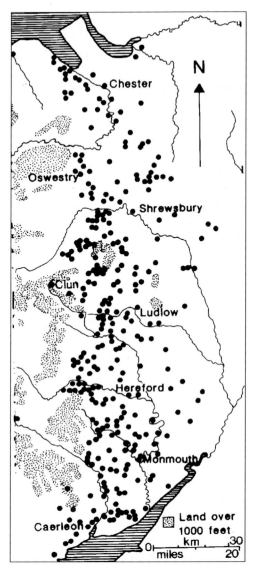

*40 Distribution of castles in the Welsh
Marches dating primarily from the
twelfth century*

against enemy forces. The distribution of
these castles was to some extent determined
by the locations of the various uprisings
against Norman control, for instance in the
south-west of England and the Welsh
Marches. But underlying this distribution
there is a pattern of political centralisation,
not merely in response to specific uprisings,
but also as a means of intimidating any
potential unrest in the form of an
unambiguous statement of Norman
superiority.

For these purposes the motte and bailey
design was ideal. The motte (a Norman-
French term for mound) was normally
conical in shape, and could range in height
from 9-90ft. The mound was surrounded by
a ditch from which the material making up
the motte was extracted. There would have
been a wooden bridge leading from the
castle bailey (the enclosure attached to the
motte) to the motte, which was capped by a
tower, initially constructed of timber. The
bailey was also surrounded by a ditch or
ditches and a rampart, on top of which a
palisade was built. Inside the bailey there
were various buildings, such as a hall, chapel,
stable, smithy and buildings for storage.

Motte and bailey castles appear to have
developed from the seigneurial enclosures
with tower gatehouses that were found in
north-western Europe during the
Carolingian (pre-Norman) period, and, as
we have already seen, castle-like structures
had already been erected in the Marches by
the Normans prior to 1066. In England the
intermediate stage in private fortification
appears to have been a tower and a circular
area enclosed by a bank, but no mound — the construction of such castles has often left
distinctive earthworks known as ringworks. The success of the practice of piling earth
around the base of the tower to prevent its being burnt down easily may well be the reason
why the motte developed as the principal feature of early Norman castles in England. The
Bayeux Tapestry depicts an attack on a motte tower in Brittany which was on fire,
underlining the point that firing fortifications was an important part of siege warfare and

that wooden towers were vulnerable to burning. The tradition of constructing ringworks continued into the twelfth century in the Marches, but the decision to build a ringwork rather than a motte seems to have reflected nothing more than the personal preference of the local lord or his castle builders.

The beauty of these early earth and timber castles was that they were relatively easily and rapidly built using materials that were readily to hand. This type of construction avoided problems of finding quarries or masons, and arranging for the transportation of stone. All that would have been required were a number of carpenters and a force of men to dig the defences. In William's England this was not a difficulty, as the Normans could command an endless supply of labour. Thus, in troubled areas, the Crown or its representatives could rapidly establish a formidable presence capable of withstanding an all-out attack. The chroniclers recorded that castles were thrown up in just a few days (it has been suggested just 15 days were required to build the castle at Hastings), and although there are doubts about the accuracy of these accounts, it is quite possible that the basic structure could be erected within a very short time.

Apart from the advantage of speed in the construction of this type of castle, the capacity for rapid rebuilding following destruction was also an important factor in its success. At Hen Domen (Montgomery) a motte and bailey castle was constructed between 1070 and 1074 as a base for an attack on Cardigan by Hugh, son of Roger de Montgomery. The Domesday Book notes that the castle was built in an area of 'waste' used by three Saxon thegns as a hunting ground. During the next century and a half it was besieged on several occasions and changed hands frequently before a stone castle was built at a new site in Montgomery town after 1223. Philip Barker, the excavator of the castle, demonstrated that wooden buildings within the bailey which have left only ephemeral traces were repeatedly destroyed or dismantled and then rebuilt. Moreover, the bridge from the bailey to the motte is of the 'gangplank' variety so graphically depicted on the castles of the Bayeux Tapestry.

In the whole of England and Wales by far the densest concentration of earth and timber castles was in the Marches, where the earthwork remains of several hundred motte and bailey castles reflect the troubled conditions which existed there up to the end of the twelfth century. A number of the more strategically important timber castles were later rebuilt in stone, to add to the company of stone castles already in existence. However, mottes were not always easily converted to accommodate stone towers, and there are records, such as those for Shrewsbury Castle, which tell of the collapse or slippage of masonry on the mound following such an attempted conversion. A compromise solution was to ring the top of the motte with a roughly circular or polygonal curtain wall following the crest of the mound, creating what is known as a 'shell keep'. A particularly fine example of this design is to be found at Snodhill, in Peterchurch parish in western Herefordshire.

Norman castles were part of the apparatus of war and suppression, but despite their longevity in the landscape, many Border castles had only relatively short active lives. As Norman dominance of England was cemented, so the need for private defence on such a scale declined and those timber castles that were not rebuilt in stone fell into decay. Resident lords sometimes built themselves more comfortable manor houses close to their former castles, while others moved out of villages altogether and built their homes on completely new sites, often maintaining a semblance of defence in the form of a water-filled moat. Nevertheless the earthworks of the motte and bailey castle remain the most tangible and indelible element of the Norman contribution to the landscape. The sheer size of most mottes has ensured their survival even though they lost their original function many centuries ago. They are not readily converted to alternative uses or easily eradicated from the landscape. With a few notable exceptions such as at Hereford, where the castle mound was destroyed in the nineteenth century, mottes of all shapes and sizes have survived into the early twenty-first century, and into an age when they are protected for their historical importance. Like prehistoric hillforts their very presence in the landscape has influenced what has come after them, and the subsequent morphology of town and village alike has been affected by these monuments to Norman confidence and energy.

The new Norman Marcher towns

The castle in conjunction with the town proclaimed the Norman domination of England and the Marches. The impact of the construction of castles in towns is graphically recorded in Domesday Book, where many early castles destroyed large areas of Saxon housing. Prior to the Conquest the normal unit of settlement in Wales and the Marches was the isolated family homestead or small hamlet. Groups tended to be self-sufficient, and there was little inter-community trade to stimulate the growth of market centres. The conditions necessary for urbanisation were therefore not present. The coming of the Normans changed this situation and it was soon found that the combination of a castle and a borough formed an economic unit of considerable vitality. The castle attracted merchants with its promise of protection and guarantee of a local monopoly of trade.

In Wales, trade in each lordship was confined to the newly established boroughs, since it was a monopoly of the burgesses (town merchants) who paid the lords a fixed sum annually in return for the right to collect the town dues and elect their own officers. These privileges were set out in the town charter under which the town was governed. The country folk of the locality were permitted, on payment of a toll, to trade their produce in the street at the weekly market. At the town fair, held for several days once or twice a year, itinerant traders also offered their wares for sale. The castle garrison would have provided the merchants and artisans of the borough with a basic market and eventually the borough would have provided for the material needs of the castle, as well as bringing the lord a substantial revenue. The combination of castle and borough possessed a strength and unity which the combination of castle and rural manor never exhibited.

The Normans quickly realised that such communities were most effective in the settling and control of newly conquered or disputed areas. The scale of town creation, in Wales and the Marches unparalleled since the Roman period in Britain, reflected what was going on at the same time in the rest of England and indeed in many parts of western Europe. In the Marchlands, however, the movement towards the creation of new towns and market centres was even more feverish than elsewhere. The territorial jigsaw of the Welsh border country, in the form of a mixture of baronies, lordships and earldoms,

1   *View of the River Wye at Symonds Yat, Herefordshire*

2   *The Black Mountains, which form the boundary between Herefordshire and Gwent*

3 *Arthur's Stone, the surviving core of a neolithic long barrow. Such Megalithic monuments were often associated with Arthurian legendary characters*

4 *One of a group of Bronze Age round barrows on Ludlow Racecourse, which lies in Stanton Lacy parish. In the nineteenth century each barrow had a tree planted on top of it for landscaping purposes*

5   The multi-valate iron age hillfort at Hopesay, Shropshire. The fort was forested until 1986 when storms destroyed many of the trees. The earthworks of the fort that were revealed as a result are particularly well defined, as they have not been subjected to erosion by livestock walking over them

6   The massive fortifications of the hillfort referred to as the Hereforshire Beacon, which clings to the southern summit of the Malvern Hills. In the centre is a probable medieval castle known as The Citadel

7 *Aerial view of the excavated area of Wroxeter (Viriconium); the main feature is the 'Old Work' standing wall which leads into the bath suite*

8 *Aerial view of The Berth near Baschurch, a prehistoric fortification surrounded by marshy land. It is the possible site of Pengwern, the Dark Age centre, which was occupied after the final collapse of Viriconium*

9 (right) Aerial view of Offa's Dyke at Bubbington in north-west Shropshire. The straight line of the dyke is emphasised by hedges and woodland which follow it

10 (above left) The motte and bailey at Ewyas Harold, Herefordshire. It is believed that a castle was built here by Normans invited into the Marches by Edward the Confessor, well before the Norman Conquest. The existing castle, however, is probably post-conquest. Tree-covered mottes are a feature of a large number of Marcher villages

11 William Fitz Osbern's great hall/keep at Chepstow. This was the earliest stone keep in Britain and probably closely resembled the palace/hall of Normandy. Its site on the estuary of the River Wye formed a base for the Roman conquest of south Wales

12 The elegant ruins of Tintern Abbey in the Wye Valley. A monument that has inspired artists and writers, including Wordsworth, for over two centuries

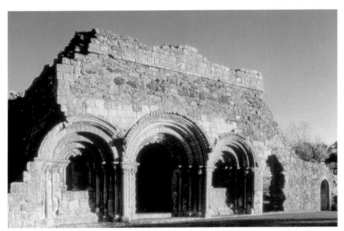

13 The late Norman arches of the chapter house at Haughmond Abbey

14 The sturdy walls of Goodrich Castle, a building which was strengthened in the thirteenth century

15 The gatehouse of Wigmore Priory, all that remains of the Mortimer foundation in Herefordshire

16 The great Norman nave of Hereford Cathedral

17 The surviving church at Abbey Dore

18 (left) The romantic buildings of Stokesay Castle viewed from a distance. The best known fortified manor house in England is a monument to the medieval Ludlow wool merchant, Lawrence of Ludlow

19 (above) View of the earthworks of the prehistoric hillfort and failed town at Cefnllys

20 Half-timbered merchants houses in
     Ludlow High Street; the stone building is
     the Butter Cross

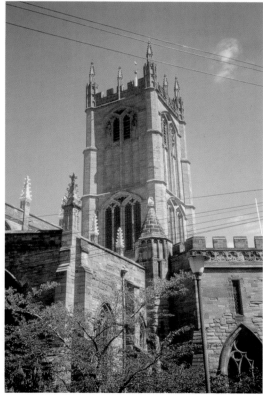

21 The fifteenth-century tower and porch of
     St Lawrence, Ludlow, a church built on
     the prosperity of the Ludlow merchants
     and the Palmers Guild. It is the largest
     parish church in Shropshire and the
     closest building to the cathedral to be
     found in that county

22 *The church of St Mary Magdalene, Battlefield, which was founded by Henry IV as a chantry to pray for the souls of those that died in the battle of Shrewsbury (1403). The church is now used just once a year: a service is held on 21 July every year to mark the anniversary of the battle*

23 *The River Severn at Bridgnorth, the location of a busy river port until the mid-nineteenth century*

24 *Attingham Hall, built 1783-5, with the River Tern on the right. Thought by many to be the most elegant country house in the whole of the Welsh Marches*

25 *Aerial view of the extensive landscaped park and lake at Walcot, created for Lord Clive of India in the mid-eighteenth century*

26 The relics of lead mining at Shelve in the 1970s. The old waste tips have now been grassed over

27 Forge Bridge over the River Teme at Bringewood in Herefordshire. Built in 1772 for the Knight family's industrial activities in the vicinity, it was designed by an accomplished local surveyor, Thomas Farnold Pritchard

28 Restored bottle kiln at Coalport for the production of ceramics. The kiln now forms part of the Ironbridge Gorge Museum

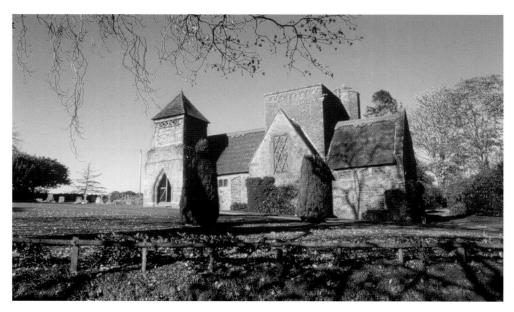

29 All Saints church at Brockhampton by Ross, built (1901-2) by W.R. Lethaby. The church formed part of a fundamental landscape redesign in the parish

30 *The riverscape at Shrewsbury from the English Bridge. The dominant building was the nineteenth-century Shrewsbury Infirmary, which has now been converted into a shopping precinct. St Mary's Church spire can be seen in the distance*

31 *The viaducts at Chirk over the River Ceiriog in north-west Shropshire. The earlier of the two was designed by Thomas Telford to carry the Ellesmere Canal and was completed in 1801. The larger of the two bridges was built to carry the Shrewsbury-Chester railway line in 1846-8. Both viaducts are still in use today*

32 *The Wye Forest to the west of the River Severn near Kidderminster lies in Shropshire and Worcestershire. It was a Royal Forest in the Middle Ages, and today has largely been taken over by the Forestry Commission*

33 *Wenlock Edge showing the damaging impact of mechanical quarrying in recent years. The quarried limestone is used largely for road building and construction. In the far distance the distinctive landmark of the Buildwas Power Station cooling towers can been seen*

*34 Prairie farming
on the North
Shropshire Plain
near Newport*

35 Telford New Town

*36 Ironbridge Power
Station was built
in the 1960s to
replace a smaller
generating plant.
The station
dominates the
wooded slopes of
the Ironbridge
Gorge which lies
beyond it*

provided fertile ground for the establishment of new towns. Each unit of new political order needed central places where trade, law and government could take place. The logical focal point where these functions could be safely encouraged lay in the shadows of the walls of scores of new castles founded between 1066 and 1200. The new towns were largely inhabited by people from the surrounding districts, but there is some evidence to suggest that in the first instance Normans or Frenchmen were brought in as settlers. Domesday Book indicates that the greatest concentration of Frenchmen in 1086

41 Montgomery town and castle, showing the regular layout of the town, which was created in the shadow of the new castle (started in 1223). For many centuries Montgomery was a shire capital until local government reorganisation in 1974

was in the Border counties of Cheshire, Shropshire and Herefordshire. There were, for instance, 43 French burgesses in Shrewsbury alone and such a large number does indicate that a deliberate policy of bringing French settlers into urban centres had been adopted; the French burgesses of Shrewsbury accounted for 17 per cent of total recorded population in 1086. Furthermore it is implied that they were exempt from tax.

It should be stressed that most of the new 'towns' were very small, often with only 100 or so burgesses, and sometimes considerably less. Towns ranged in size from less than an acre within the walled area, as at Longtown, Herefordshire, to over 80 acres in the case of Ludlow. Their legal status also varied considerably: some were granted borough charters while others never achieved borough status — they did, however, all have common urban aspirations. Frank Noble, who made a special study of the Border boroughs, identified four phases of borough creation in Herefordshire; these reflect the uneasy consolidation of the Welsh border and the various advances into Wales by the Norman lords. In the first phase, which dates from within a few years of the Conquest, new castles were built at Wigmore and Clifford and the pre-Conquest castles at Hereford and Ewyas Harold were rebuilt. These four castles were intended as bases from which to attack Wales and had boroughs attached to them at an early date. Chepstow, Ludlow, Clun, Bishop's Castle, Caus, Oswestry and Monmouth probably also date from this period.

During the second phase of borough creation, which dates from the late eleventh to the early twelfth century, castles and boroughs were established by lesser Marcher lords. The de Lacys created a borough and castle at Weobley, which can still be identified from its large open market square, although the settlement here does not appear to have been fully defended. The de Lacys also established a new borough beside their castle at Grosmont. At White Castle there are hints of a borough beside the castle, and further south at Trelleck the village has a grid plan indicative of an undeveloped borough. Although there is no documentation of a borough at Dorstone, from the village topography and the castle it seems probable that there was an early borough plantation there as well. It is also possible that the earthwork enclosure adjacent to the castle which incorporates the remarkable Romanesque church at Kilpeck, Herefordshire, dates from this phase.

The third phase dates from the later twelfth century, with the establishment of boroughs at places such as Huntington (between 1174 and 1190) and Hay, at Brecon and in the Black Mountains at the ridge-top and the shrunken site of Longtown (1185-95). The fourth phase dates from the thirteenth century, when we have the consolidation of market boroughs in western Herefordshire at places such as Eardisley in 1233 and Pembridge in 1240. Another of these, Ploughfield, described as a borough in 1273, is today only a hamlet in Preston-on-Wye parish. In Shropshire there was a similar process with attempted town plantations at Baschurch in the late thirteenth century and close by at Ruyton-Eleven-Towns, which was granted borough status in 1308 (Ruyton did not finally lose its municipal status until 1886). Burgage plots can still be identified in the property boundaries which lie along the broad high street running westwards from the church and along the northern extension of the town. There appear to have been several other attempts to graft new towns or, more frequently, new market areas on to existing settlements. Robert Burnell, for instance, attempted to extend Acton Burnell in the late thirteenth century: by 1315 there were 36 burgesses living here, but because of its comparative isolation this embryonic town did not flourish and had been absorbed back into the rural landscape by the later Middle Ages.

Although the vast majority of the borough towns were Anglo-Norman creations, by the later thirteenth century there were attempts by the Welsh to establish towns comparable to those of their English neighbours. Llewellyn ap Gruffydd was proclaimed Prince of Wales in 1258, and in 1267, by the Treaty of Montgomery, Henry III recognised Llewellyn's title and conceded to him the territory of Cedewain. This included much of the area that was to be incorporated into the county of Montgomeryshire in the sixteenth century. Llewellyn proposed to build a castle with a borough at Dolforwyn, a wild site on the upper Severn overlooking Montgomery. The idea met with considerable English opposition and following Edward I's invasion of Wales in 1277 Dolforwyn was besieged and taken, and granted to Roger de Mortimer. With the acquisition of this new territory the Mortimer empire occupied a considerable part of the central Welsh borderland well into Wales; and continuing the Mortimer tradition of borough creation, Newtown (Llanfair Cedewain) was developed.

The creation of the towns of the Welsh Marches is closely related to the persistent westward expansion of the territories of the Marcher lords. Of the many towns in the region created in the late eleventh and early twelfth centuries Brecon illustrates, perhaps more clearly than most, the relationship between the westward advance of the Norman frontier and the planting of towns. By 1110 the army of Bernard de Newmarche had overrun the whole of the Dark Age Welsh princedom of Brycheiniog. In his wake three new towns, Brecon, Builth and Hay, were created. Brecon was planted at the junction of the River Usk with its tributary, the Honddu, draining in from the north.

The first element of the Norman settlement at Brecon appeared on a steep western bluff overlooking the two rivers in the form of a motte and bailey castle constructed in 1092. Outside the north walls of the castle the foundations were laid for the church of St John, a church which later became a priory and is today a cathedral. Facing the site of the castle on the east bank of the Honddu the new town of Brecon appears to have been implanted at the same time as the building of the castle. Traditionally it is believed to have been created by Bernard de Newmarche. Bernard was also the benefactor of the monks at Battle Abbey in Sussex, and gave St John's church to them as well as lands in the town. Bernard himself came from Neufmarche in Normandy, a name whose literal meaning is Newmarket.

We can still see today the elements of the Norman town engraved on the townscape. The centrepiece is the market place, in the form of a triangle which, as so often with successful new towns, was later encroached upon. The oval-shaped defences of the walled borough, once crowned by 10 equally spaced towers, can also be traced. It is believed that stone for the Norman defences was obtained from the Roman fort at Brecon Gaer, which lies three miles west of the town. Today minor changes of level and a curving street pattern that follows the inner line of the walk betray the presence of the former ditch. In the thin parallel backyards of the backstreets of Brecon

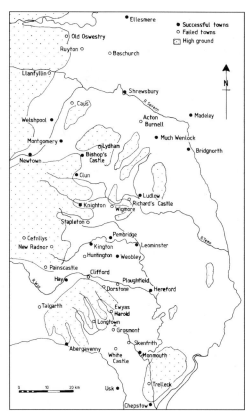

42 Medieval towns in the Welsh Marches

the shapes of the original burgage plots can still be identified. Both Builth and Hay also retain clear indications of their Norman origins in their street plans, and it is reasonable to assume in all three cases that the towns were laid out soon after the building of their castles.

With this consolidation of power by the Marcher lords in the late thirteenth century, the urban geography of the Welsh border was largely complete. There were few attempts at borough creation during the remainder of the Middle Ages and further urbanisation did not occur until the Industrial Revolution. The economic forces which had enabled towns to be created throughout the Borderland had begun to deteriorate in the fourteenth century, and by the time of the creation of Newtown some of the earlier town plantations were already in decline. The truth is that town creation in the Welsh border had gone too far. It had been partly a response to the strategic situation and had partly mirrored the general process of town plantation throughout England in the early Middle Ages. From 1300 onwards, however, the economic tide had turned and whereas previously the climate was right for new and expanding towns, afterwards the position was different and both towns and villages were being abandoned rather than created. Town desertion in the Welsh border country appears to have occurred at a considerably higher level than elsewhere in the country.

43 *The substantial stone remains of Hopton Castle in southern Shropshire sit on a low mound, which appears to be the vestiges of an earlier motte and bailey castle. The keep dates from the twelfth century. Hopton saw bloody action during the Civil War when it was the scene of violent reprisals by the Royalists against a band of Parliamentarians whom they massacred*

The reasons for the success or otherwise of a border town appear to have been linked to the town's ability to change its function from military to economic, and a small minority of new towns enjoyed considerable success during the Middle Ages. A prime example of a successful new town is Ludlow, founded by Roger de Lacy in the late eleventh century. Ludlow was able to combine its military function happily with thriving commercial activity. By the middle of the fourteenth century it was rated as one of the most prosperous towns in England. Monmouth and Chepstow fall into the same category of prosperous regional commercial capitals. Less successful were a line of towns further to the west: Welshpool, Montgomery, Bishop's Castle, Clun, Knighton, Kington and Hay enjoyed only moderate prosperity as minor market towns. Montgomery, however, remained a county town until local government reorganisation in 1974. Oswestry and Clun were both Fitz Allen creations and, despite their size, acted as important centres where Welsh and English cultures were able to meet and mingle. Most of these towns, however, barely outgrew their medieval form, and this can still clearly be seen in their street plans and the lines of their defensive fortifications. Some, of these places, such as Clun, have decayed since the Middle Ages while the basic topography of small market towns such as Pembridge and Weobley appears to have changed hardly at all over the centuries.

Failed boroughs

Today the landscape of the Marches is littered with places that were once granted market charters and burghal rights, and that have since failed completely. A rectangular-shaped field where sheep and cattle now graze, as at Huntington, may be the sole visual evidence of a former market place. Narrow high-hedged fields, as at Richards Castle, mark the plots that attracted the burgesses to a newly founded borough eight centuries ago. Deep lanes and foot paths indicate the lines of former streets; the once formidable castle of a forgotten founding Marcher lord is now no more than an overgrown mound, steep to ascend and defended by brambles, nettles and scree.

Some of the most evocative landscapes in the Borderland have been produced by these once proud and dominant towns. At Caus in the parish of Westbury, in the foothills of the Long Mountain, only a few miles from Shrewsbury, there are the earthworks of a massively fortified town and castle created by the Corbet family. The place name of the new town echoes the name of the Norman homeland from which the founder, Roger Corbet, came — the *Pays de Caux*, which lies to the north of the Seine estuary. Sited on a high ridge, Caus commanded the valley road from Shrewsbury to Montgomery. Today the ruins of an enormous earthwork and stone castle with outer fortifications have to be disentangled from the undergrowth; nothing except earthworks and the odd chunk of masonry remains of the borough. The town was created by Roger Corbet in 1198, and it is recorded that by 1349 there were 58 burgesses living here. In the mid-fifteenth century much of the town was burnt down during a rebellion by Sir Griffith Vaughan; by the time a survey was made of the site in 1521 the castle was recorded as being in 'grete ruyne and decay'. Thus the borough of Caus faded away in the later Middle Ages and now only its earthworks, its place name and a single farm remain. In the words of Maurice Beresford, Caus was like 'a prehistoric monster crushed beneath the weight of its own armour', unable to adjust to the new economic conditions of the later Middle Ages. The great tree-covered motte and bailey and the line of the town ramparts can be clearly identified, and here and there are more subtle remnants of this once locally important town. Tucked behind one of the farm's outbuildings are two great stone buttresses that originally must have reinforced the massive town wall. In the inner bailey of the castle a stone-lined well can still be found, and at the northern entrance tree roots, and the passage of animals through the centuries has revealed part of the town wall over 8ft wide. Prehistoric pottery found underneath the wall here suggests that the town was originally the site of an Iron Age hillfort.

A failed town with a similar history lies further into Wales beyond New Radnor. This town, Cefnllys, was planted within another reoccupied hillfort. The site of Cefnllys stands on a rocky spur 300ft above the wooded gorge of the River Ithon. The Mortimer family built a

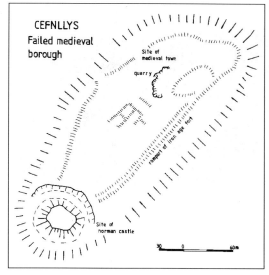

*44a Plan of Cefnllys failed town (see **colour plate 19**)*

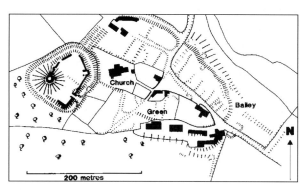

44b Plan of Richard's Castle failed town

101

*45 The castle and shrunken borough at Longtown, just to the
east of the Black Mountains. The medieval castle in the
foreground occupies a massive earthwork fortification.
Beyond the castle the straggling vestiges of the medieval
town can be seen. Abandoned burgage plots of former town
dwellers appear as parallel linear earthworks on the left-
hand side of the principal road*

castle here between 1240 and 1246, at the same time as they constructed other outposts at New Montgomery and Paincastle. It is recorded that in 1332 Cefnllys had 20 burgesses and a survey of 1360 records it as a borough. But this highly exposed settlement had little chance of subsequent success and was already in decline by the time that Edward I led his attack on Wales. By the late fourteenth century there were only 10 burgesses at Cefnllys. Like other border boroughs of its type the earthworks of the actual town are difficult to disentangle. Only a short stretch of street with possible burgage plots can be identified within the ramparts of the Iron Age fort, and like so many of these lost towns it has been fairly extensively plundered for its stone. Like Wigmore and Richards Castle it is dominated by massive motte and castle defences. At the close of the sixteenth century the antiquary Campden described Cefnllys as a 'lonely ruin'. Surprisingly, however, it survived as a rotten borough into the early nineteenth century. In 1832 the parliamentary boundary commissioners' report showed that there were still 16 burgesses there who had the right to return a member of parliament, but they were living in just three farms and one cottage.

Moving south-eastwards we come to Huntington whose borough was created in the late twelfth century as part of a policy of political reprisal. In 1173 after a rebellion against Henry II, the honour of Kington, a nearby planted borough, was suppressed and absorbed into the new Marcher kingdom of Huntington. This was granted to William de Braose and as a result Kington castle was abandoned sometime before 1230 and the government of the lordship moved to Huntington. The outlines of the new borough were sketched out between the castle mound and the church. Ironically Huntington failed to make any real progress and the really successful town in the area was Kington-in-the-Fields, which had been laid out in a valley bottom some distance away from the old borough of Kington. Huntington is today one of the most spectacular of the failed border boroughs occupying as it still does a small territorial enclave of England which projects into Wales; the boundary of the borough is still marked in a conspicuous indentation in the boundary between England and Wales. The earthworks are in the form of the castle ruins and an extended outer bailey marking the town precinct, and the lumps and bumps that remain of the medieval settlement indicate former town houses. Its situation, however, is so essentially rural that it is difficult to imagine that the settlement ever harboured urban ambitions.

Another site where today it is difficult to imagine there ever having been a town is Richards Castle, near Ludlow. This site was important even before the Conquest as a Norman, Richard le Scrob, was given land at Orleton and built a castle at what is now Richard's Castle. By the beginning of the next century a small town known as Richards Castle had developed. Although no trace of a borough charter survives, there is little doubt than an urban community flourished here for some three centuries after the Norman Conquest: a document of 1304 records over 100 burgesses living here. However, like Huntington, Caus and Cefnllys, Richards Castle went into a decline in the later Middle Ages. Today the only remnants of the ancient town are the church of St Bartholomew, noted because of its detached tower, and the outlines of the borough which still survive in the form of earthworks, providing us with one of the most interesting examples of a failed borough anywhere in the Borderland. As in many of the border boroughs there is a triangular green at Richards Castle which marks the site of the former market area. The reasons for its failure are familiar ones: the town's inability to change from a military to a trading community, and its location on an inaccessible high bluff looking eastwards. It was an inappropriate site for a market town relying on the ready access of people and goods. In contrast, Ludlow was well located on a bridging point of the River Teme, and on a major north-south routeway. As Ludlow's fortunes waxed in the later Middle Ages so the commercial fortunes of Richards Castle declined. A new village carrying the name of Richards Castle was created, at a later date, down in the valley on the road leading from Ludlow to Leintwardine. A little to the west, Wigmore occupies a very similar location and although a village survives here, together with its market place, only the enormous earthworks of the castle give some indication that this was the capital of the great medieval Mortimer kingdom.

The castle-dominated settlement was not limited to just urban or proto-urban centres, but was to be seen in small villages as well. For instance, the renowned Romanesque church at Kilpeck lies adjacent to the earthworks of a large castle and at the apex of a rectangular-shaped defended enclosure, now identifiable only in earthwork form. Similarly at More, near Bishop's Castle, the earthworks of a defended deserted village lie immediately to the west of a ringwork castle. The documentary evidence suggests that the settlement here was a post-Conquest creation contemporary with the castle and church. More, which was carved out of the great Saxon manor of Lydham, was granted a charter by Grand Searjentry in the reign of Henry I; this service is described by the nineteenth-century antiquary Eyton as follows:

> The Lord of More, as a Constable of the King's host, to assume the command
> of two hundred foot-soldiers whenever the King of England crossed the Welsh
> Border in hostile array. The said Constable was to march in the vanguard of the
> army, and with his own hands to carry the King's standard.

The topography of the surviving settlement, with the earthworks of the castle at the west end and the church at the east, clearly demonstrates its planned origins. The church has a squat Norman tower, typical of the Clun region, which almost certainly performed a military role during the early Middle Ages.

46 *White Castle, Gwent. The most remote and formidable of Hubert de Burgh's 'Three Castles'. Most of the standing building dates from the thirteenth century when White Castle was in the front line of the English defences against the Welsh leader Llewelyn ap Gruffyd. There appears to have been some form of urban community adjacent to the castle*

Places to visit

Chepstow, Gwent

Chepstow was founded as a frontier town in the later eleventh century at the lowest defensible point on the River Wye, on the border between England and Wales. Soon after his coronation on Christmas Day 1066, William the Conqueror granted the Welsh Kingdom of Gwent (the Marcher lordship of Striguil — from Ystraigyl, meaning 'the bend in the river' in Welsh) to William Fitz Osbern. Fitz Osbern was one of the Conqueror's principal Norman barons and was created Earl of Hereford soon after the Battle of Hastings. Fitz Osbern died in 1071, and his son, Roger of Breteuil, forfeited his lands to the King four years later. Thus the great stone keep at Chepstow can lay claim to be the first masonry castle in Britain, earlier even than the White Tower of the Tower of London. It still dominates the greatly extended castle, which crouches along the crest of the limestone cliff above the swirling waters of the River Wye, presenting an appearance of utter impregnability from the English side of the river. William Marshall, who gained possession of Chepstow in 1189 by marriage, extended the castle considerably. It was Marshal who introduced a feature of contemporary French fortification — the drum tower — into the castles of Wales and the Marches. He built at least four such towers at Chepstow and it is now believed that he was also responsible for the outer gatehouse with its two round towers.

William Marshall died in 1219 and was succeeded by a sequence of sons, the last of whom died in 1245. During this period much new building was undertaken, not only to extend its defences but also to provide elegant accommodation. Two gifts by the king of oak trees are documented for these buildings, the first to the eldest brother, William, in 1228 for work on the 'turris', presumably the hall-keep, the second to the third brother, Gilbert, in 1234. The final major phase of construction was that of Roger Bigod III, Earl of Norfolk, who inherited the Marcher lordship of Striguil in 1270. A series of receivers' accounts for the lordship

47 The huge earthworks and masonry ruins of the castle at Huntington. The castle occupies a small territorial enclave which projects into Wales. During the thirteenth century it formed the apex of a medieval borough, which was never really successful, and was always subsidiary to nearby Kington. In 1403, the Countess of Stafford was ordered to fortify the castle and rebuild a tollgate destroyed by the Welsh; by 1521 the castle was reported to be derelict, except for a tower in which prisoners were kept

indicate that in about 1271-2 he added the tower in front of the west gateway of the barbican; that between 1278-87 he built a hall and kitchen range immediately within the gatehouse of the lower bailey, and that from 1286-93 he further embellished and strengthened the lower bailey by constructing Marten's Tower thus providing a self-contained residence which could be isolated from the rest of the castle. Finally, between 1293-1300, the eastern two-thirds of the keep were heightened.

In the sixteenth century the castle was in the hands of the Earls of Worcester and during the Civil War the fifth Earl held it for the king. In 1645 and again in 1648 the castle fell to Parliamentary forces, the south curtain wall being badly breached. After the war Cromwell himself held the castle, and strengthened the south wall with embrasures for cannon along the top. Such fortifications however were unnecessary as the castle, though garrisoned until 1690, became a prison, Marten's Tower taking its name from one of the executioners of Charles I, Henry Marten, who was imprisoned there for 20 years by Charles II. The castle remained the property of the Dukes of Beaufort until the early twentieth century, and in 1953 was conveyed as a guardianship monument to the Ministry of Public Building and Works. It is now in the care of CADW: Welsh Historic Monuments.

William Fitz Osbern also founded a Benedictine priory a quarter of a mile to the south-east of the castle. All that remains is the nave of the priory church, which was taken over by the town for its parish church after the Dissolution.

The planned town which lies adjacent to the castle basically consists of one elongated road, High Street, then Middle Street, then Bridge Street, down the slope from south-west to north-east between castle and priory, to the river bridge. The town wall (Port Wall), constructed between 1272 and 1278 across the high ground to protect castle, priory and town on the peninsular, largely survives.

Post-medieval Chepstow was important as a river port and as a centre for ship-building and repair. A graving dock was constructed in 1759. The town became a tourist centre in the second half of the eighteenth century as the Wye Valley became one of the most fashionable haunts of the Picturesque traveller (see chapter 10).

48 Clun Castle and town — a place where the English and Welsh met over the centuries to trade and, occasionally, to fight. The town appears to have been planned within the shadow of the massive Fitz Allen Castle. Note the faint traces of a 'pleasance' (ornamental garden) adjacent to the castle

Shrewsbury Castle, Shropshire

Between 1067 and 1069 Roger de Montgomery constructed a large motte and bailey at Shrewsbury in the narrow neck of the loop of the River Severn. The loop of the river is so close here that there are only 300m left to guard. The sixteenth-century Shropshire poet Churchyard said that Shrewsbury Castle was built 'in such a brave plott that it could have espyed a byrd flying in every strete'. Domesday Book records that 'the Earl's castle has taken over 51 dwellings and 50 other buildings are unoccupied'. This represented 40 per cent of the recorded dwellings in Shrewsbury in 1086. This remarkably high number of empty buildings may represent an attempt to create a clear area adjacent to the castle for security reasons, or it might have been caused by an earlier uprising. In 1069 'the Welsh, with the men of Cheshire, laid siege to the king's castle at Shrewsbury aided by the townsmen under Eadric the Wild'. The castle survived the ordeal successfully until the town was relieved, at which point the insurgents burnt down the town and retired. The castle was rebuilt in stone under Henry II, but by the thirteenth century, in common with many other Border Castles, it was in decay. An enquiry of 1255 found that the motte had been undermined by river erosion, a condition attributed to the recent construction of a mill by the Abbot of Shrewsbury. The great tower on the motte collapsed sometime during the 1270s. During his campaign in north Wales (1277–83), Edward I made Shrewsbury the seat of his government and rebuilt the castle. In 1790 Thomas Telford converted the castle, then in ruins, into a residence for Sir William Pulteney: among his additions was Laura's Tower, a red sandstone octagonal structure that overlooks the castle and town. The castle now houses Shrewsbury District Borough's council chamber. (See chapter 10 for further details on Shrewsbury.)

Clun, Shropshire

Clun lies at the heart of one of the least populated parts of the Welsh Marches. The area has been known since the Middle Ages as the Clun Forest, but it is now hardly wooded at all. The famous lines 'Clunton, Clunbury; Clungunford and Clun are the quietest places under the sun' are frequently attributed to A.E. Housman, but they are actually a traditional jingle which he used for a preface to one of his poems in *A Shropshire Lad*. The castle at Clun, which today is a picturesque if somewhat precarious ruin overlooking the little town of Clun and the Clun valley, began life as a motte and bailey. There is a large oval motte, with two baileys, the smaller of which is today used as a bowling green. It was rebuilt in stone in 1195-6 by the Fitz Allens (later Earls of Arundel) after the battle of Radnor, when we hear that Prince Rees had besieged Clun Castle and reduced

49 Bishop's Castle was a medieval borough planted by the bishops of Hereford between the remains of the castle (top) and the church of St John the Baptist (bottom). The town is still largely contained within its medieval layout, with the parallel lines of the burgage plots still surviving in the form of property boundaries

it to ashes. To the right of the river on low-lying ground below the castle is an unusual complex of earthworks, representing the remains of a medieval 'pleasance' or pleasure garden and an attached complex of square moated enclosure which would have consisted of one or more pavilions ranged around a central formal garden. The adjacent banks and depressions represent former fishponds, which like the 'pleasance' provided for the needs of the nearby castle. This unusual survival emphasises the role of the medieval castle as a private residence as well as a military stronghold, in this case belonging to one of the great baronial families of medieval England. The ruined castle is thought to have been the inspiration for Walter Scott's Garde Dolourense in *The Betrothed* (1825), where the scene is set in the Welsh Marches.

There was also an attempt to stimulate a town community here and the grid layout of the town clearly demonstrates its deliberately planned origins. This Norman settlement lies to the north of the River Clun on a site that was laid out on waste ground — the ancient centre of Clun appears to have been around the church of St George on the opposite side of the river.

The attempt at urbanisation here was only partially successful, for although Clun was an important meeting place for Welsh and English, its vulnerability and remoteness meant that it never really flourished. This is reflected in a borough rental of about 1300, which records

50 An oblique air photograph of the 'classic' medieval planned town of Ludlow emphasises the essentially rural nature of Marcher Towns. The castle (centre left) and town walls are clearly visible, as is the regularly laid out street pattern

that some 60 tenements were lying empty and worth nothing.

The church has a squat Norman tower, typical of the region, but may have been added to an earlier Norman cruciform church, presumably itself sitting on the site of an earlier Minster church. The bridge which crosses the River Clun and joins the ancient centre with the Norman plantation is a medieval saddleback with five arches. Otherwise the town is not particularly well endowed with historic buildings, although the splendid Holy Trinity Hospital, a group of seventeenth-century almshouses with a chapel, is well worth visiting.

Bishop's Castle, Shropshire

Not far from Clun is Bishop's Castle, another castle town which has similarly enjoyed only modest success. The castle was erected by the Bishop of Hereford in 1127 in the western part of the 18,000-acre parish of Lydbury North. The latter is now a small village three miles to the south-east of Bishop's Castle. The castle lay at the top of a hill with a long central road running down to the church of St John Baptist, originally a chapel belonging to Lydbury North. The town was developed between the church and castle. The solid squat form of the Norman church tower, a characteristic of several churches in this area, suggests that it played a role in the defence of the community. Ironically, the castle which gave its name to the town has all but disappeared and doesn't feature in the modern townscape of this delightful little settlement except in the form of a bowling green. Apart from this, Bishop's Castle has hardly changed in shape or size since it was created, and until 1967 could boast of being the smallest borough in England. However it still maintains its other claim to fame, The Three Tuns, a seventeenth-century inn which has a widespread reputation for its home-brewed beer.

Ludlow, Shropshire

In contrast, a few miles to the south-east of Bishop's Castle lies Ludlow, a Norman castle town whose plantation was an unqualified success. Ludlow Castle, which was begun by Roger de Lacy in 1085, was constructed in local sandstone. The castle soon acquired a remarkable round Romanesque chapel in the middle ward — part of the improvements made in the 1130s by Sir Joyce de Dinan, an enemy and rival claimant to the Lacy castle. The two turbulent decades of his occupancy and the heroic recovery by the Lacys of their home are described in graphic detail in the thirteenth-century romance *Geste of Fulk Fitzwarine.*

Subsequently five generations of Mortimers lived there, and it was probably they who were responsible for the impressive fourteenth-century buildings of the north front.

The castle later became the seat of the Lord President of the Council of the Welsh Marches. The most illustrious of the Lord residents was Queen Elizabeth's favourite, Sir Henry Sidney, father of Philip. The building of the gatehouse on the north side in 1581 was part of the extensive architectural improvements carried out under his tenancy. Originally the entrance to the castle had been through the Norman keep where its infilled outline can still be clearly traced. During the seventeenth century the castle became a cultural centre. Samuel Butler (1612-80) wrote part of his satire, *Hudibras*, in his rooms above the castle gateway during the time he was steward to the Earl of Carbery (1661-2). Milton presented his pastoral entertainment *Comus* at Ludlow in 1643 as a spectacular last act to close the castle's long active history. Although the castle was not seriously damaged in the Civil War, almost immediately afterwards the defences were dismantled. Vandalism in the reign of George I, when the lead was removed from the roofs, contributed to its decay which continued throughout the nineteenth century.

Ludlow town, which is laid out adjacent to the castle, has long been recognised as a classic example of Norman town plantation. In his book *New Towns of the Middle Ages* (1964) Maurice Beresford demonstrated how a large number of English, Welsh and French towns were deliberately laid out during the Middle Ages, their plans still reflecting their origins. Over half a century earlier W.H. St John Hope had drawn attention to the planned nature of Ludlow's layout. Even earlier, however, Mr Hudson Turner, in his book *Some Account of Domestic Architecture in England from Edward I to Richard II* (1853), wrote a description which could have been based entirely on observations of Ludlow:

> There is, however, still another class of towns which were entirely founded in the Middle Ages, built from their foundations on a new site for some specific object, which have not been specifically noticed. These towns are more regular and symmetrical than most modern towns, and are built on an excellent scientific plan, combining very close packing with great convenience for individuals, while the principal streets are wide, open and straight, crossing each other at right angles only. There are always two parallel streets at a short distance one from the other and connected by short streets at frequent intervals; between these principal streets and also in parallel lines are narrow streets or lanes corresponding to the modern mews and employed for the same purpose: by this means each plot of ground for building on is of a uniform size and shape, a parallelogram with one end facing a principal street and another a lane. In some towns each building plot, or when built upon each house, was also divided by a narrow passage or court leading from the principal street to the lane, serving as a water course and surface drain. Sometimes when a large house was required two plots were thrown together and the passage omitted; in some towns these narrow passages were not used at all.

The town of Ludlow was created by the de Lacys in the eleventh century, immediately after the castle had been built. The new town lay in the parish of Stanton Lacy, and ancient parish boundaries to the north of Ludlow clearly demonstrate how the land was divided between St Peter's church, Stanton Lacy, and St Lawrence's, Ludlow, and later St Leonard's, Ludlow. Up until the late nineteenth century part of the keep of Ludlow Castle still lay within Stanton Lacy parish.

The wide High Street which extends eastwards from the castle gates was laid down in the twelfth century and formed the original market place. The terraced shops at the eastern end of the High Street were originally temporary market stalls, but were effectively 'fossilised' when they were converted into more permanent structures. Such encroachments rarely have any land attached to them and as in this case often give the appearance of having grown out of the street along which they sit. Old Street does not conform to Ludlow's regular grid plan and may pre-date the town. It could have been the original north-south routeway that crossed the River Teme some 200m to the east of Ludford Bridge, the present crossing point. Ludford Bridge lies close to the medieval St John's Hospital, which dates from the fifteenth century.

Mill Street and Broad Street have a slightly bow-shaped street form, characteristic of medieval town plantations. Such a design provided the maximum amount of market area within the new town as well as enabling control of the narrow entrances and exits, where tolls could be exacted. West of Mill Street the plan has been considerably altered, but a narrow lane, originally known as Christ Croft, ran parallel with it towards the river. This was part of the original road plan, and on its western side sits the twelfth-century chapel of St Thomas of Canterbury. There is a strip of ground between this lane and Mill Street extending north and south, which itself is now divided into gardens and was apparently one of the original town streets. The abandonment of streets like this was a consequence of the addition of the new outer castle bailey at the end of the twelfth century. The new bailey cut off the western end of the High Street, making redundant those roads immediately to the south of the castle.

St Lawrence, the largest parish church in Shropshire, was given a block of land to itself in the original town grid, to the north-east of the High Street. The present church was built between 1300-1500 by the wealthy wool merchants of the town and by the Palmers Guild. The imposing church and tower cannot be fully appreciated from within the town, and later medieval infilling in the High Street has completely obscured the fine southern porch. However, when approached from the north, it is the church along with the castle that dominates Ludlow's skyline. St Lawrence's has many fine architectural features including a set of late medieval misericords depicting scenes from everyday life.

There is no doubt that the plantation at Ludlow was successful, for by 1377 there were over 1000 taxable householders here. Not only had there been a considerable movement of population to the new town, but Ludlow had also taken over the important north-south route previously controlled by Stanton Lacy. Ludlow maintained its prosperity throughout the Middle Ages, and later many of the fine medieval timber houses were encased in brick. As the majority of standing buildings are ostensibly Georgian the overall impression that Ludlow gives today is that of a fashionable late eighteenth-century town; indeed there were plans at one stage to turn it into a Salopian version of Bath. Ludlow is in many respects the most pleasant and best preserved of Border towns. None of the other new Border castle towns was as successful as Ludlow, and although places such as Hay on Wye,

51 The striking earthworks of a fine motte and bailey castle at Culmington, surrounded by the ridge and furrow of medieval agriculture. The castle earthworks appear to sit on top of the ridge and furrow, suggesting that it occupied an area of arable cultivation in the early Middle Ages. The rectangular hollow of a medieval fishpond can be seen on the left-hand side of the photograph

Knighton and Montgomery enjoyed a modicum of prosperity, today they carry an air of detached obscurity compared to the hustle and bustle of Ludlow.

Hubert de Burgh's Three Towns, Gwent

Among the undulating hill country between the main valleys of the Wye and Usk in the former county of Monmouthshire we find the remains of a number of failed urban experiments. The construction of White Castle began in 1184-5 in the parish of Llantilio Crossenny. White Castle is traditionally associated with Gwyn ap Gwaethfoed, who is said to have been a native princeling of the region. The name White Castle was in use as early as the thirteenth century, and must refer to the plaster coating of the castle walls, of which fragmentary remnants can still be seen. The castle stands about one mile from the village of Llantilio Crossenny on the summit of a high west-facing hill. This hill was the strategic centre of the region enclosed by the northward bend of the River Monnow.

In 1201 King John granted White Castle and the castles at Grosmont and Skenfrith to Hubert de Burgh, an officer in the royal service who later distinguished himself in a prolonged defence of Chinon during wars with France. In 1205 the castles were transferred to William de Braose, a local magnate who already held the neighbouring lordships of Brecknock and Abergavenny. William fell from royal favour and lost his lands in 1207, but his son regained White Castle and other neighbouring strongholds during the ensuing confusion and civil war at the end of King John's reign. In 1219 the king's court once more confirmed that the three castles belonged to Hubert de Burgh, then at the height of his power as effective Regent of England.

Eventually Hubert de Burgh fell from royal favour and was forced to surrender the three castles in 1232. Their custody was granted to Peter des Rivaux, a nephew of the Bishop of Winchester, who subsequently acquired a key position in the royal administration, but who fell from power in 1234, when the three castles once more reverted to the Crown. The castles were then placed in charge of a royal officer, Waleran the German. Matthew Paris, the medieval historian who recorded the fall of the once all-powerful Hubert de Burgh and his surrender of the three Monmouthshire castles, states that these were the most prized of his possessions, on which he had spent immense sums of money.

Waleran was still in charge of the three castles in 1244, when a new hall, buttery and pantry were erected at White Castle. In 1254 the three castles were granted to Henry III's elder son (later King Edward I). In 1267 they were transferred to his younger brother Edmund Crouchback, Earl of Lancaster. It was in this period that a serious threat to the western Marches developed. Llewellyn ap Gruffydd, the Welsh ruler who had succeeded to a united principality, which has been built up by his grandfather Llewellyn Fawr, moved on to the offensive during the English civil war between Henry III and Simon de Montfort. The Welsh tenants of the Border lordships rose in 1262 and a report to the King in the following spring records the loss of many of the English-held castles, stating that the frontier then held by Llewellyn lay only a league and a half beyond Abergavenny. It became clear that should that castle fall, White Castle would constitute the next line of defence. The Lord Edward is known to have been raising money in that year for 'certain urgent business' of the King in the Marches. Even when the English civil war was over and peace returned the threat remained: the Treaty of Montgomery (1267) recognised the Welsh conquests, and Abergavenny remained a frontier fortress. Only in 1277 was English control in this area finally re-established. The campaign of that year forced Llewellyn to surrender his conquests and the subsequent advance and the subjection of the Welsh a few years later robbed White Castle of its primary strategic role.

Even after the Edwardian conquest of Wales, White Castle remained an administrative and financial centre. It was the place at which levies for the Scottish wars were mustered and where the rents and dues from the extensive manor were collected. White Castle continued in the possession of the Earldom, and later Duchy, of Lancaster until it was taken over by Henry IV. Thereafter the castle appears to have been neglected and was described as roofless and derelict in a survey made in the sixteenth century. Medieval records refer to 'town merchants' at White Castle, but the small town failed to develop and has left no trace apart from earthworks in the field adjacent to the castle, which conceal the house-plots of its former burgesses. Today White Castle is a delightfully lonely place — the rather menacing calm which prevails provides an appropriate memorial to its turbulent history.

Skenfrith lies on the west bank of the River Monnow, on a site which commanded one of the then main routes from England to Wales, and a small town appears to have been created about 1200. The borough of Skenfrith scarcely added to the primary elements of church and castle in the centuries after its foundation. Despite its favourable valley-based

52 *The Norman keep of Goodrich Castle. The original entrance was at first floor level. The keep was probably built during the war between King Stephen and the Empress Matilda from 1138-53 (The Anarchy), when the area was disputed between the Earls of Gloucester and Hereford. The castle looks out over a crossing point of the River Wye, and is close to the line of the Roman road from Ariconium to Blestium (Monmouth). The village of Walford across the river takes its name from the Welsh ford, possibly an indication of the survival of a British community into the late Saxon period*

location, Skenfrith probably failed to take off as a market town because of competition from its neighbours on the Monnow, Monmouth and Grosmont.

Scarcely three miles above Skenfrith on the Monnow, the ruined keep of the castle at Grosmont stands perched on a precipitous river cliff. Castle building had started at Grosmont in Henry II's reign, about the same time as the foundation of the other strong points of the defensive triangle. As the head of a Marcher lordship, Grosmont had acquired the right to hold markets and fairs; its status as a borough lapsed only in 1860. It is possible to recognise in Grosmont all the basic elements of the medieval townscape. Between the castle and the church lies a rather forlorn market place and a nineteenth-century market hall. The parish church of St Nicholas bears witness to the declining population and prosperity of Grosmont over the centuries. Most of the church building dates from between 1200 and 1400 and its elaborate cruciform plan and fine octagonal tower suggests a busy and prosperous settlement here. However, for centuries St Nicholas has been too big for the dwindling population of Grosmont, which since the fifteenth century has found sufficient accommodation for its ecclesiastical needs in the chancel and has used the abandoned nave as a graveyard. Around the market place the cottages stand on narrow rectangular strips of ground, the burgage plots which were sketched out early in the thirteenth century when Hubert de Burgh established his new town. Some of these plots lost their buildings long ago and are now used as allotments.

Montgomery, Powys

Shortly after the Norman Conquest Roger de Montgomery, who had been left in Normandy as co-regent, received grants of large tracts of territory in Sussex and in

Shropshire. Roger was created the Earl of Shrewsbury, where the castle already established by the Conqueror in 1069 became his principal seat. Roger came from Sainte Foy de Montgomery in the department of Calvados in Normandy. Sometime between 1070-4 Roger built a castle in what was then the Shropshire hundred of Witentreu (whose name which may survive in Whittery Farm and Whittery Bridge in Chirbury parish), and named it after his ancestral home in Normandy. This appears not to have been on the site of the present castle, but it has been argued it lay at Hen Domen one mile north of the town, where there is a motte and bailey castle. Any reference to Montgomery prior to 1223 may therefore refer to this site, known as the Domen (the Old Mound), and not to the present castle. However, the site of Domen has a number of disadvantages as the location of a major early Norman fortification and it may yet transpire that the site of the early Montgomery Castle lies close to or even underneath modern Montgomery.

Earl Roger died in 1094 and was succeeded by his son Hugh. During Hugh's tenure the castle was sacked in 1095 by the Prince of Powys. Hugh was killed in Anglesey in a battle against the Norwegians in 1098 and was succeeded by his elder brother, Robert. Robert sided with Duke Robert of Normandy against his brother Henry I, and as a result was deprived of his estates in 1102. After a turbulent career, he died as Henry's prisoner in Corfe Castle in about 1131. The castle at Montgomery was then granted to Baldwin de Boulers, whose son, Stephen, and grandsons, Robert and Baldwin, succeeded him. The lordship was eventually sold to Thomas de Erdington, of Erdington (Warwickshire), in 1214-15 and although this sale was confirmed by King John he handed the lordship to Gwenwynwyn, Prince of Powys, in 1216. Gwenwynwyn was almost immediately driven out by Llewellyn ap Iorwerth (Llewellyn the Great), Prince of Gwynedd.

In the autumn of 1223 the royal army under Henry III, which had relieved the de Braose castle of Builth from siege by Llewellyn ap Iorwerth, advanced through Hereford, Leominster and Shrewsbury to Montgomery, where it arrived on 30 September, the eve of the young King Henry's sixteenth birthday. The chronicler Matthew Paris wrote that it was at this point that the young Henry III was shown, probably by Hubert de Burgh, 'A suitable spot for the erection of an impregnable castle' on the high rock a mile south of Hen Domen. Orders had already been given to the chief forester of Shropshire to admit the King's carpenters into Shirlett Forest for the purpose of making brattices, or wooden palisades, to fortify Montgomery 'when the need shall arise . . .'. Orders were also issued for the dispatch of 20 miners from the Forest of Dean to work on the new castle. By November work was sufficiently advanced for the King to refer to his 'new castle of Montgomery' and to make arrangements for mass to be said in its chapel. A castle erected so swiftly can only have been of timber, and the purpose of the autumn building campaign of 1223 must have been to erect a temporary castle which could subsequently be replaced by a stone one. In 1224-6 £2000 was spent on the castle, including the wages of the garrison and the cost of clearing the surrounding area of trees and undergrowth.

On 27 April 1228, the King granted the castle to Hubert de Burgh for life, with 200 marks (about £130) a year for its upkeep. The still uncompleted castle was attacked by the Welsh prince Llewellyn ap Iorwerth in August, but he failed to take the castle. Llewellyn failed again in a subsequent assault in the summer of 1231, though on this occasion he did succeed in burning the new town which had been laid out below the castle. The castle was again attacked without success by Dafydd ap Llewellyn in 1245.

In 1229 Hubert received a further grant of £166 13s 4d towards 'enclosing' the castle. The work probably included 'the new bailey running from the road to Bedewin [i.e. Cedewain] to the castle'. This new bailey was most likely the complex outworks which lie between the present farm building on the site and the middle ward. In the autumn of 1223 'The Tower' was roofed in lead, probably marking the completion of the castle, but by then it was no longer Hubert's. In the previous year, when Hubert lost the King's favour, he also lost Montgomery together with his other Marcher castles. In 1249 a survey listed the castle 'within le donjon' and a number of brattices, together with chapel, granary, stables, penthouses 'which cover the timber without the five brattices', a tower outside the gate, the house of the arblaster, or crossbow master, and a guest-house.

Llewellyn ap Iorwerth had died in 1240 and much of his work for the unity of Wales was undone by the treaty of Woodstock in 1247, but his grandson Llewellyn ap Gruffydd reversed the course of events. The Treaty of Montgomery, confirmed by the King at Montgomery on 19 September 1267, marks the high water mark of Llewellyn's fortunes. This treaty secured the King's acceptance of his considerable territorial gains and of his title Prince of Wales. He also formally recognised his status as feudal lord over most of the smaller independent Welsh rulers.

In 1272 Prince Rupert had ascended the throne as King Edward I. The first few months of the new reign brought new trouble in the Marches. Llewellyn ap Gruffydd started to build a stone castle at Abermule, four miles south-west of Montgomery. On 15 June 1273 he was ordered to stop this work; he felt strong enough to ignore this command and it was not until 1277 that the English attacked and captured the new castle. It was called Dolforwyn, and sat on a commanding hilltop high above the left bank of the Severn at Abermule. All this led to a strengthening of the defences of the town and castle at Montgomery, by replacing the wooden palisade around the town with a stone wall in 1279-80. With the Edwardian conquest of Wales, Montgomery lost its importance as a frontier fortress, and the centre of castle building transferred to north Wales. In 1299 Montgomery was granted to Margaret, the second wife of Edward I, but was transferred to the Prince of Wales in 1301.

The antiquary John Leland, whose tours in Wales extended from 1536-9, visited Montgomery on more than one occasion. He observed, which he said had been 'defloriched by Owen Glindour', that 'great ruines of the waulle yet apere ad vestigia of gates thus cawlyd, Kedewen Gate, Chyrbyry Gate, Arthur's Gate, Kery Gate. In the waulls yet remayne broken towerets, of the wiche the white towre is now most notable.' But he speaks of the castle itself as 'now a late re-edified'. This 're-edification' was due to the energy of Rowland Lee, Bishop of Coventry and Lichfield and President of the Council of the Marches in Wales from 1534-43. The castle site was later occupied by a brick-built mansion house which was home to the Herbert family. This fine building, which enjoyed an unrivalled view over the Vale of Montgomery, was destroyed after the Civil War in 1649. The poet John Donne was a lifelong friend of Lady Magdalen Herbert and was staying at the house in 1613 when he wrote his poem, *The Primrose, being at Montgomery Castle*. Montgomery Castle was an overgrown ruin until 1960, when the Welsh Office undertook a vigorous programme of clearance and restoration. The site is in the care of Welsh Historic Monuments (CADW) and is open to the public.

7 The early Church in the Marches

The late Saxon Church

At the time of the Norman Conquest, the Church in the Marches was relatively weak. The scale of Anglo-Saxon monasticism was limited, there were few religious houses in the Marches, and the process of parish church creation, which in other parts of the country was well advanced, was still in its infancy in the Borderlands. The degree of survival of Romano-British Christianity in the Marches is difficult to determine. It is clear, however, that Anglo-Saxon Christianity began to penetrate the region in the seventh century. A number of important ecclesiastical centres were founded, possibly sited close to already existing religious establishments. In addition to the cathedral at Hereford, there were two very important monastic institutions in the region, one in Shropshire at Much Wenlock and one in Herefordshire, at Leominster. The history of these two ecclesiastical centres runs in parallel. Both appear in the records for the first time in the middle of the seventh century, both were endowed with extensive estates, which may well have incorporated Romano-British or sub-Roman territorial elements. During the later Saxon period both were involved in ambitious programmes of land colonisation and were active in the creation of subsidiary parish churches. Both, too, were afflicted first by Danish and then by periodic Welsh attacks.

Early in the eleventh century there was an attempt to revitalise the monastery at Leominster by Earl Leofric and his wife Godiva, but by the middle of the century it had been 'dissolved for its Sins'. Indeed, the Anglo-Saxon Chronicle for 1046 recorded that

> in this year Earl Sweyne marched into Wales . . . when he was on his homeward way he had the Abbess of Leominster fetched to him and kept her as long as he pleased, and then let her go home.

Nonetheless the secular importance of Leominster is recorded in Domesday Book as one of the largest manors in England; it consisted of some 80 hides divided into six scattered manorial units, undoubtedly reflecting the wealth of the monastery. A new Benedictine priory was established here when Henry I granted the manor of Leominster to Reading Abbey in 1153. The nave of the great priory church, which still serves as Leominster's parish church, was consecrated in 1130. At Wenlock the state and status of the monastery during the early part of the eleventh century is far from clear, although it retained its extensive estates in south Shropshire and Herefordshire. In 1066 Wenlock seems to have been operating as a typical Borderland minster church, with an extensive parish worked by a number of peripatetic canons who followed their own particular rules. Roger de Montgomery established a Cluniac house (a daughter house of the great French abbey at Cluny) at Wenlock between 1079 and 1082, when he granted most of the lands of the former Saxon minster to

53 A watercolour drawing of the church of St Milburgh at Stoke St Milborough by the Reverend E. Williams, 1791. The church here created a considerable number of daughter chapelries in the late Anglo-Saxon period, including that at Heath

the new establishment. Roger asked the abbot of Cluny in Burgundy for monks to house the established monastery and a number of monks from the Cluniac house at La Chairté sur Loire were sent to Wenlock in around 1080. The French monks supervised the construction of a new church at Wenlock with a large triple apse at the east end, similar to that at Cluny.

There were other minster churches which catered for the pastoral needs of large parishes in the late Saxon period including Bromfield, Morville and Stanton Lacy in Shropshire, and Bromyard, Hereford, Withington and Moreton in Herefordshire. Minster churches at Chirbury, Maesbury and Oswestry also performed a similar role. Chirbury manor had two churches, one of which was St Michael's in Chirbury itself. The other was a daughter chapelry at Church Stoke, which now lies on the Welsh side of the Border. 'Stoke' is a place name normally applied to daughter churches or chapels that were dependent upon a mother church. Chirbury parish was originally very large, constituting almost the whole Domesday hundred of Witentreu. Such extensive parishes were commonplace in the western part of the Marches prior to the Conquest. Writing of Clun before 1086 the antiquary Eyton noted, 'Here was one of those great Saxon foundations whose parishes we hardly venture to define for fear of falling short of reality'. Such parishes covered large tracts of forest and open heathland on the edge of the Welsh massif. Subsequent to the Conquest Chirbury founded other chapels at Montgomery, Snead, Forden and Hyssington. As we shall see, this was a process followed elsewhere in the Borderland.

In addition to places where churches were specifically recorded in Domesday Book such as Shrewsbury, which is attributed with five churches, priests without churches were also recorded in a considerable number of Border manors. It is assumed that such a reference implies the existence of a pre-Conquest church or chapel. Even so, in the case of Shropshire, out of a total of 630 entries in the Domesday survey, only 50 churches are recorded, while in Herefordshire, out of 313 places recorded, only 41 had priests or churches attributed to them in 1086. Even given the relatively immature parochial structure in the Borderlands, it would seem unlikely that as few as 10 per cent of settlements had some permanent form of place of worship. It is clear that much information is hidden in the blanket assessments of Domesday Book, where large tracts of land containing many settlements are often bundled together for the sake of administrative convenience. It becomes even clearer that this is a considerable underestimate when we look at those churches which contain elements of late Saxon architecture. Indeed outside the *burhs* the most important visible Saxon legacy in the Marches is that group of churches which were built before the Norman Conquest. There is a

54 Christ's entry into Jerusalem as depicted on the unique mid-twelfth-century Norman tympanum at Aston Eyre

remarkable assemblage of such churches in south Shropshire — these include St Peter's, Diddlebury, St Giles's, Barrow, and St Andrew's, Wroxeter. The most notable of these, however, is St Peter's at Stanton Lacy in the Corve Dale. In the case of St Eata's, Atcham, the church not only contains Anglo-Saxon architecture, but it is known that the historian Ordericus Vitalis was baptised there in 1075, even though there is no church recorded at Atcham in 1086.

The new Norman Church

The Normans came to England not only as conquerors but also as latter-day missionaries. The Conquest itself had been perceived as a holy war by the Normans, blessed by the Pope. In return for papal support William had agreed to reform the English Church, and after his victory at Hastings he sent the Pope the banner of the defeated English King Harold. The transformation of the church in England by William the Conqueror was an important feature of the Norman takeover. The establishment of a new church securely in Norman hands was meant as a demonstration of Norman power. Therefore the massive transfer of land following the Norman Conquest was accompanied by the refounding of monasteries such as Wenlock and the creation of a new Benedictine abbey at Shrewsbury by Roger de Montgomery. Other Border barons followed suit and founded new monastic establishments at places such as Wigmore and Abbey Dore, while minsters such as Chirbury were refounded as monasteries or priories. The second stage of monastic foundation in the Marches was the most important. All the new houses were established within a few miles of existing communication routes, normally in wooded regions that were just being opened up for cultivation. The new foundations were granted large estates in the Marches and became some of the principal landholders in the region. These monasteries helped to meet some of the needs which arose as the result of the transformation of the Saxon Church. The old minsters had served scattered chapels in huge parishes, and they also provided hospitality along the main routes and in centres of local government. Both the abbey at Buildwas and Shrewsbury's dependent cell at Morville were expressly founded with an obligation to provide hospitality. There seems to have been a similar obligation at Bromfield, where a dependent cell of Gloucester Abbey replaced an older collegiate establishment in the early years of Henry II's reign.

When they arrived the Normans did not like what they saw of the established Anglo-Saxon Church and they immediately set about its reformation. Quite apart from its administrative structure they disliked the archaic Roman liturgy, the Anglo-Saxon

118

architecture and its incomprehensible learning. Initially the Normans also had little respect for the English saints, of whom Archbishop Lanfranc wrote:

> These Englishmen among whom we are living have set up for themselves certain saints whom they revere. But sometimes when I turn over in my mind their own accounts of whom they were, I cannot help having doubts about the validity of their sanctity.

At Evesham Abbey Abbot Walter (1077-1104) burned the saints' bones to test their authenticity; only those that survived were deemed to be genuine. The hostility towards the English saints did not, however, survive the first generation of Norman clerics: the writings of contemporary chroniclers did much to re-establish the reputation of the most famous English and Celtic saints and the Church began to appreciate the economic importance of their relics in attracting pilgrims.

William the Conqueror's attitude to his English bishops was the same as his attitude to his English secular leaders — he needed men in place he could trust. He therefore delayed only a few years before undertaking a radical re-staffing of the English Church, and, prompted by clerical involvement in the northern risings, William set about the systematic replacement of the upper sections of the Anglo-Saxon Church hierarchy. So complete was the eventual foreign 'takeover' that William of Malmesbury, writing about 1125, claimed that:

> England has become a residence for foreigners and the property of aliens. At the present time there is no English earl, nor bishop nor abbot; strangers all, they pray upon the riches and vitals of England.

In the case of the See of Hereford, however, there was no dramatic change in leadership, for in 1060 Edward the Confessor had already installed a French bishop there — Walter of Lorraine, chaplain to Edward's wife, Queen Edith. In 1079 he was succeeded by a fellow countryman Robert Lorraine (Losinga), who was responsible for the rebuilding of the cathedral in the new Norman style. The policy of appointing Norman bishops and abbots in England and drafting monks from Normandy was accompanied by a strong Norman influence on English architecture. Despite the fact that many English churches had been rebuilt in the tenth or early eleventh centuries, the Normans considered Anglo-Saxon architecture inferior and missed no opportunity to construct new buildings. Almost inevitably, as soon as a Norman prelate had taken charge of an English see or monastery, work on a new church began. Such was the scale of rebuilding started in the eleventh century that it prompted a contemporary, Raoul Glaber, to write in another context: 'One would have thought that the world was shaking itself to cast off its old age and was clothing itself in a white robe of churches.' The Conquest presented an opportunity to start afresh, and with the arrival of the new school of Norman Romanesque, these elements combined to produce one of the great periods in English architectural history.

Worcester was one of the very few cathedrals to retain an English prelate and some at least of its English customs; nevertheless the cathedral was rebuilt. Wulfstan had survived the political upheavals and ecclesiastical reforms associated with the Norman Conquest, and had been bishop for over 20 years before he turned his attention to any major building work. The Worcester Annals (compiled in the early fourteenth century) state: '1084. The beginning of the work of Worcester Minster by St Wulfstan.'

The circumstances surrounding the new work are detailed in a charter issued by the bishop in 1089. It reads:

> I Wulfstan, by the grace of God, pontiff of the church of Worcester, desiring to enlarge the monastery of the holy Mother of God, Mary, built in the episcopal see by my predecessor of pious memory, that is by blessed Oswald — to enlarge it with greater honour and dignity, not only in the building and adoring of the church, but indeed also of the monks serving God there, I have sought to enrich it by an augmentation of property.

The charter indicates that Wulfstan on his appointment to the see in 1062 had founded a small community for whom the old cathedral buildings were probably quite adequate. However, after the Conquest he had set about reforming it according to the conventions of Lanfranc's wider reform movement. By 1070 the size of the community had increased to nearly 50 monks, which must have rendered the old buildings practically unusable. St Oswald's church of St Mary was to be replaced by the new building to which the dedication was transferred. By May of 1089, the new building was sufficiently far advanced for the monks to move into it.

William of Malmesbury gives further historical information about the state of the works around 1089 and, perhaps more interestingly, provides an insight into Wulfstan's own views about what he was doing. This information he derived, as he says, from Nicholas, who was an eyewitness at the time, and who became prior of Worcester in about 1113. William writes that

> when the work of the main church, which he had begun from the foundations, had advanced to that stage of growth that now the monks might move into it, the old church which blessed Oswald had built was ordered to be unroofed and destroyed.

William goes on to record that Wulfstan

> yet then completed the new church, and you could not easily find the ornament that did not decorate it, so marvellous was it in single details and singular in all parts.

The move into the new church in 1089 was accompanied by the removal of the relics from the old church of St Mary and their reinstatement in the new. The most important of these relics were those of St Oswald, and William of Malmesbury records that Wulfstan contributed 72 silver marks towards embellishing the shrine which contained them and other relics. Worcester was the earliest major church to be rebuilt after the Conquest in the Severn valley. Richard Gem has pointed out that the main source of inspiration for the new cathedral at Worcester lies in what had been built in the previous decade at Christchurch and St Augustine's, Canterbury. In turn Worcester, as the foremost Romanesque building in the area, influenced other new churches in the Marches such as Great Malvern Priory (founded *c.*1085), the abbey church at Gloucester (begun 1089) and the great abbey church at Tewkesbury (founded in the early twelfth century).

New parishes

In the century and a half following the Norman Conquest the process of parish creation continued at a rapid pace. This process was in some cases initiated by monasteries, in others by large wealthy mother churches. Typical of this process was the minster church at Morville in Shropshire, which according to Domesday Book was the only church in the whole of the Saxon hundred of Alnostreu. In the late Saxon period it had been served by eight canons, who were working over the whole hundred. In the century following the Conquest, new chapels were planted in Morville's territory, at Billingsley, Oldbury, Taseley, and Aston Eyre, all before 1140.

The latter chapel contains a remarkable tympanum showing Christ's entry into Jerusalem. This work is considered by many to be one of the finest pieces of Norman sculpture in the whole of the Marches. Further chapels were founded in Morville parish, at Aldenham, Underton, and Astley Abbots. The latter was endowed with 'assart' land, indicating that chapel creation was in some instances associated with woodland clearance. The term 'assart' or 'essart', comes from the Old French *essarter*, which literally means 'to grub up', but was extensively applied in the early Middle Ages to land which had been cleared of wood and scrub in order that it could be cultivated. It is commonly found as a field or place name in the Marches, often in marginal areas. The original chapel at Bridgnorth Castle, too, was dependent upon Morville. Although all traces of the chapels at Underton and Aldenham have disappeared, along with the hamlets which they served, the rest of these chapels all emerged later as full parish churches.

In many other large parishes there was a similar burst of activity. St Mary's church at Shawbury founded chapels at Acton Reynald, Moreton Corbet, Grinshill, and Great Wytheford. A certificate of Bishop Roger de Clinton dated 1140 tells of the time when these manors were without chapels and that he himself had consecrated three of them. In the more hilly districts chapels were planted along river valleys and a line of such chapels, later to become parish churches, follows the county boundary between Herefordshire and Shropshire along the Teme valley at Bedstone, Bucknell, Stowe and Llanfair Waterdine.

A considerable number of these early medieval chapels simply disappeared in the late Middle Ages with the desertion and shrinkage of the settlements they served. Duke, in his *Antiquities of Shropshire* (1854), records some 105 lost chapels in the county. One of these, at the deserted hamlet of Bold in the parish of Aston Botrell, was later incorporated into the outbuildings of the surviving farm and was drawn by the Reverend Williams at the end of the eighteenth century in one of his striking watercolours of Border churches.

55 *The substantial nave and chancel ruins of the Norman church of the Cistercian monastery at Buildwas, on the banks of the River Severn close to the Ironbridge Gorge*

Monasteries in the Marches

After the Conquest there was a steady stream of new monastic foundation, while four centuries later all the monasteries in the Marches were dissolved, most of their buildings destroyed and their estates sold or handed on to new secular landlords. The impact of both events on the landscape was considerable. The earliest of monastic foundations were Benedictine and include St Werburgh's at Chester and Shrewsbury Abbey, built by Roger de Montgomery. The robust abbey church at Shrewsbury which lies a little way to the east of the English bridge incorporates a substantial amount of simple but competent Norman work. The outlying abbey buildings were ravaged after the dissolution of the monasteries and the final blow came when Thomas Telford drove his A5 road through the claustral buildings. Some remains of the abbey, including the refectory pulpit, are now totally divorced from the abbey church.

Following in the wake of the early Norman foundations (which tended to be located in urban centres) the Cistercians arrived in the middle years of the twelfth century. This monastic order with its vows of poverty and simplicity normally located its houses in isolated settings well away from existing communities. The first of the great Cistercian houses in the Marchlands appeared with the establishment of Tintern Abbey in the deep gorge of the lower Wye in 1131. Tintern is a much visited site in a splendid setting, but to the north, high up in the deeply engraved valleys of the Black Mountains, lies the ruins of a monastery which exemplifies the Cistercian search for solitude even better: Llanthony Priory, built between 1175 and 1230.

Not very far away, at the mouth of the Golden Valley, lie the remains of Abbey Dore, which was founded in the mid-twelfth century. The records of this Cistercian monastery begin quite simply with the phrase, 'In 1147 was begun the Abbey of Dore'. A party of white monks from Morimond in France were sent to the Golden Valley and within 30 years the first monastic buildings had been completed. The great Abbey Dore church consists of a massive chancel and crossing, which gives some impression of the scale of the medieval foundation here. The size and the splendour of the surviving Cistercian medieval buildings at Abbey Dore reflect the accumulated wealth of the monastery, which was very active in the reclamation of wasteland and came to own the most extensive estate of any abbey in the whole of the Welsh Marches. Abbey Dore properties included 17 outlying granges, of which nine were in the Golden Valley. It is clear that this fertile corridor, isolated from the Wye valley by an irregular wooded sandstone ridge and screened to the west by the menacing plateau of the Black Mountains, owes the outline of its present rural settlement pattern to the pioneering activities of the Cistercians in the twelfth and thirteenth centuries. Granges founded in the Golden Valley include Morehampton Park Farm, a moated site close by the River Dore, New Grange, Blakemore Grange, Whitehall Grange, Hollins Grange and Backton Grange. The abbey also had estates in further flung places, including northern Monmouthshire. The wool trade provided the abbey with its wealth, and a late thirteenth-century account reveals that the Abbey Dore flock consisted of almost 3000 sheep. In an important account of the medieval wool trade, *La Patrica Della Mercatura*, it is recorded that Abbey Dore wool commanded the highest price among all the English fleeces.

The establishment of the monastic farms appears to have involved considerable woodland clearance. It is recorded that the monks of Abbey Dore were allowed to 'till, assart, enclose and deal with their pleasure'. In the early thirteenth century King John granted Abbey Dore an area of former royal forest, Trivel Wood, with permission to assart. John also allowed the monks to enlarge and dig a millpond in Trivel Wood. It is probably that this pool was the forerunner of the ornamental lake which now fills the floor of the shallow valley on the edge of Whitfield Park.

The reclamation activities of the Cistercians were not universally applauded; Giraldus Cambrensis, for example, commented adversely on the economic activities of the monasteries following his tour of Wales in the closing years of the twelfth century. He accused the monks of 'changing an oak wood into a wheat field', and implied that Abbey Dore's reclamation of the clearance of a tract of woodland because it was 'wild and rough and offered secure refuge to the Welshman and robbers', was nothing more than a lame excuse. The records of the monastic institutions show quite clearly that there were still sizeable areas of rough land available for reclamation in the Marches. We cannot be certain if this land had been cultivated in antiquity and had reverted to waste, or if it represented the residue of poorer land which had never been seriously farmed. There certainly appears to have been a larger reservoir of land available for clearance in the Marches than in Midland England just to the east. Quite apart from 'assart' place names, many field names in marginal areas carry elements such as 'marsh', 'moor' and 'heath', indicative of their unimproved condition in the early Middle Ages.

Later in the Middle Ages Buildwas Abbey, along with a number of other Shropshire abbeys, was involved in exploiting the mineral resources of the Shropshire coalfield, the basis on which the Industrial Revolution was later to develop. Buildwas' primary wealth, however, lay in the land. From a taxation document of 1291 it is clear that the monastery derived most of its income from its agricultural activities. It was assessed at the formidable figure of £113 19s 5d, of which over 60 per cent came from stock farming and over 20 per cent from arable farming. Wool was not specifically included in the valuation, but the monks were obviously exporting wool at this time and this activity must have contributed significantly to their revenue. Buildwas possessed the right to wash sheep in the River Severn at Cressage and to load barges there, which suggests that wool was being shipped downriver, perhaps as far as Bristol. Earlier, in 1264, we hear that Buildwas was one of the abbeys which was selling wool to Flemish merchants and it is the only one of the Shropshire monasteries to figure in Pegolotti's list of monasteries supplying wool to Italian traders. If the figures cited in Pegolotti's

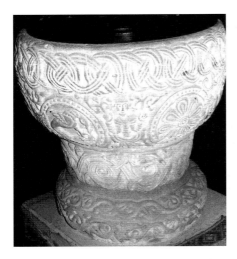

56 *The font at St Mary's Church, Stottesden, Shropshire. The carving is in the distinctive style of the Herefordshire School of Norman craftsmen who were responsible for much fine work in the region during the twelfth century. The font has been attributed to the 'Aston Master', whose work has been identified at Aston and other Herefordshire churches*

list are reliable the gross profits of the wool must have been between £150 and £200 a year, which is more than the estimated annual value of all the abbey's other income put together. The site of Buildwas Abbey is of interest because local topography determined that the claustral buildings were built on the northern side of the church with drainage towards the river as at Tintern. There is also a set of fishponds to be found to the north of the ruins of the main abbey buildings. Buildwas lies close to the River Severn, but today its hidden buildings and earthworks have to be sought out as they are surrounded by a thick belt of trees.

The Hereford School of Romanesque architecture

The Cistercian order, which was dedicated to simplicity, normally built in a plain and austere Romanesque style. However, many churches in the Borderland contain much more flamboyant Romanesque architecture. During the middle decades of the twelfth century, Norman architecture began to develop more decorative elements and a number of English regional schools evolved with their own distinctive styles and designs. Especially noteworthy are the twelfth-century carvings of the Herefordshire School, which was responsible for work in a number of churches in Herefordshire, Gloucestershire and Shropshire. The most splendid example of their work was at Shobdon in northern Herefordshire, but this church was destroyed in the nineteenth century and only a few decaying remains of the early medieval church have survived; they are displayed in Shobdon Park. In the works of this group of sculptors it is possible to detect for the first time since the Norman Conquest the strong influence of continental centres on English sculpture. The Herefordshire School is now best represented in the church of Kilpeck, where the sculpture shows that the School drew its inspiration from Anglo-Saxon, Carolingian and Viking art. Attention has been drawn to the similarity between the work of the Herefordshire School and carvings found in the great pilgrimage churches of eastern France, such as Autun and Vezelay. Their work also shows links between Marcher churches and churches along the pilgrimage route which runs along western France and northern Spain to Santiago de Compostela in Galicia.

Evidence of the pilgrimage link is to be found in the tympana at Brinsop and Stretton Sugwas, which lie about two miles apart from one another. That at Brinsop depicts St George, represented as a contemporary knight with hawks, on horseback, thrusting his spear into a dragon, whose snake-like body is being trampled on by the horse. The tympanum at Stretton Sugwas shows Samson battling with a lion, whose jaws he is forcing open. In western France there are a number of sculptures showing riders defeating enemies, which appear either in the form of dragons, serpents or in some cases infidels. The origins of this sculpture appear to be based on a Roman equestrian statue of Marcus Aurelius, but the image appears to have become confused with both Constantine the Great, who made Christianity the religion of the Roman Empire, and with Charlemagne, who features in early stories of the Christian fight against the Moors in Spain. Other work of the Herefordshire School is to be seen at Leominster priory and Rowlestone, and a considerable number of other places in northern Herefordshire and southern Shropshire have tympana or fonts which were either influenced or executed by the School. The church at Kilpeck is a little gem and still lies almost completely intact. Other churches at places such as Holdgate and Tugford also display important examples of their work.

In comparison with the Southern English School of architecture, which developed between 1120 and 1140, the Herefordshire School demonstrates an important change in patronage. The greatest works of the Southern School were found in monastic houses and they show a close similarity of style with contemporary illuminations made in the mother monastic centres, but the works of the Herefordshire School were executed for lay patrons.

A nearly complete example of a small Norman church is to be found at Heath, hidden on the plateau below Brown Clee Hill in south Shropshire. This isolated church, despite some insensitive restoration at the beginning of the twentieth century, is almost completely mid-twelfth-century. With its Norman font and later medieval box pews and decaying medieval wall paintings, and surrounded as it is by the lumps and bumps of a deserted village, Heath represents the very essence of the Welsh Border landscape. Other examples of Norman architecture are to be found scattered throughout the isolated rural parts of the Borderland, mainly in settlements which decayed during the later Middle Ages and where subsequently there was no money or impetus for rebuilding. One interesting peculiarity of the Norman Border region churches already noted are the squat square Norman bell towers, found particularly in northern Herefordshire and southern Shropshire. The most spectacular are the low squat buttress towers to be found at places such as Bishop's Castle, Clun and Lydham.

The survival of so much Norman architecture can be attributed to the quality of the original buildings and to the later comparative poverty of the area. The Normans brought wealth on a previously unknown scale and skill into the Borders, which allowed the construction of these churches. The wealth which in the later Middle Ages was gained from trading in wool and textiles on the whole found its way back into secular buildings, markets and guild halls, rather than into the construction of new churches. Places such as Leominster, Weobley, Pembridge and Ludlow all possess fine churches, paid for in part at least by the profits from wool, but with the exceptions of Ludlow and Leominster there are few wool churches on the same scale as those found in the Cotswolds or East Anglia.

57a Detail of Kilpeck, showing a warrior with foliage on one of the door jambs. The tympanum depicts the tree of life with the outer voussoirs showing grotesque heads and the signs of the zodiac

Places to visit

Kilpeck and Shobdon, Herefordshire
SO446 304 and SO 402 620

The finest surviving church of the Herefordshire School is at Kilpeck, which lies about nine miles to the south of Hereford in the former Welsh area of Archenfield. The place name 'Kilpeck' is Celtic, the first element of which means 'retreat' or 'corner'. A Benedictine priory, of which little remains, was founded here in 1135. The parish church has a wealth of sculpture on its doorway, chancel arch, corbels and windows. The doorway has been extraordinarily well preserved because a wooden porch protected it; unfortunately this porch was unwisely removed in the nineteenth century. The main arch of this doorway is carved with a series of flamboyant designs characteristic of later Norman architecture. These include beak heads, monsters and an angel, placed at the apex. There is also a chain motif, each ring of which contains birds, monsters and fishes. The doorway jambs are covered with thick bodies of twisting snakes; one of the shafts has figures of warriors intertwined with foliage, while the other is carved with foliage and a pair of doves at the base. The capitals are decorated with animals and a grotesque head and on the tympanum there is a symmetrical vine scroll.

The exterior of the church includes a richly carved west window and a magnificent corbel table fashioned in the form of grotesque heads and animals and includes a Celtic fertility symbol — a sheilah-nah-ghig. Projecting from the angles of the nave and from the centre of the west front there are a series of large heads of dragons which are reminiscent of Scandinavian art. A number of other features in the church, including some of the corbels, also suggest a strong Viking influence.

Inside the church the chancel arch is richly carved with Anglo-Norman designs, and the shafts are fashioned in a way which until the mid-twelfth century was unknown in England. Each shaft is decorated with a figure of three apostles, one above the other. The inspiration for this appears to have been the famous early twelfth-century doorway the Puerta de las Platerias at the cathedral of Santiago de Compostela in north-western Spain. In addition to the important stylistic links between the Herefordshire School and the Santiago pilgrimage route there is a remarkable document preserved in the University of Chicago that records the circumstances of the foundation of Shobdon, which contained carvings similar to those at Kilpeck. Shobdon was founded by Oliver de Merlimond, chief steward of Hugh de Mortimer, Lord of Wigmore. When the building was begun, Oliver went on a pilgrimage to Santiago de Compostela to pay homage to the relics of St James.

57b (right) Aerial view of Kilpeck showing castle, church and failed 'borough', the earthworks of which are in the form of an extended outer castle bailey

Along the route, particularly in the Poitou and Charente areas of western France and in old Castile in Spain, he came across the pilgrimage style and either made extensive drawings or more probably returned with one of the craftsmen involved in the ornamentation of these pilgrimage churches. Hence the remarkable similarity in much of the ornamentation to that found in the pilgrimage churches of France and Spain.

Just to the west of the church are the extensive remains of a motte and bailey castle, and to the east are the earthworks of a rectangular defended settlement. It would seem likely that these represent the remains of a former 'borough' laid out adjacent to the church and castle, but which, like so many of its neighbours, failed to adapt to the trading requirements of the later Middle Ages, and thus faded away.

Diddlebury, Shropshire SO 508 854

The unusual name of this Shropshire village reflects its Saxon origin. It means 'the burgh [or settlement] of Dudela', an Old English personal name, presumably that of an early lord. This village is commonly known as Delbury. St Peter's church at Diddlebury is one of a group in southern Shropshire which contains significant surviving Saxon remains. One of the reasons for the existence of substantially built churches is the wealth produced by the rich grazing land and the high quality wool of the Corve Dale region in the later Saxon period. The Saxon origin of St Peter's is evident from several notable architectural features. The infilled north door is narrow and round-headed with plain hood mouldings. The church has long and short stonework on the quoins of the north end of the chancel at the base — a common characteristic of Saxon work. The herringbone pattern of stonework of the north wall of the nave, which can be seen on the interior only, is one of the finest examples of this eleventh-century method of construction. What is particularly unusual is that the stones have been especially cut for this pattern. The church also has a number of other Anglo-Saxon features including a small double-shafted window of dressed stone, a horseshoe-shaped doorway and some interlaced sculpture. The chancel is basically Norman, although there are also a number of features which suggest that it had a Saxon predecessor. The quality of the Saxon architecture at Diddlebury is almost certainly due to the fact that it lay in Edward the Confessor's Manor of Corfham, where there could well have been a royal palace — a predecessor of the medieval castle.

After the Norman Conquest, Roger de Montgomery gave Corfham and the church of Diddlebury to Shrewsbury Abbey. Corfham stood a mile to the east of Diddlebury and by

58 The interior north wall at St. Peter's church, Diddlebury. The fine Saxon herringbone masonry represents some of the best work in this style in England; on the left is a blocked Saxon doorway with large shapeless block-like imposts

the twelfth century boasted a substantial castle belonging to the Clifford family; apart from a large field of earthworks, nothing now remains above ground. An illuminating sixteenth-century account of Corfham Castle records:

> Cofham hath been a manor of great fame, and had in it a castle compassed about with a mott and a strong cour wall, strong towers, wereof one doth remain called Rosamund's Tower, but can't long stand for it is uncovered and the lead taken away. The forsaid courts was also compassed about able to withstand any suddain invasion, but nowe all decayed, ruinated and destroyed.

Henry II gave Corfham and Diddlebury to Walter Clifford, whose daughter Rosamund was Henry II's mistress. She produced two sons, one of whom became Archbishop of York, and today a well near Corfham still bears her name. Rosamund eventually retired to Godstow nunnery near Oxford. Diddlebury is now a delightfully quiet spot in the peaceful Corve Dale far removed from its brief association with the national political intrigue of the Anglo-Norman court.

Much Wenlock, Shropshire SO 000 625

Much Wenlock was originally known simply as Wenlock. The 'Much' (Great) was added in the thirteenth century in taxation documents to distinguish the town and abbey from nearby Little Wenlock. Excavations at Wenlock Priory suggest that the settlement here may have a Romano-British or prehistoric origin. The first religious house at Wenlock was a nunnery, which was founded by Merewalh, King of Mercia, about 680 for his daughter, St Milburge. Milburge was reputedly a gentle lady to whom miracles were attributed in her lifetime. Milburge came to Wenlock in 687, when she became abbess; the Monastery was then a double house of monks and nuns. It is believed that the monks' church lay at the crossing of the later priory church and that the nuns' church was on the site of the present parish church of The Holy Trinity. This nunnery was destroyed by the Danes when they raided Mercia in the late ninth century. The second foundation at Wenlock was a minster built by a friend of Edward the Confessor, Leofric, the powerful Earl of Mercia. In addition to Wenlock Leofric founded several religious houses in the mid-eleventh century

59 Aerial view of the surviving ruins of the Cluniac priory at Much Wenlock with the large cruciform church (centre left). An attempt was made to save the church at the time of the dissolution, by recommending that it should form part of a new joint bishopric with Chester; it was eventually demolished. The prior's lodging (centre right), which dates from c.1500, was turned into a magnificent private residence (see 70)

including Coventry, Stow, and Leominster. In 1086 in Domesday Book it is recorded that Earl Roger 'has made the church of St Mildburg into an abbey. The same church holds Wenlock and held it in the time of Edward the Confessor.'

The refounded monastery was dependent upon La Charite in France and was well endowed with lands in southern Shropshire. A small number of monks came from La Charite to take possession of the lands of the church of St Milburge and the newly installed monks decided 'to open the silver shrine which was believed to hold the body of St Milburge'. The story relates that the shrine was empty, but soon afterwards a servant of the monks called Raymond was working in the monastery of the Holy Trinity, and there found an old box on an altar. Inside it was a document which stated that the saint's body was buried before the high altar of the church of the Holy Trinity. The monks then asked for advice from St Anselm, Archbishop of Canterbury, who divined that this had happened 'not by the will of man'. He told them to dig up the ground and search and as a result they found the bones. The monks deposited the bones in a new shrine and subsequently miracles followed to confirm the truth of the discovery.

By 1169-70, the monks of Wenlock had become so numerous that they were able to send a prior and 12 monks to found the Cluniac monastery of Paisley in Scotland. They also sent a prior and a small number of monks to three small dependent priories, Dudley, St Helen's in the Isle of Wight, and Church Preen. The latter lies a few miles from Wenlock and is one of only four English churches once served by Cluniac monks still used as a parish church.

Dramatic events at Wenlock are recalled in a letter written in about 1163 and addressed to the prior of La Charite from the prior and monks of Wenlock. This recalls a local uprising by the priory's agricultural tenants.

> The villeins who held lands by rendering of feudal service had rashly lifted up their heel against us and wished to depose the prior and put another in his place . . . They carried their complaint to the king's court, and although they met with little favour, a writ was sent to the sheriff to inquire into their grievances

. . . The prior offered an inquiry by the tenants in chief and his own free tenants. At last the villeins were convinced of their error and they took a solemn oath over the body of St Milburga that they would be faithful in all things to the priory. But the next day they went back on their oath and their last error was worse than the first when they threw down their ploughshares. It was Tuesday in Whitsun week . . . and as was our custom we went out from our church in procession carrying the shrine of St Milburga and with a great company of men and women following us. After a sermon had been preached to them we put forth a sentence of excommunication against those who wrong the church. When our villeins heard that sentence they hastened back to Wenlock before us and beset the three doors of the church, and when we came back they barred our way crying out, 'Seize the unjust man and kill him.' By the mercy of God and with the help of the knights who accompanied us we escaped them, but they threw stones and cudgels after us and some of our monks and servants received severe blows. After this outrage they consented that six monks and four knights should hear their grievances, and both they and the prior would accept the decision of these judges. This was done. The villeins submitted and on the morrow they intended to come back and plough the land. But the messengers whom they sent to you to complain of our prior have come back from La Charite with a letter from you. The villeins have gone back on their pact and lifted their horns. Saving your reverence you have acted incautiously, for judgement is not to be given in absence. If you have any mercy, if any virtue of charity, if any bowels of compassion restrain the rage of these wolves while there is time . . . We would rather die than give in to them.

We do not know how this story of an early version of the Peasant's Revolt ended, but calm seems to have returned to Wenlock fairly rapidly. The oldest parts of the buildings to survive are the twelfth-century chapter house and lavatorium. The blind arcading in the chapter house and the carved scenes on the side of the lavatorium are some of the finest architectural features in the whole of the Marches. The church was rebuilt in the first half of the thirteenth century, and the priory received many gifts of money and materials for the work. One such gift was timber from Henry III, who was several times a guest of the priory. In 1295 when once more war broke out between France and England, alien priories like Wenlock came under suspicion because of this allegiance to a foreign house. For the next 100 years Wenlock was subject to severe restrictions and heavy taxation, which only came to an end when the links with La Charite and Cluny were finally broken in 1395. At this point Wenlock, along with all the other 'alien' priories in England, was placed under the Benedictine rule.

The monastery was dissolved on 26 January 1540. There were proposals for using the church and revenues for a new diocese; another was that there should be a see of Chester with Wenlock, and another linked Shrewsbury with Wenlock. However, these plans came to nothing and most of the buildings were destroyed. The eastern block, however, which contained the prior's lodging (*c.*1500), was converted into one of the finest private houses to be created out of a monastic building anywhere in England.

As well as the remains of the priory, there is much to see in Wenlock. The parish church of Holy Trinity, for example, incorporates a Norman nave and chancel. Elsewhere there is a mixture of building styles and building materials closely packed along narrow streets. The town appears to have been laid out at the abbey gates, in the form of a market square and a street of burgage tenements. It is possible to identify the original regulated medieval town plan in the modern property boundaries. The sixteenth-century half-timbered guildhall is a building of considerable charm, with its open ground floor. It is still used as a court and also houses the parochial council chamber.

Much Wenlock is an unlikely place to search for the origins of the modern Olympic Games, yet here in 1850 Dr William Penny Brookes founded the Wenlock Olympian Society and staged annual Olympian Games from that date. Despite the presence here of some of the country's leading athletes in the 1870s and 1880s the contribution of Dr Brookes to the Olympic movement was all but forgotten until relatively recently. The achievement of Dr Brookes and the Wenlock Olympians is particularly remarkable when the background to his life and work is considered. The population of the small, declining market town of Much Wenlock was just under 2500 in 1841. Its character was primarily agricultural, and although it was the largest non-county borough in England, Kelly's Post Office Directory of 1864 characterised Wenlock as:

> . . . chiefly agricultural, but there is a considerable trade in malting and tanning, and in lime and limestone for which this neighbourhood is famous.

It was from this obscure and conservative background that Brookes struck a spark of the Olympic ideal, served on committees of national importance and became well known amongst Continental pioneers of organised sports.

Leominster, Herefordshire

Leominster lies in the valley of the River Lugg, just to the north of its confluence with the River Arrow, and for many centuries the town was one of the great wool markets in England. It sits a few miles to the east of the principal Roman road running from Wroxeter to Kenchester. Leominster's status during the Roman period is unknown: however, it seems to have emerged in the mid-Saxon period as one of the major political and ecclesiastical centres on the Welsh border. Its history is linked with the Saxon tribe of the Magonsaetan. It has been argued that the original pre-Roman central site in the region was the hillfort at Sutton Walls, but in the immediate post-Roman period this site was abandoned and a new one established somewhere to the south of Leominster, possibly at Maund.

A religious community was founded on the site of Leominster by Merewalh, the Saxon prince of the Magonsaete, and brother-in-law of King Aethelred. Leominster appears to have served as the ecclesiastical centre of the Magonsaete from 660 until the foundation of Hereford cathedral. Despite the transfer of ecclesiastical power to Hereford the vestiges of the original political importance of the Leominster region are credited in Domesday Book in the form of enormous estates. It is tempting to see the Domesday Book's account of the great manor of Leominster as revealing something of the territorial

60 All that remains of the large medieval Benedictine priory of St Peter and St Paul at Leominster is part of the church, which now serves Leominster. Twelfth-century Norman work can be seen in the tower, but most of the remaining visible architecture is thirteenth-century. The church is unusual in that it has three almost identically sized naves

organisation of the Lugg valley even before the Saxon settlement.

In 1123 Henry I gave Leominster to Reading Abbey, and soon after this much of the fine Romanesque work constructed of local sandstone in the nave was begun. The Norman nave was consecrated in 1130, by Robert de Bethun, bishop-elect of Hereford. In its original state, the priory was a large cruciform building. The nave of the priory was always reserved for townspeople, but this led to disputes with the monks, as was often the case with such arrangements, and in 1239 the splendid central nave was built for the parishioners. A further large extension was made in 1320, when the south nave was added and during the next century the great west window was inserted and the western tower raised to its present height. This period marked the zenith of the priory, and its gardens, orchards and fishponds must have presented an extremely attractive picture.

All this was swept away in 1539 when the monastery of Reading, with its cell at Leominster, was dissolved and dismantled. The last Abbot of Reading, Hugh Cook, was hanged before the gates of his own monastery, but the fate of John Glover, the last Prior of Leominster, is not known. Immediately after the dissolution the work of destroying the monastic buildings began and the whole of the eastern end of the priory, together with the central tower, was demolished. The parishioners, however, were eager to maintain their rights, and they erected the present eastern wall to safeguard the fabric of the naves, so that now the church, curiously, consists of three naves, each about the same size.

The earliest surviving part of Leominster's street plan seems to date from the early Middle Ages when a community developed outside the western entrance to the church. Corn Square appears to have been used as a market square and New Street and Burgess Street to the west show signs of deliberate extensions during the late Middle Ages. Quite apart from its central geographical position, able to attract trade from northern Herefordshire and Central Wales, Leominster's wealth developed on the wool trade. Leominster Ore, as the local wool was called, had gained an international reputation for its quality by the late Middle Ages. The town hall, now the offices of the district council, and the market hall were built by the local architect, John Abel, in the late sixteenth and early seventeenth centuries. These buildings provide obvious signs of the prosperity brought to the town by the wool trade. The great rebuilding of the seventeenth century in particular is demonstrated by the sheer number of timber-framed buildings to be found in the town, especially in the area of Corn Square, Drapers Lane and School Lane.

Stanton Lacy, Shropshire
SO 496 788

Stanton Lacy was a centre of considerable importance before the Norman Conquest; in fact it was the predecessor to Ludlow. The affix 'Lacy' was added after the Conquest, incorporating the name of the Domesday estate holder, Roger de Lacey. St Peter's church was built to a cruciform design and although reconstruction, halted through lack of funds, took place in the thirteenth century, it still has some fine Saxon features, including pilaster strips and Saxon carvings. Indeed it is the finest of all the Saxon churches in the Marches. Built of local limestone, the west end looks particularly beautiful in the light of the evening sun.

61 The west end of the Saxon church of St Peter at Stanton Lacy. The vertical sections of parallel stonework known as pilaster strips may be an imitation of timber work in contemporary or earlier churches

Llanthony Priory, Gwent SO 289 279

A group of Augustinian monks formed a community at Llanthony in the Honddu Valley at the beginning of the twelfth century, but disturbed local conditions drove them away and they formed a new house called Llanthony Secunda, near Gloucester. A fresh start was made in the Vale of Ewyas in about 1175 but there was continued rivalry between the old and new establishments. The two eventually became independent in 1205, but it was the Gloucester community which flourished, and in 1481 it received royal authority to take over the older priory, by then almost deserted. Llanthony continued as a dependent cell until the Dissolution, when it passed to one of Henry VIII's servants, Nicholas Arnolde. In the eighteenth century the abbey ruins were sold to a Colonel Wood who converted the south tower as a shooting lodge. In about 1807 the estate was bought by the poet and essayist Walter Savage Landor. He was a romantic who landscaped the estate

133

and intended to live there as a model country gentleman. However, a quickness of temper brought him into conflict and litigation with his neighbours. He was refused permission to restore the priory and in 1814 Savage left Llanthony and his mother took over the management of the estate.

The revival of interest in Gothic ruins from the late eighteenth century onwards led an increasing number of people to visit Llanthony along with the picturesque site of Tintern Abbey in the lower Wye valley. For three centuries the buildings at Llanthony had been neglected, but gradually care and conservation were applied; yet it was not until the 1930s that a systematic programme of restoration was started. The buildings were bought by the artist Eric Gill in 1924, who intended setting up a community of fellow artists. However, perhaps because of the poor communications in the Honddu Valley this venture also failed. The west range now houses a small hotel and the monument, one of the most picturesque in the whole of the Marches, is in the care of Welsh Heritage (CADW). The place name Llanthony is derived from Llanddewi Nant Hoddni, that is 'the church of St Dewi on the River Hoddni'.

Tintern Abbey, Gwent SO 000 534

Tintern is one of the most picturesque monastic sites in Britain, despite the untidy surrounding car parks and gift shops. It is located on a narrow terrace close to the River Wye, and is surrounded by steep tree-covered slopes. Its siting has made it an object of artistic and architectural interest since the eighteenth century.

The Abbey was founded by the lord of Chepstow, Walter de Clare, who established a colony of Cistercian monks from L'Aumôse in northern France at Tintern in 1131. Tintern was only the second Cistercian house to be founded in Britain (Waverley, Surrey was founded in 1128) and was the first in Wales. Little above-ground architecture survives from the original foundation and most of the visible remains date from a massive programme of rebuilding dating from the thirteenth and fourteenth centuries. This work was funded by a series of generous grants by successive lords of Chepstow, in particular William Marshall in 1223-4 and Roger Bigod in 1301-2. The reconstruction work started in 1269 and the first mass was said in the presbytery in 1288. The new church was consecrated in 1301, but work continued for several more decades. The abbey was constructed almost entirely in local Old Red Sandstone, which contributes to the striking dark silhouette of the monument as it is approached from the south.

In 1536 at the time of the dissolution Tintern was the wealthiest abbey in Wales. The abbey with its estates was granted to Henry Somerset, second Earl of Worcester and lord of Chepstow. In the 1540s the lead was stripped from the roofs and the remainder of the buildings robbed. The absence of any significant nearby settlement seems to have saved some of the monastic fabric, particularly the skeleton of the formidable church. This isolation together with difficult road access would have deterred casual stone robbers but later workers from the ironworks in the nearby Angidy Valley appear to have colonised the ruins for a while.

By the middle of the eighteenth century the site had become valued for its aesthetic qualities as the Wye tour began to become popular. The Duke of Beaufort cleared, levelled and turfed the interior of the church, but the ruin did not please the doyen of the

62 The dramatic ruins of the Infirmary at Haughmond Abbey, close to Shrewsbury. The abbey was founded by William Fitz Alan for Augustinian Canons c.1135. Only footings of this building survive and the ruins date largely from later in the twelfth century. The abbey has an unusual plan, as its east end abuts so closely onto Haughmond Hill that some of the walls have their lower courses shaped out of solid rock

picturesque, William Gilpin, who in 1783 judged the ruin to be 'ill-shaped'. He proposed that 'a mallet judiciously used might be of service in fracturing' the gable ends and transepts. Sir Richard Colt Hoare writing in 1798 was more impressed:

> No ruins I have seen in England has so striking effect on the mind and sense as that of Tinterne when the door first opens and presents the whole extent of this most beautiful Gothic aisle, overhung with ivy in the most picturesque manner, and terminated by the magnificent eastern window through which is seen a distant hill covered with copse wood, on which fortunately there are no buildings or breaks to disturb the repose and tranquillity of the scene.

Despite this eulogy, a new turnpike road (now the A466) was carelessly driven through the Abbey precinct.

In 1901 the ruins were brought by the Crown from the Duke of Beaufort and the site gradually cleared, ivy and all. The much-visited abbey ruins are now in the care of CADW.

8 Woodland, Park and Forest

Over the centuries man's activities had diminished the natural woodland cover of the Marches to the point that even in Roman times there was relatively little virgin forest surviving. Indeed, woodland became an important commodity — both as a refuge for game and as a building and fuel resource. Measures were required to preserve the woodland used for hunting, and coppicing was introduced as a device to ensure a regular supply of timber for domestic and industrial uses. Woodland was also important for the retention of game and for hunting activities. Norman kings created a number of hunting reserves in the Marches. For example, the Brown Clee Hill in Shropshire and an area around Hereford both appear to have been designated as royal hunting reserves for the Saxon monarchy. During the reign of Edward the Confessor three thegns held land in Dene (Forest of Dean) free from rent in return for the services of guarding the woodland. Although immediately after the Norman Conquest King William began the process of

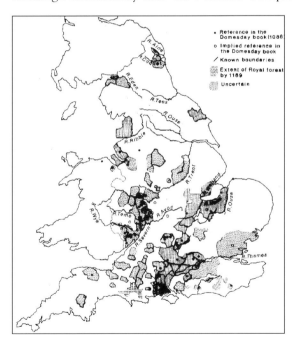

63 The distribution of Royal Forests in England by 1200, demonstrating the concentration in the Welsh Marches

Forest creation, Domesday coverage of both woodland and Forest is unreliable or ambiguous. There are, however, some hints about the nature and extent of newly created Forest areas; for instance, under the entry for Shrewsbury it is recorded that the sheriff was to provide 36 beaters when the King hunted at Marsley and Stiperstones Forest.

The term 'hay' (enclosure) occurs with some frequency in Domesday Book for the counties of Shropshire, Herefordshire, Worcester and Chester, but it is found most frequently in Shropshire with over 60 hays recorded. Hay, a term used only in the Marches, literally means hedge, but Domesday hays seem to have been enclosures used for the control of deer. Two manors, Lower Churton and Stretton, had five hays each. Two others, Wentnor and Worthen, had four and there were five hays at

64 The upland plateau of Brown Clee Hill lies in the foreground. All this area formed part of the Clee Forest and later Clee Chase in the Middle Ages. The regular fields in the centre were created by parliamentary enclosures in the eighteenth and nineteenth centuries

Clunton. These enclosures were constructed for the purpose of capturing game, usually roebuck, or in some cases for rearing game. At Corfton Manor the Domesday survey expressly stated that the hay was 'for the taking of roe deer', and at Lingen in Herefordshire, a heavily wooded area in 1086, there were three hays used for the same purpose. At a later date the term 'hay' was used in the Welsh border context to refer to larger enclosures, particularly in connection with debased Forests — for example, the Hay of Lythwood, immediately to the south of Shrewsbury, and the Hay of Wellington, which formed the residue of the forest of Mount Gilbert (based on the Wrekin), frequently appear in contemporary documents.

It would appear that there were still substantial areas of woodland in the Marches during the Middle Ages, and Marcher timber, particularly that from Shropshire, is often mentioned in connection with building operations in other parts of the country. When Abbot Faritius (1100-35) rebuilt his abbey at Abingdon, we hear that

> for all the buildings which the abbot made he caused beams and rafters to come from the district of Wales, for he had six wains for this purpose, twelve oxen for each of them, six or seven weeks was the journey coming and going, for it was necessary to go as far as Shrewsbury. The timber from Shropshire used in the south of England was sometimes referred to as 'Walschborde'.

Throughout the Middle Ages there was a consistent demand for Marcher timber for a variety of uses. The building and repair of castles, churches and houses required enormous quantities of wood, and there are numerous references to these activities. For instance in 1213 William Cantelupe was licensed by the Crown to take timber from Aconbury Wood for the purpose of fortifying and repairing Hereford Castle. In 1286 Edward I licensed Robert Burnell, Bishop of Bath and Wells, and Hugh Burnell, his brother, to fell and take away whatever great and small timber they required for their manors within the bounds of the Forest of Shropshire. Industrial activities required a regular source of timber and although oak trees were reputed to be 'the weeds of Herefordshire', eventually conservation measures had to be taken to maintain timber supplies even in that county. Thus in 1226 Henry III ordered a temporary cessation of the work at the iron forges in

Penyard Wood in order to prevent its complete destruction. Court rolls contain persistent references to infringements of local conservation regulations. As late as the sixteenth century one defendant at Lingen was accused of having 'felled and carried away for his own use (in his pottery kilns) 500 great oaks and saplings', over a period of seven years.

Royal Forests in the Marches

Quite apart from the building of castles, churches and new towns, the Norman Conquest had a dramatic effect upon the Marcher landscape in another way — the creation of Royal Forests. The Anglo-Saxon Chronicle for 1087 bemoans that:

> The King, William, set up great protection for deer and legislated to that intent that who so ever should slay hart or hind should be blinded . . . He loved the high deer as if he were their father.

After the Norman Conquest much of Shropshire, parts of Herefordshire and a large portion of Gloucestershire in the Forest of Dean were designated Royal Forest. Forest in this context was a legal term applied to areas in which the Crown and its delegates had exclusive hunting rights. Although the forests of Wyre, Morfe, Brewood and parts of Long Forest were heavily wooded, Royal forests were not necessarily tree-covered. The establishment of such forests would frequently incorporate villages and fields, but did not involve the expropriation of private property, and initiated the imposition of a special code of Forest Law on its inhabitants. At one stage in the twelfth century, up to a third of England was designated Royal Forest and subject to the Norman Forest Law. It is, however, doubtful whether the Forest Laws were ever quite as harsh as described by some contemporaries. By the thirteenth century a considerable degree of lassitude had crept into the implementation of Forest laws largely because of the difficulty of enforcing them over such vast tracts of land. Many of the fines for encroachment in forest land were in reality no more than an annual rental, and fines imposed for tree felling represented a form of timber trading.

At the height of forest creation at the end of the twelfth century, more than half the county of Shropshire was operating under Forest Law and was collectively known as the Forest of Shropshire. The area of Royal Forest in Hereford covered a considerably smaller area and consisted of two principal forests, a section of the Forest of Dean and an area of indefinite limits to the west and north of Hereford, possibly created as a physical buffer between the Marches and Wales. This latter area was subsequently broken up into a number of remote chases known as Mocktree, Deerfold and Bringewood. The forests which saw the most royal activity tended to be in southern and central England, adjacent to royal palaces such as Woodstock (Wychwood Forest) and Winchester (New Forest). It is difficult to believe that the Norman Kings thought they were ever going to use the Marcher forests regularly for their own hunting. It is probable therefore that the draconian imposition of Forest Law in the Marches was intended as a form of royal control on remote areas about which the Crown and the court had little first-hand knowledge.

The Crown's interest in the forests was in the first instance principally, but not exclusively, for the 'deer' (wild pigs and hares were normally classed as deer). The forests also provided other resources such as timber, underwood and, in the case of the Forest of Dean, minerals. In 1237 the Constable of St Briavel's was ordered to

> cause to be erected mobile underwood forges [and] to sustain those forges . . .
> with thorn, maple, hazel and other underwood; so that no oak, chestnut or
> beech be cut down; and to cause the area felled and allocated . . . to be well and
> sufficiently fenced lest any deer or other beast be able to get in to browse there.

The status of many woodland areas is far from clear at times during the Middle Ages, as they appear under different descriptions at different times. For example Brewood Forest was 'taken out of Royal Forest' in 1209, when it was recorded that the knights and men of Brewood in Shropshire gave the king 100 marks 'to secure the disafforesting of that part of Brewood Forests for themselves and their heirs'. Yet in 1256, 6000 oak trees in Tong Wood, which had recently been taken out of Brewood 'Forest', were felled. Another Royal Forest which enjoyed a short life was the Stiperstones, a prominent landmark in western Shropshire which was granted by Henry II to Roger Corbet, and was subsequently used as a private hunting chase by the Corbet family.

The Long Forest, which took its name from its shape, extended along the continuous ridge of Wenlock Edge, and also covered the whole of the Domesday hundred of Condover, and large portions of adjacent hundreds. There were also three 'hays' in the Long Forest. Another extensive medieval Forest was that of the Wrekin, normally known as the Forest of Mount Gilbert. It embraced nearly the whole of the Domesday hundred of Wrockwardine and extended into the liberties of Shrewsbury. The forest was divided into two areas, known as the Bailiwick of Haughmond and the Bailiwick of Wombridge, both post-Conquest ecclesiastical monastic foundations. By the mid-fourteenth century the hay of Wellington was all that survived of the former Forest; nevertheless in the 1260s it had a fully paid-up hermit — Nick de Denten. In 1267 the Crown granted him six quarters of corn 'to give the hermit greater leisure for his holy exercises', and in 1273 he was given a further grant; but subsequently he was involved in some misdemeanour and was obliged to quit his post.

The Forest of Shirlett, which abutted on to the Long Forest, was originally very extensive and remained partly under royal control until the sixteenth century. Shirlett appears to have been the original 'shire forest'; the name means a 'share of the shire' and it may have performed the same role as the Forest of Dartmoor did in Devon, providing common grazing and other rights for a whole county. In 1233 two of the King's carpenters were sent to Shirlett to make bottices to fortify Montgomery Castle 'when the need arises'. A decade afterwards oak trees were sent throughout the county as 'the men of Llewellyn were in many places rising'. Wood from Shirlett was regularly sent to Shrewsbury Castle and jail for repairs and fuel. A survey of Shirlett in 1235 noted a great amount of recent timber felling and recorded

> The custody is good as regards oak trees and underwood, except that great

deliveries have been made by order of the king to the Abbeys of Shropshire, Buildwas and Wenlock . . . there is small abiding of beasts except in coming and going from other forests.

A fine roll of Shropshire forests for 1179 demonstrates that there were a range of other activities within forest areas. The Abbey of Lilleshall paid a mark for a mill within the forest bounds, and there are references to encroachments, house building, assarts, the enclosure of wastes, and the cultivation of newly cleared land. The crops raised on these new enclosures are listed as winter rye or oats. On the same roll there is a reference to the sale of the King's lead obtained from within the forest, which was sold for the considerable sum of £55, when the total income from all other sources only amounted to £45. Other interesting, if somewhat incidental, information about the operation of Forest Laws in Shropshire comes from the Forest Pleas of 1209, when it was reported that a hart had entered Bridgnorth and guards took it to the castle. When the news reached the forest officers they demanded that Sheriff Thomas de Urlington, then in charge of the castle, should report on the fate of the hart. He acknowledged the offence and promised that his men would appear before the justices; in the event the whole town of Bridgnorth was fined for this violation of Forest Law.

Another interesting case involved the question of the use of these remote areas as sanctuary, and relates to the forests as the resort of criminals and heretics:

> Richard of Hotton, Wilkin of Eastlegh, Hulle of Hinton and Hulle Roebuck, the serjeants of the county, found venison in the house of Hugh le Scot. And Hugh fled to the church and when the foresters and verderers came thither, they demanded of Hugh whence that venison came. And he, and a certain other person, Roger of Wellington by name, acknowledged that they had killed a hind from which that venison came. And he refused to leave the church, but lingered there for a month, and afterwards escaped in the guise of a woman. And he is a fugitive, and Roger of Wellington likewise. It is ordered that they be exacted; and unless they come let them be outlawed.

Deerfold Forest in western Herefordshire seems to have been used regularly as a place of refuge, and it is recorded that anchorites (hermits) settled here in the early Middle Ages. It has been suggested that some of these became the first nuns at the nunnery at Limebrook, which was founded by Robert de Lingen in the late twelfth century. During the early fifteenth century Deerfold became known as an area where persecuted Lollards (religious reformers) could take refuge. Sir John Oldcastle, who led an abortive Lollard rebellion in 1413-14, hid at Chapel Farm for three years before his capture and execution.

The royal forests were at their most extensive in the late twelfth century, but by the mid-thirteenth century they were already in decline. Although the process by which the forests were disbanded, known as disforestation, was a protracted one extending over several centuries, many of the legal and administrative trappings of the Forest survived throughout the Middle Ages. Nevertheless the true royal forests were relatively short-lived features of the landscape; it was only the Norman kings at the very height of their authority who could impose and maintain such a system effectively. Few physical traces of royal forest survive today, but as the forests gradually fell out of royal control, in many places the monopoly of hunting rights was taken over by individual lords who created chases or parks for their own sport; for instance, a line of such private deer parks was created out of the Long Forest in the thirteenth century, along the dip-slope of the Wenlock escarpment.

The record of forest offences shows that red deer were the dominant animal in the thirteenth century in Shropshire. In one year alone charges concerning the illicit killing of 22 harts, 9 hinds, 3 roe deer and 3 fallow deer were heard. In April 1274 an order was given by Edward I to the Sheriff of Shropshire for all the venison taken from the forest for the King's use to be carried without delay to Westminster and deposited at the King's larder. A Crown licence was issued in 1279 to Adam Atwell 'to take foxes throughout the Forest of Shropshire, by traps or other means and to carry them away'. Two years later Roger de Mortimer obtained a licence to hunt the fox and hare with his own hounds in all the forests of Shropshire outside the coverts, providing he took none of the King's great game or deer. In the same year there is a reference to Peter Corbet obtaining authorisation to take wolves by the aid of man, dog or traps, wherever they could be found in Shropshire Staffordshire, Gloucestershire, Worcestershire or Herefordshire, and the bailiffs and minsters of the forest were to give him all the assistance he required. This thirteenth-century reference to wolves is one of the last in England.

The process of disforestation was erratic, but in Shropshire by the middle of the fourteenth century only the forests of Morfe, Shirlett and the hay of Lythwood survived as royal forests. A survey taken a century later by Geoffrey Lee of all the King's and Queen's woods, forests and chases in the county of Shropshire showed that the Forest of Morfe covered some 1200 acres. Morfe was one of the longest surviving forests in the Marches outside the Forest of Dean, and originally it occupied the area where the counties of Shropshire, Stafford and Worcestershire converge in the Severn valley. Ranolf, Earl of Chester, Sheriff of Shropshire 1216-23, sold 1700 oak trees from Morfe Forest during his period of office and is also recorded as supplying timber for the fortifying of Bridgnorth. By the early fifteenth century records show that the Forest was being systematically coppiced for timber.

The process of clearance and colonisation within the forest is shown clearly, indeed somewhat touchingly, in a map of 1582. This was drawn as evidence in an enquiry about grazing rights, and shows the remnant of the forest consisting only of saplings and stumps. During a further enquiry into the extent of the forest held in 1615, John Hatton of Claverley said that he knew the

> great waste common called Morfe Wood reputed to be a Forest but he never
> did knowe any deare to be there in his memorie, neither is theire any woode
> or underwood, but few trees in many miles compass.

Some of the destruction had been on a large scale, for at an earlier enquiry in 1592 a witness recalled the cutting of 4000 oaks for Lord Dudley and 4000 for the Queen. He also commented that when the Council of the Welsh Marches met at Bridgnorth, 200-300 cartloads of timber at a time were sent from Morfe to the town.

Morfe was important for its grazing to those settlements around its edge as well as to those that developed within the forest. At yet another enquiry, held in 1589, witness William Potter listed the numerous villages and hamlets that had rights of grazing, some lying within and some without the forest. According to another witness, John Billingsley, each of the inhabitants of the named places holding a yardland was entitled to graze 100 sheep, 12 cattle and two horses and to take three loads of fuel. From these records it is possible to trace the extension of arable farming into the Forest. By the late thirteenth century the assart land in Claverley totalled as much as 631 acres. In the forest proceedings there are many references to newly assarted land which had been planted, usually with oats. In 1272 Hereward de la Syche held small assarts like this at Claverley, Bobbington and Nordley, and the Abbot of Haughmond had an acre at Beobridge. Buildwas Abbey was also involved in the clearance of woodland here. Much of the dispersed character of the communities within the once wooded parts of the Royal Forest must be attributed to the settlements of the assarters, and their names provide a vivid reminder of their work — William atte Mor, Robert atte Ok, Robert atte Lee, Richard atte Feldehouse.

The remnants of the waste left after medieval assarting and Tudor destruction were finally enclosed about 1812. The resulting pattern of regular fields, often enclosed by quickset hedges, can be seen clearly today, as for example along the A458 between Bridgnorth and Enville. This regular pattern contrasts with the parts of the forest which were settled earlier, with their winding, deep-cut lanes, isolated farms and irregular fields representing elements of a more ancient landscape.

The Forest of Dean

The Forest of Dean represents one of the most important survivals of the royal forests of England. During the reign of Henry II, its boundaries extended from Gloucester, via Newent, to a point a little south of Ross to the north, and to the confluence of the Severn and the Wye at Chepstow to the south, forming a rough triangle bounded on the east and west by these two rivers. Encroachment and disforestation steadily reduced the forest area, and successive records of the perambulation of the forest boundaries clearly demonstrate this process. By the time of Edward II the Royal Forest had been reduced by more than half. The earliest record of interest in the protection of the Forest of Dean on the part of the Crown is contained in Domesday Book, which states that Edward the Confessor had exempted the forest from taxation. Domesday Book also contains reference to ships 'giving to the wood' when dealing with the lands beyond the River Wye. Under the earlier Norman kings the forest was administered by the Constables of St Briavels Castle, who were also Wardens of the Forest of Dean. Wood from the forest was used on a large scale for the smelting of iron, for mining as well as for domestic purposes.

The Constable of the Forest presided over the Court of the Hundred of St Briavels, for the laws of the forest were superimposed on those of the civil administration. Furthermore, he presided over the Mine Law Court, though this was rarely held. The Verderers had their Court of Attachment before which offenders against the vert (any clearance of growing wood) of the forest were brought for preliminary examination.

Suspected felons were sent for trial before the Forest Justices at Gloucester, where the Foresters-in-fee and other witnesses gave their evidence. The carvings on tombs at Newland Church illustrate the costumes of some of these officials. The justice rolls of the thirteenth century tell us of the corruption of many forest officials. They also tell of offences against the 'king's beasts' by, among others, the clergy, even the Canons of Hereford, who stole venison and took it to their house at Lydney. It appears that much of the venison and timber stolen from the forest went to Bristol.

During the Edwardian wars of the thirteenth century, St Briavels became a major armaments centre. The industry was in the hands of the Malemort family for three generations, when they specialised in bolts for crossbows, and developed a considerable export trade to Scotland and the Continent. It was the abundance of iron and timber for smelting that made this industry possible, and more than 70 forges are recorded as having been working at this time. Nails were also being produced, and, at a later date, pins. The George Inn at Mitcheldean was formerly the location for making pins and shot, while Guns Mills, near Flaxley, derives its name from the cannons made there in the seventeenth century.

The iron industry made serious inroads on the timber of the forest, and from time to time the Crown bargained over rights to forest woodland with forge owners, such as Flaxley Abbey. It was in this way that Abbot's Wood, near Cinderford, came into being, granted as it was to the abbey in exchange for a right to cut timber in the forest. There were other woods which were granted by the king to individuals or religious houses, but such grants were carefully monitored in order to protect the King's game. At first the royal concern was mainly for the preservation of game cover, but in the course of time, timber acquired increased importance for iron-smelting and shipbuilding and, as the coal-mining industry developed, for pitworks.

Outcrops of coal were being worked in the Forest of Dean from at least as early as the thirteenth century. Ochre, used for textile dyes, was also quarried in the forest from the Middle Ages onwards. The Free Miners of the Dean Forest are first mentioned in a record entitled 'The Laws and Customs of the Miners in the Forest of Dean', compiled about the year 1300. Until recently they retained privileges in the opening and working of the small shallow collieries that are scattered throughout the coal-bearing areas. Between 1668 and 1777 a unique Court of Mine Law met at intervals to deal with disputes amongst the miners. It was presided over by the Constable of St Briavels Castle, with the Gaveller and Clerk of Court attending and verdicts being given by a jury of 12 miners. The Gaveller, whose office still survives, superintended the opening of the mines, and kept an eye on the King's interests there. An example of court procedure is given in the following extract from *The Book of Dennis*:

> Ye Miner shall present the debtor in the Mine Law w'ch is Court for the Mine and there debtor before the Constable and his Clarke the Gaveller and the Miners and none other Folke to pleade onely the Miners shall bee there and hold a sticke of holly and then the said Myner demanding the debt shall putt his hand upon the sticke and none other with him and shall sweare his Faith that the said debt is to him due.

In the seventeenth century Dud Dudley experimented here with coal, as distinct from charcoal, for smelting iron. Late in the following century the invention of the steam engine and the development of a nationwide road system opened the way for a large-scale trade in coal from the forest.

During the seventeenth and eighteenth centuries the forest was rented out from time to time to royal favourites. The office of Constable survived, but forest management under this regime was never rigorous. Timber from the Forest of Dean had acquired a reputation as being good for shipbuilding, and there was considerable interest in the forest at the time of the Spanish Armada. John Evelyn, the diarist, in his classic work on forestry, *Silva* (1662), mentions that he had heard

> that in the great expedition of 1588 it was expressly enjoined the Spanish Armada that if, when landed, they should not be able to subdue our nation and make good their conquest, they should yet be sure not to leave a tree standing in the Forest of Dean.

From the Tudor period onwards the history of the forest was largely one of exploitation and mismanagement by successive court favourites. There was a change of heart by the Crown in 1638, when a survey demonstrated the parlous condition and stocking of the woods, and some 17,000 acres were ordered to be enclosed. This scheme developed, however, into the notorious sale of the forest to Sir John Winter by Charles I in 1640. Winter's patent was annulled by the Commonwealth, but during this period there was extensive felling and the timber was sold for the benefit of the government. In 1656 a bill was passed for the preservation of the timber in the forest. Reafforestation was, however, fiercely resisted by the local inhabitants, and little permanent good seems to have been done. Winter's 'rights' were restored to him by Charles II, greatly to the displeasure of the neighbourhood. At this time a new survey showed that the mature timber in the Forest was reduced to 25,929 oaks and 4204 beeches. By 1667 hardly any trees remained. In the meantime a committee of the House of Commons had been appointed to investigate local complaints, and they came up with the following proposal:

> Imprimis, That 11,000 acres of the waste soil of the forest of Dean, whereof Lea Bayly and Canopp to be part of the said waste, may be enclosed by his Majesty, and discharged for ever from all manners of pasture, estovers and pannage; and if ever his Majesty, or his successors shall think fit to lay open any part of the said 11,000 acres, when to take in so much elsewhere, so as the whole enclosure exceed not at any one time 11,000 acres.

In the following year the Crown was empowered to enclose common waste of the forest for timber, provided that the total area enclosed at no time exceeded 11,000 acres, and this limit still holds. The enclosures authorised were free from common rights, and when the trees had grown up beyond damage the areas could again be thrown open for grazing and an equivalent area enclosed elsewhere. In 1675 the forest was divided into six walks or districts; six lodges were built and for each walk a keeper was appointed. It is stated in a return made in 1691 that, except in 'Lea Bayly', where the fences had been thrown down by dissatisfied commoners, the plantations were 'generally very well grown'. In 1705 it was reported that the woods were full of young trees, two-thirds of which were beech and were overtopping the oaks. By 1788 the actual area still enclosed had dwindled to 765 acres. From the days of Charles II until 1808, the total area of the Forest of Dean suffered no appreciable reduction. In 1808 measures were again taken to ensure a supply of oak timber for the Navy. At that time the Forest of Dean covered some 18,500 acres, together with between 600 and 700 acres of freehold land also held by the crown. The rest of the forest had a sparse tree cover and it was estimated that only 24,000 old oaks remained on the ground, and that many of those cut were used for naval construction. Few of the old oaks survive today, but there are still about a dozen standing in Churchill enclosure, and a few others elsewhere. Tree felling for the Navy finally ceased in 1863, by which time iron was supplanting oak as the material used for the construction of warships.

Medieval parks

The royal forests may be viewed as a dramatic, but relatively short-lived, interval in the story of the management of wild animals, but as the forests went into decline so deer parks became increasingly common. The park was a far more effective means of controlling animals, although the creation of medieval parkland could involve considerable capital outlay on behalf of the park owner. Medieval parks were primarily intended for the retention of deer: at first roe and red deer, but later exclusively fallow deer. Just as the greatest nobles aspired to the ownership of forests and chases so, too, the acquisition of a park became an important status symbol which penetrated to lower levels of the social strata. From the late thirteenth century the Crown granted a large number of licenses to empark. Such licenses had to be bought from the king and represented a valuable source of income to the crown. Lucrative fines were imposed when the system was bypassed, as in 1251 when the Prior of Wenlock was obliged to pay £200 to retain his unlicensed park at Oxenbold in the Corve Dale of south Shropshire.

The medieval park differed from the forest in that it was normally demarcated by a boundary consisting of a ditch and wooden pale, or in certain areas a stone wall. Parks varied in size from just a few acres to well over 500 acres in size. Most of the medieval parks have subsequently been cleared and enclosed for agriculture, but their curving linear earthworks survive as modern boundaries, and place names such as Park Farm, Park End or Park Lodge often indicate the site of a former deer park which has long since disappeared. For example, Park Farm, close to Heath in south Shropshire, was created out of a medieval deer park, and its boundaries are still identifiable on the ground. In 1334 there was a reference to the King's parks in Herefordshire at Stretton Sugwas, Ledbury, Donningwood, Colwall, Bromyard and Ross-on-Wye, but by the late fourteenth century the vast majority of parks were in the hands of private individuals.

There are numerous references in medieval documents to Marcher parks which have disappeared without trace. For example, in 1336, two parks at Wigmore are recorded as containing 'many great woods and great oaks', while a lost park with deer and a watermill

65 The ruins of the late thirteenth-century fortified manor house at Acton Burnell. The castle formed the centrepiece of an extensive medieval deer park which measured some four miles around its circumference

is recorded at Asperton in the same year. Other parks survived into the post-medieval period and were converted into landscaped estates attached to country houses. Many of these parks feature on Saxton's sixteenth-century maps and include Hodnet Park, which is first referred to at an inquest held in 1275. The enquiry found that it would not be to the public detriment if Sir de Hodnet enclosed two footpaths which ran through Hodnet Park, on the condition that he provided alternative footpaths around the park. Saxton also marks two parks close to Hodnet, at Stanton and Shawbury. At Shawbury, Giles de Erdington received a licence, in 1253, to make a deer-leap into his park. In 1297, Edward I licensed the Abbot of Haughmond to enclose 20 acres of his wood in the Bailiwick of Haughmond, and Edward II, in 1313, extended this licence to 60 additional acres in the same forest. These grants probably marked the origin of the large park at Haughmond which also featured on Saxton's map.

On the borders of Shropshire and Cheshire, Saxton marks four adjacent parks: Blakemere, Ightfield, Shavington, and Adderley. The last of these still exists; it was emparked by Walter de Dunstanville, Lord of Adderley, by permission of Ralph, Abbot of Shrewsbury, between 1175 and 1190. Blakemere, which originally belonged to the Le Strange family, is described thus by Leland, when making his progress through the county:

> From Whitchurch a mile and a half, I cam by the pale of the large parke of Blakmer longying to the Erle of Shrewsbiri, wherin is a very fair place of loge. The Park had both red deer and falow. In the park (as I herd say) be three fair poles, of wich I saw by the pale the largest. caullid Blakem, whereof the park is named.

At Ightfield, Leland records that

> Syr Richard Manoring, chefe of that name, dwelleth a three miles be est from

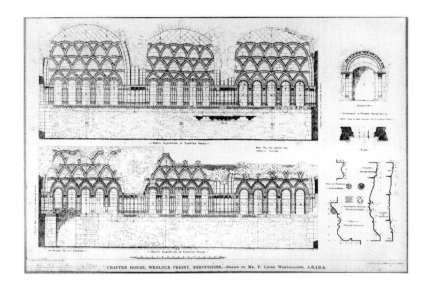

66 Romanesque blind arcading in the Chapter House at Wenlock Priory as it appeared in a drawing for The Builder in 1888. This represents some of the finest Norman architecture in Britain

Price village at a village cauleld Hightfelde, having a Parke and great plenty of wood about hym.

To the south of the Severn, both Leland and Saxton record a park at Willey, on the bounds of the Forest of Shirlett, and south of this Saxton marks a park at Upton Cressett (discussed in chapter 10). In the centre of the shire, but south of Shrewsbury, Saxton shows parks at Langley and at Plaish and another at Rowton, eight miles west of the county town. In the south of the county other important parks are at Oakley, to the west of Ludlow, and Stoke St Milborough, a little to the north of Ludlow; also Dean Park, near Burford, on the Worcestershire boundary, and the large park of Cleobury in the south-eastern part of the Forest of Wyre. Before the First World War there were 11 deer parks in Shropshire, four of which had ancient origins and were on the sites of early forests.

Places to visit

Forester's Lodge, Millichope, Munslow, Shropshire SO 522 893
An interesting reminder of the nature of forest landscapes in the early Middle Ages is provided by the Forester's Lodge at Upper Millichope on Wenlock Edge. This twelfth-century building has the appearance of a medieval chapel from the outside with a single round-headed doorway on the entrance side, with no windows (apart from a later insertion). It lay within the Long Forest and may have acted both as a lodge for a royal Forester and as a jail for poachers and others who broke Forest Law.

The place-name, Millichope, is Anglo-Saxon and means 'remote valley associated with Milla'. The lodge is in private ownership.

Brown Clee Hill, Shropshire

The Clee was one of the smaller Shropshire Forests; it was no more than 24,000 acres in extent, and it remained under the direct control of the Crown for only a short time. The Clee ceased to be true royal forest in 1155, but it was later operated on the lines of a royal forest by the Cliffords from Corfham Castle in the Corve Dale. Its history, however, illustrates aspects of landscape history which are significantly different from the true woodland forests. The Clee Forest, constituting Brown Clee Hill and its surrounding area, was at one stage originally joined with the Long Forest to the north and Shirlett Forest to the east. The name Brown Clee does not appear until the fifteenth century, before which the hill and forest were known as 'Les Clivas'. The name Clee is probably derived from *cleo*, which in Old English means 'ball-shaped massif'. Brown was later added to distinguish this hill from neighbouring Titterstone Clee and is an obvious allusion to the reddish-brown soils of the area.

It is possible to reconstruct the boundaries of the original forest from early parish boundaries, which radiate from the three most prominent points on the Brown Clee, giving each foothill township a proportion of wood and wasteland on the hill. Where these boundaries run as straight lines they presumably reflect unexploited woodland or heath, which had not been subject to territorial control before then or at any rate had not been physically demarcated. Earnstrey Park, now in Abdon parish, was part of the forest and the medieval 'hay' there probably represents the residue of a Saxon park, the boundaries of which can clearly be identified on the ground today in the form of a linear park boundary. Apart from the manorial woodland attached to each village, most of the remaining timber was cleared during the early Middle Ages, principally by Wenlock Priory and Shrewsbury Abbey. In 1465, such was the shortage of local timber that when a new fence was required for Earnstrey Park, the wood had to be bought outside the forest and by the time Leland visited the area in about 1540, he observed, 'There is no great plenty of wood in Clee Hills.'

A most interesting document of 1612 called *A Description of Clee* demonstrates the persistence of the common rights of all the townships that had lain within the ancient forest. Common rights on Brown Clee included agistment and pannage (grazing rights for livestock), turbary (right to cut and collect turf) and estovers (right to take wood for repairs and fuel). These rights, however, were reserved for those townships that actually lay on Brown Clee, the inhabitants of the old Forest area being allowed common rights of considerably less importance. In return for these privileges, the 'out-commoners' were subject to a modified form of Forest Law — in particular they were to refrain from disturbing deer found among their crops. The out-commoners had to follow very precise routes from their townships to the grazing areas on the Clee. These roads were known as 'drift-ways', 'straker ways' or 'outracks'. The name 'outrack' is still given to a sunken road in Ditton Priors leading to Brown Clee, and other outracks survive on the Long Mynd and in other hilly parts of the Marches. The term 'straker' probably refers to the method of calling the inhabitants of the forest by a horn (Middle English *strake* means to blow a horn as a summons). Gough in his *History of Myddle* refers to 'streaking' in connection with similar movements of animals to common land. Many of the straker roads became deeply entrenched and can still be traced as sunken or 'hollow' ways. These routes were still in use in the seventeenth century when it was claimed that 'the driftways are long and tedious because the strakers were to drive the lands and commons belonging to other lordships before they could reach Clee soil'. An interesting footnote to this story was that at the time of parliamentary enclosure (1809), Thomas Mytton, Lord of Earnstrey, tried to obtain extensive allotments on Brown Clee as 'lord of the Clee Chace'; in reality this was an attempt to claim rights from the Royal Forest which had been disbanded some six centuries earlier.

The Brown Clee remains a fascinating place to visit. It incorporates the remnants of three major Iron Age hillforts as well as extensive areas of open moorland. It is best approached from Heathamgate on the west side of the hill which gives ready access to common land and the well-preserved hillfort at Nordybank.

Limebrook Nunnery, Lingen, Herefordshire SO 375 662

The site of Limebrook Nunnery is not a place to visit for its architectural glories, as today all it consists of is a few stumps of its former buildings. It does, however, occupy an immensely attractive site, located in a beautiful position on the narrow level floor of the valley of the Lingen Brook in the former Deerfold Forest with steep hills rising from each side. In the area around wild strawberries reputedly grow and the surrounding woods are said to contain herbs grown originally for medicinal purposes. The nunnery, which was Augustinian and dedicated to St Thomas Becket, murdered in 1170 and canonised in 1173, was reputedly founded in 1189 but there is no positive evidence to confirm this date. A group of six nuns lived in this peaceful spot and the records of the nunnery suggest that although it frequently claimed poverty, the nuns were not particularly poor. Throughout its history the nunnery gradually acquired property, much of it on the best farming land in the area. In 1536 when, strictly speaking, under the terms of the dissolution of the monasteries it should have been dissolved as being valued under £200, the nuns purchased 'perpetual continuance' by payment of £53 6s 8d, which hardly seems the act of a body of poor nuns. However, in 1539, Limebrook along with all the remaining religious houses was dissolved and the nuns pensioned off — their payment had prolonged their existence for only three years. A survey of Limebrook Nunnery property in places such as Aymestrey, Brimfield, Croft, Lingen, Pembridge, Stoke Bliss and Wigmore suggests that its houses, many of them of late medieval 'cruck' construction, were quite large. The antiquary John Leland, writing in the early sixteenth century, records that there was a stone bridge over the River Lugg at Limebrook; this lay a kilometre or so to the south of the nunnery, where the Lingen Brook joined the Lugg.

9 The later Middle Ages

During the later Middle Ages, Shropshire and Herefordshire enjoyed mixed fortunes. The various attempts by medieval kings to subdue Wales had resulted in the tide of national conflict moving further west, leaving hundreds of castles high and dry. During the thirteenth and fourteenth centuries, however, the Marches were the backdrop for important events involving the English crown, and Wigmore Castle came to represent a power base of national significance. Added to which periodic Welsh raids occurred right up until the time of the Union with England in 1536 and baronial conflict was endemic in the Marches. During the Baron's Revolt of 1321, it was recorded that Roger de Mortimer 'seized wools, meat, grain, livestock and other goods valued at more than £141 from the unwilling villagers in Herefordshire'. Other acts of barely disguised piracy were common, although as the number of fully functioning castles decreased, so the offences tended to be of a more petty nature.

Battles in the Borderland

Occasionally the Marches featured on the stage of national politics. At the battle of Shrewsbury in 1403, Henry IV defeated Sir Henry Percy (Hotspur). The battle, which is perhaps principally remembered today as forming the climax of the first part of Shakespeare's *Henry IV*, took place on 21 July 1403 between an army led by the Lancastrian King Henry IV and a rebel army led by members of the Yorkist Percy family. In July 1403 Sir Henry Percy and about 200 men, including some former Scottish prisoners, rode south from the Scottish border. Travelling by way of Northumberland and Lancashire they reached Chester on 9 July. Here Sir Henry stayed at the home of Petronilla Clark who, along with other inhabitants of Chester, eventually lost her property for siding with the rebel. Indeed most of the rebel army was raised in Cheshire and both city and county were later heavily fined for their support of the losing side. The other rebel leaders came from north Wales, Lancashire, Shropshire, Herefordshire, Northumberland and Yorkshire.

Ironically, Henry IV was on his way to the Scottish border to aid the Percys against the Scots, and it wasn't until he reached Nottingham that he heard that the Percys had risen against him. Henry then moved rapidly westwards by way of Derby to Lichfield. After an abortive attempt at a negotiated peace at Saniway in Cheshire, both armies reached the vicinity of Shrewsbury on 19 July. Shrewsbury was the principal town on the route taken by the Percy army and was important both as a major crossing of the River Severn and as a potential source of supplies. The rebels' intention was to join up with another group of Welsh dissidents led by Owen Glendower.

67 Rowley's Mansion, Shrewsbury. This massive sixteenth-century half-timbered building houses the town museum (it also contains a collection of material from Roman Wroxeter). It was built by William Rowley, a wealthy town merchant. The austere brick building attached dates to about 1620 and was the work of his son; it was the first significant brick building in the town

The Percy army arrived first with the intention of fighting for Shrewsbury and stopping Henry's army from crossing the river. They were preparing to attack the town when the banners of the King's army were seen approaching from the east. The early arrival of Henry caught the rebels by surprise and Percy retreated a little to the north and spent the night at Berwick. According to one story, Percy was upset at leaving his sword at a place where it had been foretold he would die. The royal army apparently forded the Severn at Uffington on the night of 20 July and drew up in battle array near Haughmond Abbey. On the morning of 21 July, the Percy forces marched east towards the enemy. The precise site of the battle has not been identified, despite many attempts to locate it. Indeed such an attempt was made by Charles Darwin, a native of Shrewsbury, who reported finding 'a surprising number of iron arrowheads . . . in a grass field . . . on the northern side of the Severn'. On 21 July the two armies faced each other for several hours while remaining out of arrow-shot; in the meantime negotiations took place to see if a bloodless settlement could be negotiated. The envoys included the Abbots of Shrewsbury and Haughmond, for the royal side, and the Earl of Worcester, from the rebel army. Finally, however, two hours before sunset the peace talks broke down, partly because the King feared that the talks were being protracted to allow time for rebel reinforcements which were expected the following day.

After the King gave the battle order the royal vanguard moved forward under the Earl of Stafford to meet the rebels led by the Earl of Douglas. The archers dismounted and opened fire 'so thick and fast that it seemed to the beholders like a thick cloud'. The Percy archers were more effective that the royal ones during this initial contest, for, as one chronicler wrote, the royal vanguard fell 'like apples falling in the autumn, when . . . stirred by the south-west wind'. After the arrows were exhausted hand-to-hand fighting began. Percy and the Earl of Douglas led a mounted charge apparently aimed directly at the King himself and succeeded in killing the Royal Standard Bearer, while the Earl of Douglas was severely wounded. After the initial Percy successes the royal army counter-attacked. One account says that the tide of battle turned when Prince Henry (later Henry V) joined the battle with his troops. But the decisive moment appears to have been when the rebel army learnt that Henry Percy had been killed. The precise circumstances of Percy's death are not known and there are several versions, all of which emphasise his bravery. A considerable number of his supporters died with him and some important rebel leaders, including the Earls of Worcester and Douglas, were captured. The battle had lasted for only just over two hours and when it ended many did not even know which army had won. The survivors were scattered over several miles of Shropshire countryside, 'they sank down in all directions, a chance medley of weary, wounded, bruised and bleeding men'. The contemporary chroniclers emphasise the exceptional number of casualties, and one wrote 'Now those who were present said they never saw or read in the records of Christian times so furious a battle in so short a time or of larger casualties than happened there.' Estimates of the casualties vary; one charter of 1445 mentions burials over an area of three miles, and other chronicles record the dead as numbering from 5000 to 9000 men. One unusual feature of the battle is the exceptionally high proportion of casualties suffered by the victors. There were 16 Royalist and 8 rebel knights killed. Sir Henry Percy was buried at Whitchurch in Shropshire; it is reported that before he was buried King Henry wept at the sight of his body. Nevertheless, soon after, the King gave orders that the body should be put on show to prevent rumours that Percy was still alive. The body was exhumed and displayed in Shrewsbury and was later cut into quarters. The quarters were then displayed at Newcastle, London, Chester and Bristol and the head at York. In November 1403 the remains were returned to Percy's widow who had them buried in York Minster. There is a monumental cross at the top of Pride Hill in Shrewsbury which marks the spot where Hotspur's body was dismembered.

Monumental brasses were set up to the fallen knights in the church at Battlefield just outside Shrewsbury which was erected a few years after the battle. Attached to this was a chancery chapel where prayers were said for those who had died. During the Wars of the Roses another decisive battle was fought at Mortimer's Cross on the River Lugg to the south of Wigmore in 1461 when Edward, Duke of York (later Edward IV) defeated a Lancastrian army led by Jasper Tudor and the Earl of Wiltshire. The Lancastrian army consisted largely of Welsh, French and Irish troops, the latter having been raised on Wiltshire's Irish estates. Wiltshire landed at Milford Haven at the end of 1460 and after joining forces with Jasper Tudor moved forwards in an attempt to defeat their enemies in the Welsh Marches and then link up with Henry VI's wife, Queen Margaret, who was the effective leader of the Lancastrians. From Presteigne the Lancastrians moved towards Leominster with the intention of crossing the Severn at Worcester. However, at Mortimer's Cross they found themselves facing a Yorkist army which had been mustered in Hereford under the command of Edward, Earl of March.

On 2 February 1461 the Yorkists won, but little is known of this important battle apart from the report of a strange apparition seen in the sky when:

There were seen three suns in the firmament shining full clear, where the people had great marvel, and there of were aghast. The noble Earl Edward them comforted and said, 'Be of good cheer, and dread not; this is a good sign . . .'

Edward, who was only 18 years old at the time of the battle, later took the 'Sun in Splendour' as a personal badge and was proclaimed and installed as King Edward IV on 4 March 1461. Following the battle of Mortimer's Cross, Jasper Tudor and the Earl of Wiltshire escaped. However, Owen Tudor, who had accompanied the Lancastrian forces on the march through Wales, was captured and taken to Hereford, where he was beheaded.

Edward's ancestral home was at Wigmore, just a few miles away from Mortimer's Cross. Had the Percy-Glendower alliance been successful, schemes afoot to dismember the kingdom into three parts — one each for Glendower, the Percys and the Mortimers — could have dramatically changed the course of British history. Wigmore Castle is today a massive ruin sleeping quietly in the Herefordshire countryside, and only its size hints at the momentous historical events with which it was associated.

The Welsh Marches also featured prominently in the ultimate phases of the Wars of the Roses, when the Tudors fared considerably better. On 1 August 1485 Henry Tudor sailed with an expeditionary force from Harfleur in Normandy for Wales. He landed just to the north of Milford Haven on 8 August and marched up the western coast of Wales collecting followers on the way. By 13 August Henry was at Welshpool close to where he met up with a contingent led by Sir Rhys ap Thomas; the combined armies spent the night on the Long Mountain in western Shropshire. The following day the army marched on Shrewsbury, taking Montford Bridge, about four miles west of the town, and Forton about two miles north of the Severn. Messengers were sent to Shrewsbury requesting admission, but the town's senior magistrate, Thomas Mytton, refused entry and closed the town gates. However, the next day, following further negotiations, Henry was allowed into the town and recruited more troops there. The bloodless taking of Shrewsbury provided a major morale boost for the Tudors. Just one week later Henry's army, having continued their eastwards thrust, successfully confronted Richard III at Bosworth Field and effectively ended the civil war.

The end of the Marcher castles

The status of the Marcher lordships who enjoyed legal independence from the Crown had long made them offensive in the eyes of the English sovereigns. Their demise came when the Crown acquired Marcher lands during the later fifteenth and early sixteenth centuries in the wake of the Wars of the Roses, thus effectively making the King the most important Marcher lord of all. The battle of Bosworth brought Henry VII not only the English Crown, but also the extensive estates of the House of York around Ludlow and Wigmore and further westwards into Wales. In 1495 Chirk, Bromfield and Yale were forfeited and in 1521 the fall of the Duke of Buckingham gave Henry VIII further extensive Marcher lordships. As a result by 1530 most of the larger Marcher lordships were in royal hands, and the way was clear for the Act of Union which extended English common law to Wales and divided the Welsh parts of the Marches into shires on the English model. In order to maintain order in what hitherto had been a notoriously disorderly part of the country, the Tudor government created the Council of the Marches with extensive judicial and administrative powers. The Council of the Marches of Wales remained in existence until the Civil War, and was not finally abolished until 1689. Throughout its history it was based at Ludlow Castle, the ancient centre of Yorkist power in the Marches. Council members made frequent journeys throughout Wales and the Marches in order to maintain order and exercise the Crown authority in a variety of matters. As they were accompanied by a considerable retinue, they required spacious lodgings. At Shrewsbury the town Corporation maintained the Council House for their use; frequently, however, they were obliged to stay in royal castles, which partly explains the survival of some of these medieval fortifications into the post-medieval period. The principal royal castles of the Welsh Marches during the later Middle Ages were Ludlow, Wigmore, Chirk, Montgomery, Brecon and Monmouth.

Bishop Roland Lee, president of the Council in 1534, deplored the state of the royal castles saying that they were 'fit for neither war or peace'. Ludlow was in such a state of decay that the Council could not stay there until repairs had been carried out. Wigmore he found 'utterly decayed in lodgings, and awful want of reparation in time'. Despite some repairs two years later further work was required at Ludlow, while at Brecon 'there is a piece of the castle fallen and another piece at Chirk, and all must be done: God send money'. The dissolution of the monasteries brought some welcome windfalls in the form of building materials: stone from Wigmore Abbey, timber from monastic houses in Ludlow and lead from Basingwerk. However, the burgesses of Shrewsbury who generally tried to maintain close relations with the Council tried in vain to save the claustral buildings of Shrewsbury Abbey. In 1540 they petitioned for the use of the abbey as 'a residence for the use of the princes grace or any other nobility of the realm that shall resort to this town'. Later, in 1590, the burgesses sent an emissary to London to petition for the 'ruinous castle to be repaired and builded, hereafter to be a place both to reserve the Council as also a convenient place for the prisoners of the Shire'.

During the seventeenth century, the only building regularly maintained by the Council was Ludlow Castle, the other ancient centres of royal authority in the Marches having been by then either passed to other owners or abandoned. It would appear that when the Council was in session both Ludlow and the castle would have been extremely lively. The winter courts were famous social occasions enlivened by a round of banquets and masques of which the most famous was Milton's *Comus*, first performed to celebrate the installation of the Earl of Bridgwater as Lord President at Michaelmas 1634. It was primarily for these functions that the medieval castle was renovated during the sixteenth and seventeenth centuries. During the Commonwealth, the Council of the Marches was in abeyance and Ludlow Castle was left to its own devices. Some work was carried out after the Restoration, but in 1689 when the Council was abolished the castle ceased to have any further political function. For a while it continued to be looked after by a resident keeper, who in the reign of Queen Anne was still being paid by the Treasury for his occasional expenditure on repairs. After this, however, it was finally abandoned and when the lead was removed from its roofs in the eighteenth century the castle rapidly fell into decay and became ruinous.

Economic decline and deserted villages

The political events which brought the Welsh Marches on to the national scene did not exempt the region from the general agricultural decline which occurred in the fourteenth and fifteenth centuries. The Black Death, which was an important, if not the prime, reason for agricultural recession, affected the Border region as badly as anywhere else in the country. The agricultural recession was accompanied by the

68 The earthworks of a typical deserted medieval Marcher village near Stottesden. The former street pattern can be identified in the form of hollow ways; internal village boundaries can also be seen. Below the village there is an area of ridge and furrow representing part of a former open field agricultural system. It would appear that the village was laid out on top of the open fields and was abandoned during the later Middle Ages

shrinkage or total abandonment of large numbers of hamlets and villages.

The arable open field system, which operated in one form or another throughout most of England, had been adopted throughout the Marches, including in highly marginal areas. This system was adversely affected by a combination of factors in the fourteenth and fifteenth centuries, including climatic deterioration and failed harvests as well as plague.

Thus over large areas of the Welsh borderland, open field arable farming was abandoned and replaced by enclosed pastoral farming at a relatively early date. In contrast to these developments a significant degree of prosperity was brought to the region by the wool trade in the later Middle Ages. The Border, with its large open moorland spaces combined with nearby lush pastures and ample water-power to treat the wool, was an ideal environment for a successful textile industry. Furthermore, towns within the Borderland such as Oswestry, Hereford and Shrewsbury benefited substantially from their ability to monopolise the trade both in Marcher and Welsh wool for many centuries.

Nevertheless, the decline in arable farming led to a rash of shrunken and deserted villages in the region. There are something like 400 settlements in Shropshire and Herefordshire which can be classified as deserted, shrunken or shifted. Not all of this movement occurred in the Middle Ages, for many settlements were abandoned later as the result of the emparking associated with the creation of country houses between 1600 and 1800. Nonetheless, a large proportion of those abandoned villages do seem to have disappeared at this time. Because many of them were originally small and because the process of shrinkage was often very slow, the identification of sites on the ground is more

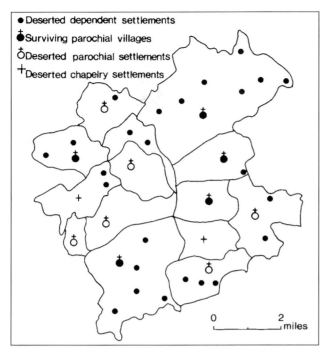

Deserted dependent settlements
Surviving parochial villages
Deserted parochial settlements
Deserted chapelry settlements

0   2 miles

69 Deserted villages in south Shropshire

difficult in the Borderland than in the central Midlands, where large areas of earthworks frequently mark the site of former villages. There are, however, a number of Marcher sites where there are earthworks to be seen on the ground. A particularly good example is called the Bold, near Aston Botterell in south Shropshire, a typical deserted Border hamlet now contained within a single modern field. An aerial photograph of the site indicates that there could have been as many as 20 families living on the site in the Middle Ages, but like so many other Border townships, the Bold gradually declined to the size of a single farm. The remains of a chapel which once served the former settlement here is incorporated into the modern farm complex. Such abandoned chapels are a common feature of deserted hamlets in this area, and Duke in his *Antiquities of Shropshire* (1854) records some 105 lost chapels in Shropshire.

A valuable source of information about village mortality in the Border area is contained in the Assessment of the Ninth (1341), a taxation record that adjusted parish tax assessments which had originally been made in 1291. The assessors tell a story of almost universal hardship throughout the region. It is true that many of the original assessments seem to have been unrealistically high, but even allowing for this and for exaggeration of the scale of poverty brought about by a natural reluctance to pay taxes, in almost every parish there was a substantial reduction. At Upton Cresset, for instance, known mainly for its fine Tudor house, the assessment dropped from 36s 8d to 17s, because it is said 'The land lay untilled and the tenants of the same have withdrawn because of penury.' Reasons given for the reduction in other parishes include taxation, pestilence among cattle and sheep, bad harvests, and the destruction of crops by storms.

The main reason normally given for the disappearance of villages was the Black Death of 1348-9. It is recorded that over half the clergy in Shropshire/Herefordshire were killed during the epidemic. In Hereford so many clergymen died that unusual arrangements had to be made for the canons to take services and the bishop complained bitterly of the 'recent unprecedented plague'. Precise references to the impact of the Black Death on rural settlements are rare, but it is clear that pestilence was a factor in undermining the village structure. Records for the year following the Black Death show that many manors were said to have been reduced in value because of plague and a few are known to have succumbed completely. For instance a small township in Stanton Lacy manor called La Yeye is last recorded in 1350 as being ruinous. Similarly, Broomcroft, a township in Kenley parish, had been depopulated by 1363 when it was said to be uncultivated because of lack of tenants.

Ecclesiastical records provide one source of information about the extent of damage inflicted by the Black Death in the area. The parish of Knill in the deanery of Leominster was one of two benefices which were recorded as falling vacant twice during the pestilence. In the deanery of Frome both the parishes of Great and Little Collington also fell vacant on two occasions and in 1352 they were consolidated. It was then stated that 'because of the pestilence the diminished value of both livings was itself hardly sufficient to maintain one priest'. One observer declared that the deanery of Archenfield 'was the plague-patch of the diocese'. Ross-on-Wye, which was an important river port in the fourteenth century, seems to have suffered particularly badly and it seems probable that the deanery of Ross was the real plague-patch of the diocese. Within four months of 1349, 13 of the 26 incumbents in the district around Morville died of plague. Two vicars of Ellesmere and one vicar of Welsh Hampton died in the same year of the pestilence. An inquisition at Lilleshall Abbey taken in 1353 found that the underwood of a park there was then worth nothing because all the customary buyers had perished in the 'Great Plague'. The inquisition also mentioned 'a certain foreign wood, the underwood of which used to be worth before the pestilence 3s 4d, and now it is only worth 12d beyond the sustentation of the house'. It also recorded that the land belonging to the abbey, which had been worth £15 in 1330, was worth only £10 after the pestilence because there were no tenants and that 'One Abbot died 1350'.

A register of loss of rents in Shropshire after 'The Great Pestilence' provides further insight into the decline of the area. At Yockleton the rents of assize of free tenants fell from £8 to 30s; at Colmere and Hampton, from £4 to 10s; in the hundred of Bradford, from £16 to £8; at Wentmore, from £5 to 40s; at Shelve, from 36s to 26s 6d; at Harleigh, from £4 to 10s; at Wyley, from 20s to 12s. All these reductions were specifically attributed to the pestilence. In 1364 the adjacent churches of Whyle and Pudlestone were united on the basis of a petition that the plague had depopulated the area. Subsequently plague was endemic throughout England and there were further major outbreaks in 1360-1, 1369 and 1379. The second of these, known as the Children's Plague, appears to have had a particularly severe impact. There is little evidence to suggest that the Marches suffered any worse than the remainder of England and Wales, but it is fairly clear that the population of the country as a whole fell by as much as half between the 1340s and the 1440s, and that endemic plague was a contributory factor to this fall.

There is little evidence to show how far the unstable political situation and periodic attacks from across the Welsh border had any permanent effect on settlement in the Marches, although it seems certain that a number of western manors were gradually abandoned because of such attrition. At Westbury, for instance, Thomas Corbet of Caus was engaged in constant warfare with his relative Gruffydd ap Gwenwynwyn throughout the thirteenth century. In 1406, following Owen Glendower's rebellion, a large number of western manors were excused taxation as they had been burnt down. One such, Burfield, today an isolated farmstead, was originally a township in the manor of Tempsitur near to Offa's Dyke. Allegedly the township and chapel were laid waste by Owen Glendower in about 1400 and thereafter it was known as the 'decayed township of Burfield'.

Plague and warfare notwithstanding, village abandonment often seems to have been a gradual reaction to changing economic, social and possibly climatic conditions. One of the abandoned Border settlements is appropriately named Cold Weston. The reason for the abandonment simply seems to lie in a poor choice of site in the first instance, lying as it does at 800ft above sea level on a north-facing slope. The village was in decline before the Black Death. In 1341 it was stated that 'there had once been an abundance of cattle here, but they had decreased because of the murrain which had hit the region', and the account concludes that 'the chapel is in a waste place and the living has been presented to four parsons within the year, but none of them would stay and there are only two tenants living by great labour and in want and others have absconded'. Today the sad and redundant little church of St Mary sits by itself in a thicket of trees, as if it were still sheltering from the cold and wind after all these centuries. Nearby lies the deserted village of Heath which is far more complete in its earthworks than the average Marcher deserted village and has more the appearance of a classic Midlands deserted village. The almost perfect Norman chapel is the centrepiece of the site, and in the surrounding fields there are extensive earthworks of the old village representing the roads, houses and even the stone-lined well of the former medieval community. In addition, close by there are the broken dams of two large fish ponds, ridge and furrow remnants of the open field system and the boundary of a medieval deer-park.

At Abdon, three miles away, the earthworks are even more spectacular. In the field to the east of St Catherine's parish church there are a number of distinct house platforms with an intersecting pattern of hollow ways, on one side of which the village earthworks are bounded by ridge and furrow. Documentary evidence suggests that Abdon, like Heath, declined slowly during the later Middle Ages. Abdon was partly reoccupied in the sixteenth and seventeenth centuries when its inhabitants were employed in quarrying on Brown Clee Hill. During the later eighteenth century, however, Abdon was deserted once more, for with the decline of the Clee Hill industries the villagers moved away. After a visit to Abdon in 1793 Archdeacon Plymley observed that 'some houses had been taken down and several seem to have fallen down', and excavations undertaken at Abdon seem to confirm this. A longhouse, which may have been the manor house, found next to the church, appears to have been abandoned about 1300 and there is no evidence of any subsequent occupation of that part of the old village. Lower down the field the base of a sixteenth- or seventeenth-century dwelling was located, but here too there is no evidence of any subsequent reoccupation.

Excavation elsewhere has revealed that not all settlement desertion was so early. At Braggington in Alberbury parish, investigations were carried out before the site was levelled. The earthworks of Braggington lay at 400ft, a quarter of a mile north-east of Braggington Hall on a north-facing slope at the foothills of the Breidden. A small stream which demarcates the Welsh border here runs eastwards at the foot of the slope, and banks and leats suggest that a mill once stood on it. Braggington is first recorded in 1255; its place name, however, with its 'ington' ending clearly suggests an earlier Saxon settlement on the site. It is therefore possible that this particular site is not that of the original community, especially as the earthworks of deserted village appeared to be sitting on top of ridge and furrow. This means that the medieval settlement was planted on ancient arable land, an indication that there was a break in the continuity of settlement. There was a population of 16 Welsh tenants living at Braggington in 1301 and the hamlet appears to have been occupied by Welsh families throughout the Middle Ages. The excavations uncovered a longhouse occupied from the fourteenth to the seventeenth centuries, as well as evidence of metal working in the form of iron slag and the bellows of a furnace. The village was abandoned before 1650 when Braggington Hall was built, and the kink in the road to the north-east of Little Braggington demonstrated that the road which originally ran to the village was diverted at about the same time, presumably in order to take the public highway away from the new country house.

Such road diversions around newly emparked areas are a common feature in the Marches. An abrupt turn in the road on the outside of a park boundary is nearly always an indication of a deserted or moved village whose presence was considered unsightly or inconveniently located by the country-house owner. Frequently, as at Braggington, the country houses which were erected were not necessarily particularly large. Another example of this device can be seen at Morville where the church of St Gregory, initially a Saxon collegiate church, now stands isolated in a field in front of Morville Hall, which was originally constructed in the latter part of the sixteenth century. The village now stretches along a road to the north of both house and former village. The road was clearly diverted when Morville Hall and its surrounding landscape were being created. Evidence of former houses and some medieval pottery has been found in service trenches in the vicinity of the church.

Many other villages appear to have shrunk considerably for a variety of other reasons during the fourteenth and fifteenth centuries. At Hampton Wafer in north-east Herefordshire there is today only a single farm, but up until the early nineteenth century the ruins of a chapel survived nearby. Deeply eroded hollow ways and house platforms, together with a pond which proved to be the flooded stock yard of a farm, mark the site of a former settlement. The excavation of several house sites revealed that occupation went back to at least the eleventh century and finished around 1300. In 1330 it was recorded that the manor passed to the Fitz Allens who held Hampton Court by the River Lugg. We know that most of their resources went into that manor and that consequently they neglected upland Hampton Wafer, thereby perhaps encouraging enclosure and the consequent transfer of the population to newly-established outlying farms. Such protracted contraction is a common characteristic of Marcher rural settlement. For example, a few miles to the west of Chepstow in Gwent lies the ruined church of St Keyna at Runston which is all that remains of the village there apart from some 25 house platforms, including a possible manor house. There were nine houses occupied in the mid-sixteenth century, while the church remained in use into the eighteenth century according to Victorian antiquaries: 'The cottages which formed the village were purposely allowed to fall to the ground, as the best way of dislodging the inhabitants who were a most lawless and troublesome set of people, subsisting by smuggling, sheep stealing, poaching and other predatory acts . . .'. Whatever the justification for these claims of lawlessness, it appears that the manorial lords, the Lewis family of St Pierre and Penlow, did much to encourage the demise of the village and that by 1878 when Archdeacon William Coxe visited the village, apart from the ruined church nothing remained.

Such high up and somewhat remote sites have tended to survive with recognisable earthworks precisely because of their isolated locations. Others, particularly in the lower parts of Herefordshire, have suffered more severely. The irregular and often unrecognised earthworks of deserted villages which contain the archaeological record of medieval rural communities are extremely vulnerable. A survey of sites in Herefordshire suggests that a considerable number have been ploughed up or severely damaged by agricultural activity over the past 30 years. Now the only surviving record of many such former settlements is to be found in the aerial photographs which were taken before their destruction.

The wool industry

Despite the arable recession and the high level of settlement abandonment during the later Middle Ages, certain areas of the Borderland prospered. The wool trade was particularly to the forefront of the Marches and Hereford, Leominster, Ludlow, Shrewsbury and Oswestry all fared well as a result of wool and the textile industry. Many of the fine half-timbered merchants' houses and market halls that grace small towns such as Ledbury and Pembridge were built, in part at least, on the proceeds of wool. The historian William Camden writing of Herefordshire at the end of the sixteenth century reported that 'for the three w's, of Wheat, Wool and Water it yieldeth to no shire of England'. At Leominster the local breed of sheep, the Ryeland, produced wool known as Leominster Ore. In Hereford the success of the wool trade in the fourteenth century was reflected in the almost continuous work on the fabric of the cathedral, in the restoration and beautification of the city churches and in the foundation of a grammar school in 1384. The city's ability to lend the King £100 in 1399, which was in part due to the wool trade, resulted in the acquisition of an important new charter.

If anything, Shropshire's wool industry was even more prosperous than that of Herefordshire. In 1273 English merchants exported nearly 1200 sacks of wool and of those over half were provided by Shropshire merchants, the largest total of any inland county. In 1294 it was recorded that 'certain English merchants, licensed by the King, crossed the sea with their wool; these ought to have been led by Lawrence of Ludlow . . .', but Lawrence, a powerful Shropshire woolman, had been drowned at sea. Draper's Row in Ludlow commemorates the wool trade and still contains some houses bought by Lawrence in the late thirteenth century. There are other monuments to the importance of Ludlow as a wool town, the most notable of which is the parish church of St Lawrence, the largest parish church in Shropshire and one of the finest in England, built in perpendicular style in the fourteenth and fifteenth centuries on the proceeds of the wool trade. The church, which is sometimes missed by visitors because it is hidden at ground level by infilling of the medieval market place, is best appreciated from the northern approach to Ludlow. Another testament to the importance of the wool trade lies a little to the north of Ludlow in the form of Stokesay Castle, probably the best-known fortified medieval manor house in England. Its great hall, whose substantial windows make it scarcely defensible, was probably built in the 1270s. Stokesay, too, was built by Lawrence of Ludlow, who received a licence to crenellate the house in 1291, when he appears to have added a second tower.

The fashion for building fortified manor houses appears in part to have been a consequence of Edward I's conquest of Wales. Robert Burnell, Bishop of Bath and Wells and Chancellor of England, rebuilt the castle at Holdgate in 1280. He was familiar with the castles of Edward I being built in north Wales and the surviving tower of this remarkable structure sitting behind a sixteenth-century farmhouse indicates the extent of his wealth and importance. But perhaps more representative of this movement is the castle at Acton Burnell, which was built after the conclusion of the conquest of Wales in 1284. It is a large rectangular house with round towers projecting at each corner; it is moatless and the entrances are all at ground level. Despite its outward appearance, Acton Burnell Castle had a thoroughly domestic function. The castle sits next to the ruins of a structure which carries the grand title of Parliament Barn, supposedly as a result of the first representative parliament being held here during a visit from Edward I. In 1420 the male line of the Burnell family died out. The castle was then abandoned and gradually fell into decay.

Shrewsbury was the most important of the Border wool towns. By the thirteenth century at least a quarter of the population was involved in the manufacture and sale of cloth. It was during this time that the great wool families that were to dominate Shrewsbury until the seventeenth century began to emerge: the Colles, the Rowleys, the Prides and the Vaughans. Such merchants built themselves imposing town houses which incorporated storage space for cloth. Vaughan's Mansion lies at the bottom of Pride Hill, its medieval street frontage having been successfully incorporated into modern shop premises (2-3 Pride Hill).

In 1326 Shrewsbury, along with Cardiff and Carmarthen, became a staple town for wool and leather for the whole of Wales, and thereafter enjoyed a virtual monopoly of trade in north and central Wales. Goods from central Wales came up the River Dovey to Welshpool and then down the Severn to Shrewsbury and the town appears to have had effective control of the wool trade in the Marches as far south as Hereford. After a drop in wool production in the early fifteenth century, trade seems to have revived by the middle of the sixteenth century. Many of the Tudor and Jacobean houses for which Shrewsbury is justly noted were built as a result of this trade revival, when Shrewsbury enjoyed its most prosperous period. Ireland's Mansion, one of the best surviving examples of Tudor architecture in the town, was built by Robert Ireland in about 1575 and exemplifies the prosperity and confidence of the Marcher wool merchants. Owen's Mansion (1592), a slightly less ostentatious merchant's house, stands nearby, facing the square. The Owens lived in another fine Elizabethan building at Condover Hall and also built the Council House gateway in Castle Street.

By 1620 Shrewsbury drapers were paying over £2000 a week for Welsh cloth, which was brought by packhorse from as far away as Dolgelly and Mawddy. Soon afterwards the drapers moved their market from Oswestry to Shrewsbury, completing Shrewsbury's textile monopoly. As a result of this shift the Merioneth clothiers had to travel an extra 20 miles each way and they were so late in arriving back home on Saturdays (the cloth was brought on Fridays) that in 1648 the rector of Dolgelly requested that the market be put back to Wednesdays. The Shrewsbury drapers compromised and agreed to buy the cloth on Thursdays. Such was the importance of the Welsh trade that Defoe on his visit to Shrewsbury noted, 'They speak all English in the town, but on market days you would think you were in Wales.'

As well as building themselves fine town houses the Shrewsbury merchants financed public buildings. Typical of these is Drapers' Hall (*c.*1580) in St Mary's Place. This was the guildhall of the powerful Drapers' Guild whose religious meeting place was the south chancel of the church of St Mary's a few yards away. A little later the Old Market House was built by the master mason Walter Hancock in 1596. Merchants were responsible for other municipal benefactions, the foremost of which was Shrewsbury School in Castlegates, founded in 1551. The old school building, which now houses the town library and has been splendidly restored, dates from the 1590s and 1630. The present Shrewsbury School, which occupies a dominating position overlooking the river and the town, moved in 1882, when it took over a building erected as Captain Coram's Shrewsbury Foundling Hospital in 1765.

The Dissolution of the monasteries

At the beginning of 1536 there were more than 800 religious houses, monasteries, nunneries and friaries in England and Wales. Four years later, by the middle of 1540, there were none. Their buildings and properties had been taken over by the Crown and given, leased or sold to new lay occupants. In 1536 an Act of Suppression of the lesser monasteries was passed which was presented by Henry VIII as a measure primarily of reform, rather than expropriation. It seems reasonably clear, however, that the King was really interested in the financial rewards of suppression rather than reforming a corrupt monastic system. Under the 1536 Act only those monasteries worth less than £200 a year were affected, and this covered some 243 houses which were suppressed. Although considerable care was taken to prepare the case against smaller abbeys and to present the dissolution as a measure of reform, the work of the suppression commissioners in carrying off church furnishings and other treasures for the King's use aroused considerable hostility towards the government. This was particularly true in northern England where the suppression of the smaller houses prompted the great rebellion of October 1536, known as the Pilgrimage of Grace. The rebellion failed, but not before some of the larger monasteries had become involved with helping their smaller brethren, the result of which was that once the rebellion was crushed the Crown's attention then turned to the larger abbeys. Almost all the greater abbeys and the smaller ones which had escaped suppression in 1536 were eventually to come into the Crown's possession as a consequence of 'acts of voluntary surrender'. The movement gathered momentum and very soon what had started out as a limited exercise in raising revenue had been elevated to a political movement against all the monasteries.

70 The Prior's House at Wenlock

The dissolution of the monasteries had a major impact on the Marcher landscape, bringing about as it did the largest exchange of property ownership since the Norman Conquest. Often it involved land passing to owners who lived far away from the Marches, and who did not earn their living off the land that came into their possession. One of the results of this was to create conditions by which large new country houses and parks could be made. The new owners did not need to cultivate their estates and were thus able to put the land to an aesthetic use. For the most part the monastic buildings were sold off and demolished. In a few cases, such as Abbey Dore, Leominster, Chirbury and Shrewsbury, the church was saved for parochial use. Abbey Dore was suppressed in 1535, and Abbot Redman was granted a pension of £13. The site and its buildings, which soon fell into ruins, were granted to John Scudamore of Holme Lacy. It was not until 1632 that his great grandson, 'the good Lord Scudamore', undertook the repair of the church, but by this time its condition was so bad that it was used as a cattle shelter and there are references to prayers being read under a sheltering arch. Restoration began with the blocking of the great arch leading to the nave and the side arches to the nave aisles. The roof was rebuilt in Herefordshire oak, 204 tons of this was used at 5s per ton, and the famous 'architector' John Abel was contracted to undertake the work. A new, rather incongruous looking tower was built and the whole still has the appearance of being half finished. Following a service of reconsecration which took place on Palm Sunday, 26 March 1634, Abbey Dore became one of the very few former Cistercian churches in England still used regularly for worship.

When in 1539 the monastery at Reading and its cell at Leominster were dissolved, the work of destruction began almost at once and the whole of the eastern end of Leominster priory, together with the central church tower, was razed to the ground. The damaged church, however, was saved for the community and today, standing in open ground, this magnificent glowing red church gives some impression of the original scale of the Benedictine building that once stood there. Chirbury was a house of Augustinian canons and throughout the Middle Ages it had enjoyed a turbulent history of conflict with the Welsh. In 1423 commissioners found the house to be 'in a state of spiritual and material

71 Lower Brockhampton by Bromyard, a fine late medieval half-timbered hall house and gatehouse. The gatehouse sits over a moat, characteristic of this area of heavily wooded Malvern foothills

collapse'. Throughout the fifteenth century the priory was suffering from constant attacks from marauders and was regularly among the houses exempted from paying taxes on the grounds of poverty. It was, however, a double church where the nave acted as the parish church and the chancel served the canons. Following the suppression of the house in 1536 the chancel and other conventual buildings were dismantled while the nave, aisles and western tower, which formed the parish church, survived to serve the community.

Shrewsbury Abbey was dissolved in 1540, when the Abbot received a generous pension of £80 and the 17 other resident monks received smaller pensions. Various alternative uses were sought for the abbey including its conversion into a seat for a new bishopric. It was also proposed as a possible residence for the Council of the Marches, or that it should be converted into a college or free school, but nothing came of these proposals and finally it suffered the fate of other Marcher houses. However, the western part of the church was preserved as the parish church of Holy Cross serving the extramural suburb of Abbey Foregate, while the remaining buildings were either adapted to secular use or dismantled. Considerable portions of the conventual buildings were still standing in 1743, but most have since been demolished by one means or another. In particular, the diversion of the London/Holyhead road from the north to the south of the church by Thomas Telford in 1836 removed many of the remaining medieval buildings. Even the abbey church suffered in the post-Reformation period and much fine Norman architecture including the clerestory was dismantled.

In most cases, however, all the buildings of the dissolved monasteries, including their churches, were destroyed, as the Borderland was already well, if not over, provided with churches. At Much Wenlock an attempt to create a new joint bishopric with Chester came to nothing and the priory complex, with the exception of the prior's lodging, was reduced to a ruin. The prior's lodgings and part of the infirmary which date mainly from the fifteenth century have served as a private house since the dissolution

72 *Late medieval bridge over the River Lugg at Lugwardine. This was on the route leading eastwards from Hereford and was of particular importance for the commercial prosperity of the town*

which has been described by Nicholas Pevsner as 'one of the finest examples of domestic architecture in England'.

The rural establishments at Llanthony, Buildwas, Lilleshall and Haughmond were largely dismantled, although the latter was converted into a private house and occupied for some years after the dissolution. Today these ruins provide tranquil and often beautiful sites to visit, a fitting tribute to the role they played in the making of the Marches, yet one can but wonder at the scale of the architectural treasures that were gratuitously lost in those few turbulent years. Other smaller rural monastic sites have disappeared almost completely at places such as Wigmore and Kilpeck, often leaving no more than a farm name as a legacy.

Within the towns the impact of the dissolution on the small institutions was just as dramatic. In Hereford the monastic buildings soon became ruinous, but in the case of Blackfriar's Priory the stone was used to build Sir Thomas Coningsby's Hospital. Henry VIII also authorised the destruction of two corn and two fulling mills belonging to the dean and chapter of Hereford cathedral: extensive trade in bread with Wales then declined and the local cloth industry was badly affected. The petition to restore the mills by Thomas Kerry a few years later talks of the cloth industry having 'utterly ceased' and of the city being in a state of 'extreme ruin and decay'. The houses of canons and the mendicant orders were similarly dealt with in Shrewsbury, Bridgnorth, Ludlow and Leominster, leaving little behind except their names and here and there fragments of medieval building.

Places to visit

Battlefield Church, Shropshire SJ 173 513

In 1406, just three years after the battle of Shrewsbury, a memorial chapel, now the parish church of Battlefield, was founded on the field of the battle by Richard Husse. He obtained a royal licence to convey to Roger Yve, rector of 'Albrygton Husee', two acres of land on which a chapel would be built. Its foundation charter made the rector and his successors masters or wardens of the chapel, with the right to nominate five chaplains. Their duties were to celebrate divine office for the King during his life and after his death for his soul and those of his ancestors, and also for the souls of Richard Husse and his wife Isolda and those who died in the battle of Shrewsbury. In a document of 1410 the site was described as being surrounded by a ditch with two 20ft entrances to the north and south, inside which many of the dead from the battle were buried. Although Battlefield began as a simple chantry chapel it developed into an important college of priests and had the right to appoint clergy to certain parishes, which allowed it to appropriate much of the income of those parishes to support the chancery. In its later years the college included a school. When in 1548 all collegiate chanceries were granted to Edward VI by parliament, Battlefield College was suppressed. Its last master was John Hussy, a member of the family which had founded the college. Its property was sold and the site was bought by the Hussey family.

Most of Battlefield church was built by 1409, except the tower which was added about a century later by Adam Grafton, then master of the college. After the Reformation, the chapel became a parish church while the other college buildings, which stood to the south of the churchyard, were demolished for the value of their materials. By the mid-eighteenth century the church had lost its roof, but this was restored in the middle of the nineteenth century when shields depicting the coats of arms of some of those who fought at the battle of Shrewsbury were added. The church is redundant, but has been restored.

Heath Chapel and Deserted Village, Shropshire SO 555 856

Heath was a part of the extensive parish of Stoke St Milborough, which in turn was originally part of the Prior of Wenlock's estate. Heath formed an upland settlement, almost certainly colonised from Wenlock in the later Anglo-Saxon period. Such dependent chapelries had the right of infant baptism, because of the very high rate of infant mortality during the Middle Ages which would have meant that a sick child would often die before it was baptised if it had to be taken to the mother church many miles away, often over inhospitable territory. The rites of marriage and burial however were retained by the mother church and Heath did not have its own graveyard until the late nineteenth century. The chapel here, which was restored at the beginning of the twentieth century, is a remarkable Norman building, dating from about 1150.

The process which created the settlement at Heath had pushed the margin of cultivation well up the slopes of former wasteland, but as the height at which arable cultivation was possible dropped quite dramatically in the later Middle Ages so it was left stranded because open field arable agriculture was no longer viable in these conditions. In 1268 the manor was leased by John Fitz Allen from Wenlock Priory, when rents were said to be valued at 49s 3d; the same valuation noted that there was a mill here. In 1327 there were seven taxable families at Heath. If this represented the total population it is a much smaller number than implied by the extensive earthworks here. A series of fifteenth-century rentals indicate that the village was slowly being depopulated. By 1407 the value of rents had fallen to 34s 9d and in the mid-sixteenth century there were only five farms in the township, all of them dispersed within a now primarily pastoral landscape. In many respects Heath is typical of settlement abandonment in the Marches; there was no sudden desertion, but rather a gradual shift to pastoral farming reflected in the slow abandonment of the settlement.

Stokesay Castle, Shropshire SO 436 818

The father of the great wool merchant Lawrence of Ludlow bought the manor of Stokesay in 1281, and nine years later Lawrence obtained a licence to crenellate (fortify) his manor from Edward I. He lived only a few more years, but before his death in 1296 he had built a strong high tower at the south end of the west front. The north tower (the oldest surviving structure in Stokesay) had been built by an earlier owner in 1240. Lawrence then added a top storey with fine projecting timber-work. Being a man of considerable wealth, he could afford to pull down the earlier hall and set up what must have been a most splendid new building 31ft wide and 52ft long with glazing in the upper windows — a sure sign of prosperity, for this was a period when glass was so expensive that families with several houses tended to take their window-panes with them from one manor to another. Though some of the timber-work may have been modified in the nineteenth century, much of it is original, and the great blackened crucks which support the roof show how it functioned as an open hall with a central fireplace. Lawrence surrounded this complex of buildings with a moat and curtain wall of stone as his outer system of defence.

The Ludlows were to hold Stokesay for more than 300 years. Afterwards it was sold and resold, but suffered only minor reverses. During the Civil War it was garrisoned for the King as an outpost of the crucial neighbouring stronghold of Ludlow Castle, but surrendered to the Parliamentarians in 1645 to avoid a damaging siege. Consequently, the damage was nominal and left the north tower intact, but without its battlements. Before this, at the beginning of the seventeenth century, an impressive timber-framed gatehouse had been built to replace the original thirteenth-century entrance. This gatehouse incorporates some fine wooden carving comparable with that on the Council House in Shrewsbury and the Reader's House in Ludlow. During the late Tudor and Jacobean period there was a renaissance in wooden carving, both on the exterior and interior of buildings in the Marches. Like the Romanesque sculptors before them, these seventeenth-century artists working in timber used a wide range of designs, including some which may have been borrowed from the Norman churches, and some which still clearly show a strong Celtic influence. The carvings are almost exclusively secular, using figures such as mermaids, serpents and grotesque heads.

Stokesay Castle's gradual decline was less damaging than it might have been. It became rundown rather than ruined and was put to various uses, as a granary and a cooper's workshop among others, but since the nineteenth century it has been well cared for and is now in the hands of English Heritage. The adjacent church of St John the Baptist incorporates a Norman door, a gallery and, most unusually, a nave which was rebuilt during the time of the Commonwealth in 1654. Stokesay castle is in the care of English Heritage.

Wigmore, Herefordshire SO 414 691

For almost 1000 years the administrative centre of the extreme northern part of Herefordshire was at Wigmore. The Romans had a fort here, east of the present Bury

73 View of Wigmore castle. Wigmore is a tranquil place today which belies its turbulent history and its association with the Mortimer family during the Middle Ages

Farm, though nothing can be seen above ground today. In the Anglo-Saxon Chronicle, it is recorded that in 921 King Edward had a fortress built at *Wigingamere*, which was unsuccessfully attacked by the Danes in the same year. Legend records that Eadric the Wild was lord of Wigmore, but this is not confirmed by Domesday Book (1086) where it is recorded that 'Ralph de Mortemer holds Wigmore Castle. Earl William erected it on the wasted land which is called *Merestun*, which Gumlert held in 1066.'

The original Norman castle was probably the small motte and bailey just to the west of the church, and closely linked to the streets of the borough, not the great mound and ruins which can be seen today further west. The earliest part of this later fortress appears to be the twelfth-century shell-keep on top of the great mound. Much of the curtain and its wall towers and gateway date from the fourteenth century. To this centre of Mortimer power came, among others, Llewellyn, Prince of Wales, Queen Isabella, Edward I, Edward III, and 'dark-eyed' Gladys, daughter of Llewellyn, who became the wife of Ralph de Mortimer. The King's Council met here and great tournaments were held, perhaps the greatest being the one held in 1330. These contests may have been the reason for the great enclosure north-east of the castle which ran down across what is now the main road and can still be traced as a cropmark today. The male line of the Mortimers died out early in the fifteenth century, but a great-grandson, Edward, Duke of York, became King Edward IV.

The parish church, with its late eleventh-century herringbone masonry, pre-dates the main castle and must have been a large Norman building. Apart from the fine roofs there are two other notable pieces of woodwork in the church — the early sixteenth-century decagonal pulpit and the stalls.

Wigmore retained its borough status for almost 800 years although it never had any parliamentary representation. The timber-framed market hall, open on the ground floor and with a meeting room above, stood at the head of the market place or 'pavement' looking down the village street until the middle of the last century. Like so many of these Marcher markets, the 'pavement', as it is still called, was triangular in shape, the main street running out at an apex and the hall standing at the base.

Wigmore Abbey, which lies two miles to the north-east of the castle near Adforton, was founded by Hugh Mortimer in 1179. It was housed by Augustinian Canons from St Victor's Abbey near Paris, who had first settled at Shobdon about 1140, then moved to Aymestrey, back to Shobdon and then finally to Wigmore. The abbey church, of which only the gable wall of the transept survives, was the burial place for generations of Mortimers. The main surviving building is the largely fourteenth-century half-timbered abbot's lodging, which is now owned privately.

Wigmore Castle is now in the stewardship of English Heritage, who were responsible for a programme of restoration in the 1990s. This work consolidated much of the crumbling stonework and made the site of the ruins more accessible to visitors.

Holdgate, Shropshire SO 563 896

Holdgate is a south Shropshire site of particular historic interest; it falls between the category of deserted village and deserted town. Holdgate sits in the very heart of the Corve Dale, the wide valley which lies between Wenlock and Ludlow, and which, in the early Middle Ages, formed an important line of communication between the Welsh frontier and the Midlands. Holdgate stands on a marl ridge at the narrowest point of the Corve Dale and during the Middle Ages it enjoyed effective control of the two major routeways running to the north and south of the ridge. All that is left of this once considerable settlement is a Norman church which contains a doorway and font executed by the Herefordshire School, a large motte and a sixteenth-century farmhouse which incorporates the tower and northern wall of a thirteenth-century stone castle. To the rear of the farm are some castle ramparts and in a field to the south is an area of recognisable house platforms, sunken ways and ridge and furrow.

In 1086 the manor was assessed at five hides, with 14 tenants; it was also recorded as having both a church and a priest, and furthermore there was a castle recorded there, one of only four castles recorded in Shropshire in 1086. It was clearly a place of some substance in the early Middle Ages, when it was held by the Knights Templar. In 1115 three royal courts were held at Holdgate and various licences for markets and fairs were granted. In 1292 the manor was highly valued at £229s 8d, and it is probable that the Bishop of Bath and Wells rebuilt the castle here about 1280. This was at the same time as he was building his mock fortified house at Acton Burnell and another remarkable fortified house at Cheney Longville not far away. As the theatre of conflict moved further westwards during the Middle Ages the settlement lost its strategic importance and it reverted to being a normal south Shropshire rural settlement. Following the pattern of many Marcher villages it gradually disintegrated in the later medieval period. Today it is a splendid, haunting place to visit with an anachronistic icehouse dug into the side of the overgrown motte and close by the gently decaying church with its magnificent Norman font.

10 The post-medieval landscape

The rise of the country house

During the late Middle Ages most of the castles in the Marches were abandoned and fell into disrepair. However, a minority continued to be occupied and their buildings were renovated from time to time to bring them up to the standards of the day. One of these was Broncoft Castle in the Corve Dale which Leland described in 1540 as 'a very good place like a castle'; today it consists of a largely nineteenth-century mock castle built out of the core of an original fourteenth-century fortification. In Herefordshire the Croft family have inhabited Croft Castle since the Norman Conquest, apart from the century after the reign of George III, when it was inhabited by a member of the Knight family. The rugged stone castle dates from the fifteenth century and now surrounds two courtyards, with sixteenth-century and later additions. It was much modified about 1765 when it was given a new internal structure with Gothic features. Beside the castle stands a small late medieval church containing the impressive tomb of Sir Richard Croft (died 1509), whose wife was governess to the sons of Edward IV at Ludlow. The park here is known for its oak, beech, lime and Spanish chestnut avenues, the latter dating back to perhaps as early as 1588.

Just over the Welsh border lies Chirk Castle, in Clwyd. This massive border fortress was completed in 1310 by Roger Mortimer, to whom Edward I had given the Chirk estates in 1282. The estate was bought by the merchant adventurer Sir Thomas Myddelton (Lord Mayor of London) in 1614 and the Myddelton family still inhabit the house. The design is in the form of a square around a courtyard. The south wing had been converted into a house by Tudor times and the outline of the Tudor gables can be traced in the infilling carried out during the eighteenth century. The park, which incorporates a section of Offa's Dyke, is entered from the little town of Chirk through some superb iron gates completed in 1721, the work of the Davis brothers. On the Welsh side of the border also sits one of the greatest castles that evolved into a country house, Powys, which is still inhabited after some 700 years. The castle dates from the late thirteenth century when Edward I granted Cruffydd ap Gwenwynwyn the baronetcy of Delapole. In 1587 the castle was bought by Sir Edward Herbert, who added the Long Gallery and did much internal remodelling. There was further reconstruction in the seventeenth and nineteenth centuries, and again at the beginning of the twentieth century. The late seventeenth-century terraced formal gardens, generally recognised as some of the finest in Britain, are believed to be the work of William Winde.

However, it was not the castle but the fortified manor house which represented the forerunner of the great post-medieval country houses that abound in the region. The undulating Border landscape with its dramatic vistas and abundant sources of running water provides an ideal setting for the country parks and houses that today still provide an

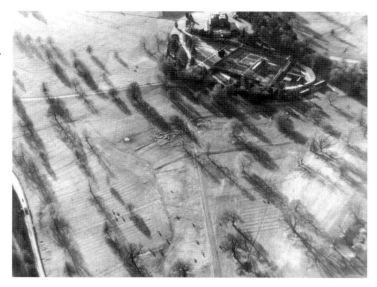

74 Aerial view of Berrington Hall and park. In close vicinity to the house are the earthworks of a deserted village and extensive remains of ridge and furrow

important element of the Marcher landscape. When Celia Fiennes visited Herefordshire at the end of the seventeenth century, she described it from the 'Pirramidy' top of the Malverns as appearing 'like a Country of Gardens and Orchards'. The great age of Marcher country houses starts in the middle of the sixteenth century, partly as a result of wealthy town merchants building themselves fashionable rural residences. Pitchford Hall was built for the Shrewsbury merchant, Adam Otley, in the 1560s, and Condover Hall for Thomas Owen in the 1590s, while the Newports built a vast mansion at Eyton-on-Severn of which only one small tower and a few small fragments incorporated into a farmhouse still survive.

There were also a considerable number of interesting smaller houses and parks created in the sixteenth century. A fine early brick house still stands at Upton Cressett, not far from Bridgnorth. This house is dated 1580, with an earlier turreted gatehouse (*c.*1540); the truly remarkable feature of the house, however, is its splendid medieval wooden hall encased in Tudor brickwork. The first reference to Upton Cressett Park was in Wolsey's Inquisition of Enclosures (1517), when it was alleged that Thomas Cressett had emparked 40 acres of arable land at Upton. The village of Upton was deserted then or possibly slightly later in the mid-sixteenth century, when the house was rebuilt and the park extended. The road running south-west from Bridgnorth was stopped and some landscaping was carried out. Later the park was broken up and today Upton Park Farm and Upton Lodge are the only reminders of its former existence. The gatehouse still stands near the Norman church, surrounded by the earthworks of the former village. Together they create a nostalgic and striking reminder of earlier prosperity and grandeur.

There is a ruined mansion of about the same period which has managed to maintain some of its former dignity at Moreton Corbet, near Shawbury. Moreton Corbet 'Castle' incorporates a medieval keep, but has extensive Elizabethan additions dated to 1579. The exterior has a facade of Tuscan columns, which provides an impression of early Renaissance splendour rarely seen in Marcher houses. Around the castle are the earthworks of the medieval defences and village of Moreton Corbet. In 1503 there were still 13 'messuages in Moreton towne', but the village appears to have been deserted at about the same time as the rebuilding of the castle, when a park was created and as usual in these circumstances the road diverted.

A major stimulus to the spread of country houses was provided by the dissolution of the monasteries. The consequences of the dispersal of former monastic land in the Border were profound. These were felt both directly after the dissolution and more gradually during the subsequent decades, when large estates came into new hands, often those of London lawyers anxious for a country seat. The estates of Lilleshall Abbey, for instance, passed to James Levisan, whose family was later actively involved in attempts to drain the Weald Moors and whose successors eventually became the Dukes of Sutherland. A particularly interesting group of country houses and associated parks was carved out of land along the back of Wenlock Edge, which had for many centuries belonged to Wenlock Priory. The dissolution resulted in the establishment of a series of smaller-scale Tudor country houses here with parks, at Shipton Hall (1587), Lutwyche Hall (1587), and Larden Hall (1607).

The creation of landscaped parks introduced a new element into the Border landscape: for the first time land was being used principally for aesthetic rather than purely economic purposes. In some cases land that had previously been farmed was enclosed into new parks, as at Longnor, which was first recorded as a park in the early sixteenth century, and where the ridge and furrow of former fields within the park pale shows that it was once cultivated arable. At Berrington in northern Herefordshire the earthworks of a deserted village together with a complete medieval field system can be seen within the park, close to Berrington Hall. Even so, many early parks still had a strictly functional side to them, and a 1682 plan of Longford Hall, to the south-west of Newport for example, shows that landscaping there was limited to a small area of formal gardens in front of the house. There were avenues of trees leading from the house, although these did not interfere with the enclosed paddocks, and some medieval fishponds which were reused as ornamental pools. Aldenham, near Morville, has a similar history, where the park appears to have been laid out at about the same time as the hall was rebuilt in 1691. The driveway, which is almost half a mile in length, gives a grand but deceptive impression of the extent of the park, a device employed in many other Border houses. In Aldenham Park, apart from the normal arable fields, coppices were grown to supply the iron industry with timber.

Many of the new parks were used for improving breeds of sheep, cattle and pigs. At Attingham Hall, for example, Lord Berwick bred Alderney, Hereford and West Highland cattle. The hall at Attingham was added to an existing building, Tern Hall, for Noel Hill, the First Lord Berwick, in the late eighteenth century. The massive entrance front, the colonnades and pavilions and the stable block were designed by George Steuart whose other major buildings, with the exception of the unusual circular church of St Chad's, Shrewsbury, have all been demolished. Humphrey Repton (1752-1818) was responsible for the landscaping at Attingham and his views on the park are expressed in his *Red Book* (1787-8), which is still kept in Attingham Hall. Repton also carried out some landscaping at Ferney Hall (1789), Condover (1803), Hopton Court (1803) and Longnor Hall (1804).

*75 Eastnor Castle, Herefordshire, built by the first Lord Somers in the early nineteenth century in
the style of a great medieval Castle. Until relatively recently the grounds were laid out in the form
of a pleasure garden. The house at Eastnor has had a profound impact on the local landscape
with its deer park and estate village*

Humphrey Repton became a professional landscape gardener in 1788, continuing the
work of the first major landscape designer to work in the Border, Lancelot (Capability)
Brown. Capability Brown improved Tong Castle (1765) and Oakley Park (1772-5), but
one of his most ambitious projects in the Borderland was at Berrington Hall, the ancient
home of the Cornewall family, built for Thomas Harley by Henry Holland. Holland
began work in 1778 and built a relatively simple house of local pinkish sandstone, which
fits well into the Herefordshire landscape — today the hall is in the capable hands of the
National Trust. The park as we see it now is a splendid example of Brown's work,
consisting of a composition of grassy slopes broken up by belts and clumps of trees, with
openings to provide wide views of the hills in the near and far distance. All this is
diversified by the glint of water from the pool and artificial lake made out of the previously
swampy ground. Brown also worked at Moccas Court, producing a landscaped park that
contrasts strikingly with the nearby deer park which consists of woodland and pasture.

Herefordshire has particular significance in the history of landscape design. The
county produced two of the great British landscape designers in Richard Payne Knight
(1750-1825) of Downton and Uvedale Price (1747-1829) of Foxley. The Wye valley has
the type of scenery which particularly appealed to devotees of the picturesque, who
followed William Gilpin on the Wye Tour like ancient pilgrims. Gilpin was a Hampshire
clergyman who in 1782 published the first of many 'observations' he made on undertaking
tours to different parts of the country, the first of which was to the Wye valley. His
observations were 'chiefly relative to picturesque beauty'. Gilpin was particularly partial to

ruined castles and rugged rocks, especially when set alongside the picturesque with a trace of the Gothic. He admired such landscapes not only for their pictorial quality, but because they also aroused an emotional response to the romance of history and the melancholy of the past. Out of that feeling grew the Gothic revival, with its attendant restoration of old buildings and the construction of new buildings using medieval designs. Gilpin looked upon scenery according to a list of rules, which he described as 'the principles of picturesque beauty'.

Capability Brown in his sketches and hints on landscape gardening, published in 1794, outlined the principles on which he worked. These were controlled by what he called the character of the scene, which in turn determined its potential or 'capabilities' for improvement, and by his search for unity in the composition of the whole scene. In the late eighteenth century there arose a school of thought which differed from Brown's now rather stereotyped approach. It was led by Price and Knight, both of whom were responsible for executing ambitious landscaping schemes in their own parks. Both were travelled, scholarly and distinguished dilettantes of the arts, and a controversy was launched in 1794 when Price published an Essay on the Picturesque and Knight a didactic poem called *The Landscape*. Repton joined the argument and a wordy yet courteous battle followed.

Price wrote when Brown embarked upon landscaping a scene:

> Adieu to all the painter admires — to all intricacies — to all beautiful varieties of form, tint, and light and shade; every deep recess — every bold projection — the fantastic roots of trees — the winding paths of sheep — all must go; in a few hours the rash hand of false taste completely demolishes what time only and a thousand lucky accidents can mature, so as to make it become the admiration and study of our Ruysdael or a Gainsborough and reduces it to such a thing as an oilman in Thames Street may at any time contract for by the yard at Islington or Mile-End . . . A good landscape is that in which all the parts are free and unconstrained, but in which, though some are prominent and highly illuminated and others in shade and retirement, some roughly and others more smooth and polished, all are necessary to the beauty, energy, effect, harmony of the whole.

Price felt that it was with this end in mind that the landscape designer should work, while Knight was particularly enthusiastic about the introduction of more exotic and flowering trees into the landscape. His ambitions were to be achieved in Victorian times when many newly discovered trees were used, particularly conifers from the Pacific coast of North America and plants from eastern Asia. Many of these trees were subsequently planted out at Price's gardens at Foxley, giving them their present luxurious appearance.

These two amateurs of taste had considerable impact upon English landscape design. They undoubtedly forced Repton to introduce greater variety into his work, while Price influenced Sir Walter Scott, both in his writing on landscape gardening and in the design and planting of Abbots Wood, which in turn had a considerable effect on the Victorian garden. J.C. Loudon, in his *Encyclopaedia of Gardening* (1827), wrote of Herefordshire, 'The county will hereafter be celebrated in gardening history as being the birth place or residence of Uvedale Price and R.P. Knight.'

To the north of Shrewsbury, at Hawkstone, the natural landscape of rugged sandstone cliffs fitted Price's theories admirably. When the improvements began here there was already a ruined medieval castle perched on its rock, presenting an ideal setting for the landscape designer with the new concepts. The improvers at Hawkstone were Sir Rowland Hill (d. 1783) and Sir Richard Hill who succeeded him. There are descriptions of the whole scheme as it was originally conceived, including over 10 miles of walks, rocks compared with the ruins of Palmyra, an effigy of the ancestor of a neighbour in the grotto, a hermitage complete with hermit 'generally found in a sitting position', a vineyard laid out

76 *Plan of Moccas Court Park in 1778 after it had been landscaped by Lancelot (Capability) Brown. Robert Adam designed Moccas Court itself (1775-80) in a severe classical style for the Cornewall family*

with fortifications and turrets, walls and bastions and an Elysian hill, an 'Awful Precipice', a menagerie, a Gothic greenhouse and so on. An obelisk with a statue on top of Sir Rowland Hill, who had been Lord Mayor of London in 1759, was added in 1795. Dr Johnson visited Hawkstone and pronounced it to be a place of 'terrific grandeur', but waspishly concluded that 'the house was magnificent compared with the rank of the owner'.

The building of country houses frequently had an impact on the landscape outside the park; gateways, lodges, stone and brick walls, and shelter belts of trees all contributed to the extramural rural landscape. In some instances the park creation resulted in the complete rebuilding of the village to fit into the new landscape. When Celia Fiennes visited Herefordshire about 1696, she described Stoke Edith as a

> very good old house of timber work, but old-fashioned, but good room for gardens, but all in an old form and mode, and Mr Foley intends to make both a new house and gardens.

77 Part of the model village at Eastnor created in the mid-nineteenth century to complement Eastnor Castle and deer park

The new gardens were staked out and 'a fine bowling green walled in and a summer house in it all new' already made. Above the house were fine woods and a 'delicate park'. In the 1790s alterations on a much larger scale were made by Repton, who drew up designs for the complete replanning of the park at Stoke Edith. On his advice the line of the turnpike road from Hereford to Ledbury was moved from its course along the hill almost immediately behind the mansion to the line of the present road. The line of this road was incorporated into a ha-ha, which divided the garden area from the remainder of the park. So deeply engraved was the road that it is some 20ft below the general ground level and requires a bridge to cross it. A new village was planned to lie around an oval green, skirted by a new road. Schools, a cider mill and a blacksmith's shop as well as cottages were planned in 1792 by William Wilkins, a landscape designer who frequently worked with Repton. The project was, however, not fully implemented. Repton himself advised against moving the whole village to the new site: the smoke, he said, arising from the chimneys of the cottages in the dell west of the mansion made a pleasing prospect against the wooded hills. Regrettably Stoke Edith Mansion was gutted by fire in 1927. Today only the walled garden and bowling green survive along with a few village houses and the lodges. Nevertheless Stoke Edith provides a notable example of a model village only partially completed and now abandoned.

A particularly good example of a surviving model village is to be found at Eastnor in eastern Herefordshire. It is a complete village of picturesque cottages built by the Somers family (founders of Somerstown in north London) to complement the house, Eastnor Castle. The castle was built in its present form in 1808 by Sir Robert Smirke, in a Baronial style but with neo-classical symmetry. The church and rectory here (1849-50) were designed by G.E. Scott; there is a drinking fountain with decorative terracotta panels standing in the centre of the village green. In addition, the school and stores were built to fit in with the overall scheme and there are a set of picturesque cottages, including a post office with a thatched roof. There had been a park at Eastnor since at least the early fifteenth century when it is recorded that Henry VI gave permission for a stone tower to be built within the park and for deer leaps to be constructed there. Eastnor Park is still stocked with deer, but unusually for the region these are red and not fallow deer.

At Brampton Bryan, Herefordshire there is also an ancient park still stocked with deer, a castle, country house and estate village. The Harley family have been there since 1309 when Sir Robert de Harley of Harley in Shropshire married Margaret Brampton. It was he who built the great gatehouse of the castle which still remains. One of his descendants, Sir Robert Harley, was the Puritan leader whose wife Lady Brilliana Harley defended the castle against the Royalists in 1643 for seven weeks. She died that October and in the following April, after a three-week siege, Colonel Wright was forced to capitulate. A few weeks later the castle, the library, its works of art and manuscripts were all destroyed. A new brick house was

78 St Mary, Stoke Edith, Herefordshire, designed as part of a model landscape for the Foleys in 1740-2. The adjoining house was burned in 1927 and the remainder of the village, designed in part by Humphrey Repton, has been abandoned

built close to the ruins of the castle in 1663 and it was this building which was incorporated into the present Georgian house in 1748.

To the south of Bridgnorth there are two model villages, Quatford and Quat. Quatford is sited beneath a mock castle in the vicinity of the putative Saxon 'burh'. All the cottages have barge-boards and latticework porches, and its neighbour, Quat, has a number of stone and half-timbered cottages situated along the roadside — even the bus-stop is designed to match. An interesting example of late landscaping was carried out at Brockhampton by Ross. Brockhampton Court was built on the core of an eighteenth-century rectory that lay close to the medieval church. It was rebuilt in a neo-Tudor style in the late nineteenth century, and the medieval church, which is now an ivy-covered ruin within the grounds, was abandoned. The creation of a small park and the building of the new church of All Saints (1901-2) designed by W.R. Lethaby came after. Lethaby was a follower of William Morris and this fine little early twentieth-century church contains furnishings by Burne-Jones and William Morris. The parish was also extensively landscaped, traces of former open field agriculture suppressed, and roads realigned as part of the overall scheme.

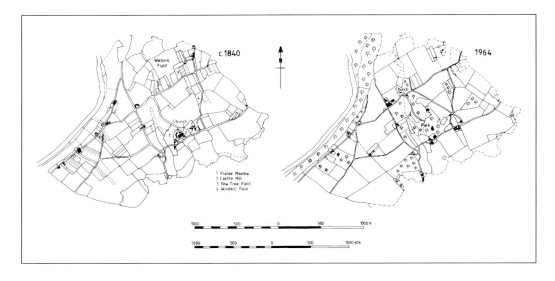

79 *Brockhampton by Ross in 1840 and 1964. Note the substantial landscape changes which were associated with the creation of a small park and the building of a new church*

New churches

Although there was a modest amount of church building and restoration during the later Middle Ages, increasingly surplus money went into public buildings and country houses. It would, however, be a mistake to believe that church building in the Marches had ceased entirely by the sixteenth century. There are many post-medieval churches of different denominations scattered throughout the region. Herefordshire in particular can boast a very wide range of parish churches. Bampton Bryan church, for instance, destroyed during the Civil War, was rebuilt in the old Gothic tradition in 1656. The medieval Gothic influence is also to be seen at Monnington on Wye, which, with the exception of the tower, was completely rebuilt by Uvedale and Mary Tomkyns in l 679. The church, which now lies at the end of a cul de sac, close to the remains of a deserted village, is worthy of a visit, not least because of its splendid isolated location on the banks of the River Wye. How Capel church was rebuilt with the exception of the medieval chancel, between 1693 and 1695, and is also medieval Gothic in style.

Many landscaping schemes involved the country house 'capturing' the parish church, but many such schemes also led to the restoration and rebuilding of the church. The pleasant church at Tyberton was built in part by the elder John Wood of Bath in the early eighteenth century, to accompany his now demolished Tyberton Court, erected for the Brydges family. The church is brick built with an attractive tower surmounted by a stone cornice, pediments and urns. Wood is better known for his design of the elegant Georgian Circus at Bath.

At Shobdon, the important Norman church was entirely pulled down except for the west tower. It was then rebuilt by John, the Second Viscount Bateman in 1752. He was a

80 The remarkable Italianate church of St Catherine at Hoarwithy, build by J.P. Seddon in the late nineteenth century

friend of Horace Walpole and had been converted to neo-Gothicism on a visit to Walpole's house at Strawberry Hill. Despite the immeasurable damage done in the destruction of the Norman architecture of the Herefordshire School here, Shobdon church is a fascinating example of rococo Gothic and is one of the most important survivals of its kind. The design was influenced by Horace Walpole's house: it has shallow transepts, the south was for the Bateman family pew, complete with fireplace, and the north was for seating the servants. The interior decoration of the church is pure rococo, including an elaborate three-level pulpit and a striking blue and white colour scheme. All that remains of the early church is the Kilpeck-type font and the arches on the hill to the north, magnificently carved, but now unfortunately badly weathered after more than two centuries of exposure to wind, rain and frost.

Not all new churches were associated with parks and houses. In the nineteenth century medieval churches throughout the Marches were ruthlessly renovated or completely rebuilt. Herefordshire has an abundance of restored churches. At Grendon Bishop, the isolated church of St John the Baptist, which is inaccessible by road, was entirely rebuilt in 1797-8, incorporating a few features of the earlier medieval church. The church marks the site of a deserted medieval village, which can be traced in the form of adjacent earthworks of a moated manor house and other building plots. At Bishops Frome the church retains its medieval tower and impressive Norman chancel arch; otherwise it was completely rebuilt in a mock Romanesque style in the late eighteenth century. At Stretton Sugwas the medieval church was demolished and a new church built on a new site close by in 1877-80. The chief characteristics of this building are the half-timbered west tower and the remarkable reset Norman tympanum, depicting Samson and the lion. Among the most unusual of this new generation of churches is the Italianate Romanesque building of St Catherine's, Hoarwithy. This building, which was personally paid for by the vicar, the Revd William Pool, adds a totally unexpected exotic element to an otherwise modest riverside hamlet. Hoarwithy was built (1880-5) by J.P. Seddon, encasing and embellishing an earlier church of 1843 which was described as a 'neat brick building'. Seddon, who practised mainly in south Wales and the West Country, was a diligent student of medieval architecture and developed a style of his own which was influenced by his love and study of the Venetian Gothic style.

With the coming of the railroad new ideas and new material were brought to Herefordshire and numerous churches had their interiors and exteriors dramatically altered. In particular there were two local architects who between them built at least 16 new churches in the county: F.R. Kempson and Thomas Nicholson, who was commonly known as 'The Destroyer'. Opinions on their work still arouse controversy. In 1883 Kempson built the nave and aisles of Holy Trinity, Hereford, which was described by one observer as 'the dullest design I have ever seen — not worth describing'.

It is perhaps too easy to dismiss the energetic works of the Victorian restorers, and a visit to the sad little unrestored church of St Andrew's in Leinthall Earls reminds us that nineteenth-century restoration must have saved many churches from ruin. St Andrew's was not subjected to Victorian updating and, although it is pleasant to see a parish church with many of its medieval and sixteenth-century features intact, the fabric has suffered severely because of lack of attention. A number of isolated churches like St Andrew's, which lies hidden on the edge of a farmyard, are in a similar condition, and some, such as the little medieval church at Wacton, are already ruined, representing nineteenth- and twentieth-century casualties, which have died partly because of the lack of remedial attention during the Victorian era.

Throughout the Marches there are of course numerous churches of other denominations. In scattered rural hamlets, particularly where there was industrial activity; brick Nonconformist chapels are common, but these, like their older relatives the parish churches, are finding times hard in the early twenty-first century. Much of the energetic work of restoration carried out over a century ago is now beginning to require attention and both parish and Nonconformist churches are becoming redundant at an alarming rate. It is only a matter of time before perhaps as many as half of the Marcher churches close their doors to their congregations for good. In most cases alternative uses may be found for them, but it would be a tragedy if this great reservoir of historical architecture were allowed to decay by default. It requires a conscientious effort to rescue this unique assemblage of buildings from destruction or unsympathetic restoration.

Enclosure — the making of the rural landscape

Open field agriculture, which was so much a feature of the English rural scene from the Norman period until the eighteenth century, appears to have enjoyed a relatively short life in the Borderland. The evidence of ridge and furrow, and cropmarkings which demarcate the strip holdings of tenants within the open field system, are to be found in patches throughout the Marches and well into lowland central Wales. They, together with documentary records, show that two- and three-field farming was operating extensively in

81 Parliamentary enclosure in the hill country of western Shropshire has left an erratic pattern of regular fields reaching up the hill slopes

the Marches by about 1300. The open arable fields in the Marches on the whole seem to have been much smaller than their Midland counterparts, and to have formed only part of the agricultural regime. Over much of the region they appear to have operated alongside pastoral farming, which remained dominant in many upland areas. The process of breaking up the open field strips into enclosures seems to have started in the fourteenth century, as gradually the open fields were enclosed by hedges, walls and fences. Sometimes, as at Clee St Margaret in south Shropshire, it is still possible to see how bunches of strips were gathered together and hedged in long narrow parallel fields at this early date.

Although a few open field systems survived intact into the eighteenth century and vestiges of open field agriculture were common, much of the Borderland appears to have been enclosed as early as 1600. In 1597, for instance, Shropshire was exempted from an Enclosure Act which encouraged the growth of corn because, 'it was best treated as a pastoral county'. During the seventeenth century some enclosed parts of Shropshire, particularly around Oswestry and Ellesmere, began to specialise in dairy produce for the growing urban market. Out of 18 livestock markets in Shropshire at this date, no fewer than seven specialised in cattle; however, some of this pastoral farming took place on land which had been cleared of woodland relatively recently in the north-west of Shropshire.

Enclosure enabled other specialisations to develop, in particular in Herefordshire where the growing of cider apples and hops became important. Hop growing seems to have started in Herefordshire as early as the thirteenth century and references to hop kilns and hop poles appear in medieval documents. In 1657 John Beale was able to claim that around Bromyard 'we make haste to be the chief hopmasters in England'. Herefordshire is a major hop-growing region, with production concentrated in the triangle between Hereford, Bromyard and Ledbury. In this area hopfields are still common; the permanent hop poles are twentieth-century — previously the constant demand for new poles was met by numerous ash plantations scattered over the county. Similarly, since the eighteenth century brick kilns have replaced wattle and daub structures.

Records of Herefordshire fruit production start in the fourteenth century and Beale in his book *Herefordshire Orchard: A Pattern for All England* (1657) notes, 'This county is reputed the Orchard of England.' He goes on to claim that fruit trees were grown by people of all stations, and even the hedges were 'enriched with rows of fruit trees, pears or apples'. By the late eighteenth century there were 15 varieties of cider apple and six of pear grown within the county. A century later Herefordshire was surpassing Devon as the premier orcharding county with a total area in excess of 27,000 acres. It is estimated that in a good season 20,000 hogsheads of cider were produced in Herefordshire, of which a considerable proportion was shipped to Bristol and London. Today the county is the fourth largest fruit producer in Britain, but in some areas such as the lower Teme valley, more than 75 per cent of land is still given over to orchards, which together with the hopfields give the modern landscape a highly distinctive appearance. Until the 1930s farm cider was common, but now it is only produced commercially, largely by the firm of Bulmers, a family who first made cider at Credenhill Rectory in 1887. Winemaking, too, is beginning to creep back into the Borderland — another tradition which began in the Middle Ages, when there were at least 35 vineyards in Herefordshire; in 1287, for example, it is recorded that the Bishop of Hereford's vineyard to the south of Wall hills yielded seven types of good white wine.

For the most part, farming remained small-scale and mixed. A survey of the manor farm at King's Pyon of 1623 sums up the character of most Border farming; it consisted of

> a dairyhouse, kiln house, storehouse, six lofts well boarded for malting and other uses, a fair stable with chambers over, a new tiled barn, and one other large barn, a large beast house, a large sheep cot, a swinehouse and a good pigeon house of stone and a hopyard with 6000 poles.

Although early enclosures did enable some specialisation to take place, large-scale agricultural improvements had to wait until the eighteenth and nineteenth centuries. There were, however, some early pioneer attempts at agricultural development. The most notable of these was Rowland Vaughan's waterwork scheme in the Golden Valley, where an elaborate system of channels and sluices was proposed, and in part built between 1585 and 1610. This was intended to irrigate the land and to provide water transport. Vaughan proposed to 'raise a golden world in the Golden Valley, being the pride of all that country with trees bordering on Wales'. He described the valley as 'the Lombardy of Herefordshire' and set out his plans for his utopia in a book called *Most Proved and Long*

Experienced Water Works. His scheme depended upon a series of irrigation works from Peterchurch to Bacton, part of which can still be identified on the ground today. This includes the remains of his first channel known as the Trench Royal. The Golden Valley works seem to have been the first of a series, as other irrigation works can be identified at the great Vaughan mansion at Hergest, near Kington, Hampton Court, Kingsland, Risbury and elsewhere. An extensive system of water meadows was constructed at Stanton on Arrow between 1660 and 1710 and another system of water meadows was dug on Lord Scudamore's estate at Holme Lacy in 1709.

Throughout the Marches the main stimulus to agricultural improvement came from the great estates, such as those of the Dukes of Sutherland based at Lilleshall. In 1812 James Loch was appointed estate steward, and he supervised a radical rationalisation of farming and land reclamation in eastern Shropshire. Roads and field boundaries were altered, new farmhouses were constructed, distinctive estate-style cottages were built for agricultural labourers, and logically planned groups of barns, cow stalls and wagon sheds were designed. These became models of their kind throughout the nineteenth century.

Although the Borderland was largely unaffected by the parliamentary enclosure of open fields, the enclosure of the surviving stretches of moor and marsh was achieved by governmental legislation in the eighteenth and nineteenth centuries. There were over 70 acts dealing with open common land in Shropshire. Of these acts 37 were brought forward during a period when the margin of cultivation was being pushed much higher as a consequence of increased reliance on home-grown food during the Napoleonic wars. The first act, which related to Newport Marsh, was passed in 1764; the final Shropshire act, concerning upland common in Llanfair Waterdine, was not passed until July 1891.

During the French wars open common land was viewed unfavourably by agricultural commentators. The prevalent attitude towards the commons is reflected in this extract from Bishton's *Report on Shropshire* (1794):

> The idea of leaving them the commons, in their unimproved state to bear chiefly gorse bushes and fern is now completely scouted except by a few who have falsely conceived that the enclosing of them is an injury to the poor; but if these persons had seen as much of the contrary effects in that respect as I have, I am fully persuaded their opposition would at once cease. Let those who doubt go round the commons now open, and view the miserable huts and poor, ill-cultivated, impoverished spots erected or rather thrown together and enclosed by themselves . . .

The process of enclosure is best observed by examining an omnibus award for 2550 acres of unimproved land in north Shropshire. In 1795 an act was passed to enclose waste and common land in the townships of Prees, Darleston, Faulsgreen, Mickley, Willaston, Moreton Say, Longford, and Stanton upon Hine Heath. Three commissioners, Henry Bowman, Valentine Vickers and Arthur Davies were appointed and were on oath to carry out their duties 'faithfully, impartially and honestly . . . without favour or affection to any person whatsoever'. Public notice was given in church of the meetings, and all claims made were subject to scrutiny and objections.

A surveyor was appointed to 'form roads which had to be at least forty wide'; and which had to be completed within two years of enclosure. Such enclosure roads in Shropshire were largely limited to heathy upland and lowland moor, particularly in the north and east of the county. The old tracks were closed and new wide, straight roads constructed in the enclosed area. The enclosure roads did not follow geographical features, but were systematically and often geometrically laid down by the commissioners. Consequently, short stretches of straight enclosure road contrast strikingly with the older winding roads; often the meeting place of the two types of road is marked by an awkward turn. Rural depopulation in some areas has meant that some of these roads now run between isolated farms. Accordingly, the metalled area of the small road necessary for modern motorised requirements occupies only about half of the available area, so that many enclosure roads in remote rural areas are accompanied by wide grass verges, set within hawthorn enclosure hedges.

The expenses of enclosure, except for fencing, were met by selling part of the commons. In all, the enclosure cost just over £3000 — £1 3s 6d an acre — in addition to which fencing for the new allotments had to be paid for by individual allotment holders.

The commissioners then divided the lands among the freeholders. They gave Sir Richard Hill and his brother John 'one full fourteenth part and also all pools and fisheries thereon', in lieu of their joint manorial rights over the common. As in all such cases the squatters on the edge of the commons were not catered for and many became homeless as a result of the 'improvements'.

Despite a series of acts passed to enclose the Clee Hills, much open common remains there today. In 1809 an act was passed to enclose the common land in Abdon and Stoke St Milborough on Brown Clee. To meet the expenses of enclosure, something like a third of the allotments were put up for public auction and realised £3803. Most plots were bought by local farmers; one exception to these, however, was Samuel Childs, a squatter coal miner who bought a small allotment next to his encroachment. It appears from contemporary accounts, however, that the Clee miners were generally impoverished and dependent upon their harvest earnings to supplement their wages. The effects of parliamentary enclosure on the landscape can be seen on the ground today. The lots sold by auction were hedged with quickset bushes, frequently interspersed with small trees or less frequently enclosed with dry stone walls. In the late nineteenth century most of the remaining open allotments were fenced and the grazing land improved. This has resulted in a striking contrast along the parish boundary between Stoke St Milborough, which has improved hedged pasture fields up to 1300 feet, and Clee St Margaret, which was never enclosed and is still open moorland. Further awards for enclosing on Brown Clee appeared in 1813 and 1841.

Despite the theoretical extinction of common rights of grazing arising from enclosure, the summit of the Brown Clee remains one of the largest areas of open common in Shropshire. Freeholders in surrounding parishes have the right to graze their animals in certain specified areas, but the wild nature of the country often makes this impossible in practice. One result of enclosure was to push the frontier of farming up the slopes of the hills, where it has remained to this day.

In the middle of the nineteenth century considerable areas of upland common in the old Clun Forest were enclosed by acts of parliament. Between 1845 and 1891, some 20,000 acres were affected. These acts covered some of the remotest country in Shropshire: for instance, in 1847 'a tract of unenclosed Common Land in the Honour or Lordship and Forest of Clun' amounting to 8600 acres was enclosed, and in 1858 a further 3580 acres was the subject of an enclosure award. As a result of acts passed in 1852, 1865 and 1880, over 2000 acres in the parish of Llanfair Waterdine alone were enclosed, and the final act passed concerning Shropshire completed the enclosure history of the parish in 1891. This area, still forming part of the wildest and most evocative countryside in Shropshire, is now traversed by fences, hedges and stone walls dating from enclosure. In the twentieth century the Forestry Commission was particularly active in this area of south-west Shropshire and many hillslopes in the Clun region now carry a dense covering of impenetrable coniferous woodland.

Townscapes

Hereford

The lack of good communications within the Marches was a major reason why some towns failed to flourish in the eighteenth and nineteenth centuries. Writing of Hereford of 1724, John Beale ascribed the basic cause of the city's poverty to 'lack of transportation'. On her visit to Herefordshire in the 1690s, Celia Fiennes talked about 'pretty long miles', and a century later Marshall reported that the roads were 'such as one might expect to meet with in the marshes of Holland or the mountains of Switzerland'. It was recorded that during the Civil War a Scottish army advancing to besiege Hereford in 1645 was able to march only eight miles a day when nearing the city because the roads were so bad.

In the summer of 1645 the Scots under Lord Leven laid siege to Hereford on behalf of the Parliamentarians. Hereford, a Royalist city, was defended by Barnabas Scudamore. The Scots succeeded in destroying the powder mill on which the garrison depended for ammunition, but the local architect, John Abel, was said to have responded by making hand mills which saved the day. In September Charles I raised the siege and granted Abel the honorary title of King's Carpenter. In October of the same year the Governor of Hereford planned to lead a force out of the city to try and capture the castle of Canon Frome, then in Parliamentarian hands. In order to do this he asked Abel to make a moveable siege engine which would be capable of being taken up to the castle walls. The machine designed by Abel is described as follows in a contemporary document:

> It was called a Sow and was carried upon great wheels to be drawn by oxen. It was made with room lofts over one other musket proof, and very strong out of which were holes to play and shoot out . . . It was so high that it could discharge it over all the works at Canon Frome, beside which a door open to bring them into the works, out of which a bridge could be drawn for entrance . . .

82 The Old Market Hall (the Grange) in Leominster, built by the famous local architect John Abel in the early seventeenth century

This strange war engine departed from Hereford for Canon Frome with 400 men. The remainder of the story is, however, an anticlimax, for when the soldiers reached a position only a mile and a half away from their destination, they halted and rested and a few of them went off to inns in Ledbury. The Parliamentary forces discovered the Sow and carried it off to Canon Frome and in the words of Webb, the chronicler of the Civil War in Herefordshire, 'Their shout of triumph made the valleys ring.'

Herefordshire was exceptionally fertile and with its cider, hops, sheep and cattle, Hereford, as the market town, should have benefited greatly. However, at a time of national growth on an unprecedented scale in the eighteenth century, it was unable to make itself much more than a local market. The River Wye was an erratic means of water transport and during the eighteenth century there were complaints that 'in plentifull yeares it choaketh up the commodities of corne and fruite'. The main causes for this were the difficulty of improving the navigation of the Wye and the fact that the cost of maintaining proper roads and bridges was too high. Although the turnpike roads did something to improve communications, Hereford at the end of the eighteenth century was still a remote county town, with no good connections to the main seaports or with the expanding industrial towns. The main market for hops was Worcester, while Ledbury and Upton upon Severn took most of the cider, perry and fruit; Ross took the wool, while Leominster, as always, remained a rival general market. Another reason for Hereford's stagnation was its lack of any substantial industrial manufacturer of its own. In 1700 gloves were the town's principal manufacture, but, as Cox observed, that is 'too poor a trade to make a place to flourish', and even this industry was in decline by the end of the eighteenth century.

Hereford's weak economic position was radically altered, however, in the first half of the nineteenth century by the completion of neighbouring canals, and by the coming of the railways. The city's population in 1757 was 5592 of which 3878 were within the walls and 1714 outside; by 1801 it was no more than 6828, but by 1851 it had nearly doubled. The coming of the railway provided important stimulus to the city, which was then able to trade much more effectively with the rest of the country. Nevertheless, at the time of the compilation of the first edition of the 2½in Ordnance Survey Map of Hereford in the 1880s,

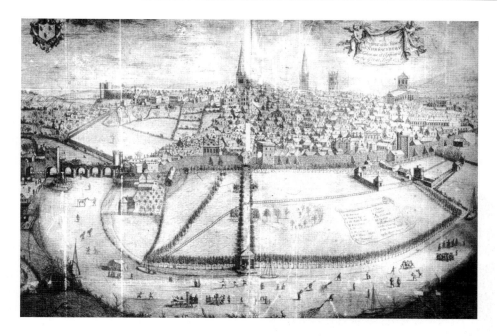

83 Plan of Shrewsbury in 1759 showing the Quarry Park in the foreground, before it was fully landscaped. The Welsh Bridge is on the left and Old St Chad's (now ruined) on the right. In the centre is the dingle, which was dug out as a municipal stone quarry in the thirteeenth century. The River Severn is frozen over and being used for a variety of winter pastimes

it was still a town largely confined within its medieval walls. During the late nineteenth century and early twentieth century, with the coming of municipal services such as gas and local public transport, the city at last broke its ancient limits and rapidly spread outwards. It now incorporates a substantial suburb to the south of the River Wye and has expanded to the point where it has swallowed up the ancient village centres of Holmer and Lower Bullingham. A considerable number of other surrounding villages act as dormitory settlements for the shire capital that has lost its county, but not its character or prosperity.

Leominster, Herefordshire

Today Leominster is a thriving market town with a large industrial estate. It continues to provide a centre for the commercial and social life of northern Herefordshire. Perhaps if its rivers, the Lugg and the Pinsley, had been faster flowing Leominster would have become a post-medieval centre of wool manufacture like Stroud. However, here, sited on a plain instead of on a steep-sided valley, the water wheels did not have the power to drive the big textile mills. Nevertheless the fame of Leominster wool was such that it prompted the poet Michael Drayton to write of 'Lemster ore. That the silkworm's web for fineness doth compare.' Despite the decline of Leominster's wool trade the borough continued to send two members to Parliament until 1885. During the nineteenth century there were a number of industrial ventures in Leominster, such as French hat-making, and cotton manufacture, but its mainstay, glove making, declined to the extent that by 1830 Pigot's Directory observed that the town 'appears to be in more of a state of decay than of improvement'. Despite the red stone of the abbey church, Leominster is essentially a half-timbered town. A short distance from the churchyard the Grange (the old Market Hall), now the offices of the District Council, is one of Herefordshire's best known timber-framed buildings, built in 1633 by John Abel as a town hall to stand at the top of Broad Street. It was offered for sale in 1853, bought by John Arkwright of Hampton Court, and re-erected on its present site. Originally it had an open ground floor which was used as a butter market, in the same way as Ross and Ledbury market halls still have their ground floors open today. When it was sold for £95 and was re-erected the ground floor was filled in with masonry. It is one of the finest timber-framed houses in Herefordshire, two-storeyed, with fine bays and adorned with elegant carvings. The windows of the upper storey project and have carvings of male and female busts. John Abel's original inscription can still be read on the frieze, in which he says his columns support the fabric as 'noble gentry . . . support the honour of a Kingdom'. This market hall is the finest remaining example of the work of John Abel (1577-1674), the leading Herefordshire craftsman of the seventeenth century. In addition to the hall at Leominster he built those at Brecon (1624) and Kington (1654), the stone grammar school at Kington (1625) and the ceiling of Abbey Dore church (1633).

Shrewsbury

The other Marcher shire town, Shrewsbury, fared somewhat better than Hereford. It continued to benefit from its position as unofficial 'capital' of north Wales as well as serving as Shropshire's county town. Shrewsbury benefited greatly from the wool trade and from its position as a major river port on the River Severn. The wool from the Welsh Borderland was generally of poor quality, but great fortunes were made by some merchants engaged in collecting and selling it for cheap clothing. One wealthy wool family was called the Prides — after whom Pride Hill is named — possibly as a nickname emphasising their prosperity. The Black Death caused a decline in population in Shrewsbury, and a disastrous trading recession followed in the fifteenth century. But fortunes revived, the population doubling from about 3000 to 6000 between 1560 and 1660. This was a period of great rebuilding in Shrewsbury, and many of the best timber-framed houses, such as the mansions of Owen, Ireland and Perche, were constructed at this time. The wealth of the town was also expressed in the continuing power of one of the medieval guilds, the Fellowship of the Drapers, with the founding of a new institution, Shrewsbury School, and the building of the market hall. 'This is indeed a beautiful, large, pleasant, populous and rich town,' wrote Defoe in the 1720s. Following the disruption caused by the Civil War, during which the castle was taken by the Parliamentarians, Shrewsbury emerged as a fashionable county town. The gentry built or rented houses in the town for the social season and in order that they could influence the outcome of both county and borough elections. These developments are reflected in the Georgian flavour of Belmont, Claremont Hill and a number of other elegant streets laid out within the town walls, adjacent to the Quarry Park.

In the last years of the eighteenth century the town finally lost control over the Welsh wool trade. However, the arrival of the canal and the railway promoted food marketing and

84 Mock medieval town and town wall at Ross on Wye dating from the early nineteenth century. In the 1830s Ross was a popular summer resort; to meet visitors' needs the Royal Hotel, overlooking the Wye Valley, was opened in 1837. The immediate vicinity of the hotel was redesigned in medieval style to be incorporated into the famous 'Prospect' of Ross

new industrial activities. Though Shropshire was at the heart of the early Industrial Revolution, Shrewsbury itself was never heavily industrialised. The saw mills, tanneries, various iron foundries and even the lead works all remained on a relatively minor scale. Shrewsbury's position was considerably strengthened first by Thomas Telford's improvements to the London to Holyhead road and later by the coming of the railways. Because of a shortage of space within the ancient town centre the elegant railway station was built (1848 and 1903-4) partially over the River Severn. For over 50 years Shrewsbury was one of the principal railway junctions in Britain. New railway towns were also created at places such as Gobowen, to the north of Oswestry, and Craven Arms, where the town streets were laid out along the lines of former medieval open field strips of a hamlet called Newtown.

The population increase was correspondingly modest in comparison to the industrial towns, but even so it doubled during the nineteenth century. A number of new public buildings were built such as the infirmary, the music hall, and a new market hall, but local political conflict tended to restrict the scale of such schemes. The main feature of the last century has been the progressive expansion of residential areas outside the loop of the river, with a limit of expansion being set by the by-pass built in the 1930s. Since the Second World War the town has continued to grow and an outer ring road built in the 1990s now effectively marks the town's limits, although the hamlet of Bayston Hill to the south is also part of greater Shrewsbury. Fortunately the post-war road improvers, intent on building an inner ring road within the loop of the River Severn, have been defeated by the local geography and a tortuous medieval street plan which, though still congested, for the most part survives with all its closeness and intricacy. The battle between traffic and the medieval street pattern is a relentless one, but the creation of a traffic-free zone in the centre of the town has made it more accessible and pleasant. A major suburban shopping complex was built at Meole Brace in the 1990s, has transformed the southern approach to the town. The Meole Brace Retail Park was built of a green-field site and covers some 30 acres; however it is quite indistinguishable from hundreds of similar sites located throughout Britain. The livestock market was moved from its riverside location in the 1960s and was rebuilt on the northern edge of the town. The Shirehall was moved from the Square in the centre of Shrewsbury to its present location at the end of Abbey Foregate in 1967. This large modern administrative building stands next to the familiar Shrewsbury landmark of Lord Hill's Column, built in 1814-16 to honour Viscount Hill, a veteran of the Peninsular War and Wellington's second-in-command at Waterloo. It was built by Thomas Harrison, and is believed to be the world's largest Greek Doric column. The statue is by Joseph Panzetta.

Ross-on-Wye, Herefordshire

Ross is aptly named from the Welsh *rhos* for a hill or promontory as it occupies a prominent hill on the eastern side of the River Wye. Much of the town, in particular its public buildings, is constructed of sandstone. The centre of town around the church is open and known as the Prospect, which was given to the town by John Kyrle (1637-1724). The market hall, constructed between 1660 and 1674, is built of red sandstone and is designed on the regular pattern of open arcaded ground floor with hall above. From here the triangular-shaped market place falls away steeply down the hill to become Broad Street. The town's ruined 'medieval walls' are an illusion, however. They, like the rest of Ross's gothic image, are a product of the 1830s. Nineteenth-century builders followed a tradition of public works, laid down by an earlier town planner. Eighteenth-century Ross was the creation of John Kyrle, Alexander Pope's 'Man of Ross'. Kyrle laid on a water supply, built a causeway to Wilton Bridge, restored the fourteenth-century church spire which dominated any view of the town and planned the Prospect Gardens. His house is now a shop in the Market Square where the open Market House stands. This is an imposing twin-gabled sandstone building, rebuilt in 1660, standing on an island in the Square. High in the eastern wall is a white stone relief picture of Charles II in full-bottomed wig, another of Kyrle's contributions to the town.

In 1830, Ross was a favourite summer resort and tourist centre. There were four Reading Societies, a Mechanics' Institute, a Horticultural Society and a Bluecoat School.

Church Street has several fine Georgian and Regency houses. There was a wide range of nineteenth-century crafts. Baskets and rope were made — the Rope Walk survives — and there were small numbers of nailers, flax dressers and weavers, glovers, braziers and woolstaplers. The town's real trade was in the market hall, its 17 inns and shops. Later the manufacturer of agricultural implements, boots and flour gave employment a growing population. Nowadays, the town makes farm machinery, plastic mouldings and other goods on industrial estates around the abandoned railway station.

In 1770 the Revd William Gilpin took a boat down the Wye as a result of which in 1782 he published his *Observations on the River Wye*. Thomas Gray and Samuel Ireland also wrote about the Wye and its natural beauty at about the same time. The cult of the picturesque had a considerable effect on Ross and the Wye below it. By the end of the century there were eight boats taking the wealthy to Monmouth from Ross for one and a half guineas or as far as Chepstow for three guineas. William Wordsworth and his sister Dorothy walked up the Wye Valley as far as Goodrich Castle in 1798, and Wordsworth's poem *Lines composed a Few Miles above Tintern Abbey, on revisiting the Banks of the Wye during a Tour, July 13 1798* was published the same year. The following year Charles Heath brought out the first edition of his *Excursion Down the Wye* — the Wye tourist industry had been born.

The cult of the picturesque affected not only Ross, but the Goodrich area to the south, where there is one of the best preserved castles in the Marchlands, located in a magnificent situation overlooking the Wye. In 1828 Goodrich Court was begun, a vast and fantastic turreted and castellated building, only half a mile from the castle. For 120 years it dominated the scene looking down the Wye — Wordsworth called it an 'impertinent structure' and wished for the power to blow it away. In fact it has now gone, with the exception of the east gatehouse on the dual carriageway from Ross to Monmouth. Round red sandstone gate towers with conical roofs and crenellations give us some idea of the appearance of the original building. Goodrich village itself still has a number of buildings inspired by Ross and the romantic movement.

Ludlow, Shropshire

The Palmers' Guild was the dominant institution in late medieval Ludlow. This was a religious guild founded in the mid-thirteenth century, which originally endowed three chaplains to pray for the dead and in honour of the Cross. The guild prospered and employed as many as eight priests, to attract members from all over the southern part of Britain, and to own many properties in the town and elsewhere. It was responsible for much of the late medieval adornment of the parish church of St Lawrence, for the founding of such charitable institutions as almshouses, and from the early fifteenth century for the administration of a school. The guild was dissolved in 1551 when its property and many of its functions passed to the town corporation.

From the mid-fifteenth century until 1689, Ludlow Castle was the main centre of administration for the Council of the Marches of Wales, a commission set up by the Crown to dispense justice in the turbulent Borderland region after the Act of Union with Wales (1536). Ludlow's role as an administrative centre generated trade and, together with the flourishing cloth trade, made it a prosperous town in the late medieval and Tudor periods. In the eighteenth century it became a town of fashion and resort, to which the moderately wealthy retired and where many landed families kept town houses. This is reflected in the many fine Georgian facades which can still be seen, most of which seem to be the work of local craftsmen. The fashionable social life of this period was paralleled by prosperity arising from a variety of industries which used the water power provided by the Corve and the Teme, among them corn milling, paper making and the manufacture of woollen cloth, blankets, and leather dress. From the last of these arose the glove making trade, which employed as many as a thousand people in the late eighteenth century.

In the early nineteenth century several of Ludlow's industries began to decline, and improved communications, first turnpike roads and then the railways, made the town more accessible but at the same time less attractive to the wealthy. It became less exclusive as a resort, although new assembly rooms were constructed as late as 1840. Nevertheless, Ludlow continued to act as an important market centre for south Shropshire and north Herefordshire and for the first time since the end of the Middle Ages began to expand its built-up area. The Victorian era was, nevertheless, a time of relative stagnation in the history of Ludlow; no large industrial enterprises were established and fortunately few of its fine buildings were destroyed.

Ludlow today flourishes as a centre of trade and administration for a wide area of the Borderland, but as in the past, its prosperity also depends on industry and on attracting visitors. Clothing and agricultural machinery are now its chief manufactures. A new livestock market replaced the Corve Street market in 1995. The Ludlow Festival, held in June and July, and Ludlow Food Fair, in September, mark the height of the town's tourist season. We have seen that several planned medieval towns over the centuries withered away to become no more than agricultural villages or less, but in spite of some periods of relative stagnation, Ludlow has continued to thrive as a centre of trade and small-scale industry and as a tourist centre. Its continuous prosperity is reflected in its many fine houses and public buildings of all periods. At the time of writing Ludlow is enjoying unprecedented popularity as a *cordon bleu* culinary centre, with a number of restaurants carrying the much-vaunted Michelin star status.

Places to visit

There are a considerable number of country houses and parks open to the public in the Marches; these include many properties owned by the National Trust. Among the most noteworthy are Benthall Hall, near Broseley, Berrington Hall, Chirk Castle, Croft Castle, Dudmaston Hall, Erddig (Clwyd), Lower Brockhampton (Bromyard), Morville, Powys Castle and Wilderhope Manor (Wenlock Edge). In this section just one of these properties is dealt with in more detail.

Attingham Hall and Park, Shropshire SJ 550 099

Attingham Hall and Park lie immediately to the east of the Severn about five miles south-east of Shrewsbury, adjacent to the village of Atcham. The present Hall was built for the First Lord Berwick in 1783-5, to the design of George Stuart. The Hall was altered by John Nash at the beginning of the nineteenth century. It was the grandest house of its time in Shropshire and certainly one of the most important Georgian buildings in the area. Nash also built the Italianate village at Cronkhill which was probably the subject of a painting called 'The Villa in Shropshire', exhibited at the Royal Academy in 1802.

It has been suggested that the original siting of Attingham Park was influenced by the presence of an earlier ironworks there. The Tern Forge stood from 1710-57 on the River Tern in what is now Attingham Park. In a list of ironworks compiled in 1717 the forge was recorded as producing 300 tons of iron goods per annum, yet virtually no trace of it remains beyond a spread of slag on the bed of the Tern. This is all the more surprising in view of the scale of the works. A letter of 1713 records how, within three years of the start of operations, there was already

> a mill for Rowling of Brass plates and Iron hoops and Slitting of bar iron into Rods for making of nails . . . a Wire Mill, forge and a furnace for Converting of Iron into steel.

In addition, workshops and housing had been built for 40 men and their dependants. Following the closing of the works in 1757, the housing and workshops were demolished to remove squatters who had quickly moved into the vacant premises.

It seems probable that Humphrey Repton used some of the ponds and pools here for his landscaping in the late eighteenth century. Repton, who was employed to improve the park in 1789, expresses the aspirations of the Georgian landscape gardeners in his *Red Book* (1797-8), which is still kept at Attingham Hall. In his critique of Attingham Park prior to the alterations, he complains that there were no trees to assist perspective and divert the eye towards the house and that barns and other outbuildings which were visible detracted from the hall. Among his suggestions for improvement were the plantation of trees to hide the park pale, the diversion of water, the construction of bridges and the growing of hedges. His general idea was to contrast wide natural views, using the Wrekin and the Welsh mountains as a backcloth, against the beautiful miniatures or set-pieces. Some, but not all, of Repton's improvements were carried out; but the importance of the *Red Book* lies in its concept of eighteenth-century landscaping.

The present approach to the house from Atcham dates from soon after 1807. About this time a number of cottages on the north side of Watling Street in the village of Atcham were demolished and the line of the Uffington road altered so that the park could be extended. Before these changes the main entrance was midway between Atcham and Tern bridges, but it did not meet with Repton's approval. He was concerned about the proximity of the house to the Tern bridge and suggested extending the park across the road and building a pair of lodges, one on each side of the road, at the eastern extremity of the park 'so that we shall induce the stranger to conceive that he passes thro' the park and not on the outside of it'. This idea was inspired by the existence of a turnpike cottage which Repton visualised as being remodelled as a classical building worthy of a nobleman's park. Only one of these lodges survives, that on the north side, which served as the entrance to the former east drive to the house, and was presumably designed by Nash.

Apart from reinforcing the planting in the park and introducing shelter-belts round it, Repton's main contribution was to make the River Tern play a greater part in the landscape. He suggested the building of a weir to the south-east of the house to maintain the water level in the upper reaches of the river and a cascade which should be visible from the house. These plans were executed, but the weir is not situated where Repton recommended. He also constructed another weir below Tern bridge in order to create a much wider river above it that would be visible from the house. However, his idea of making the bridge more monumental in its design was not adopted; neither was his suggestion that a spire should be added to the tower of Wroxeter church some two miles to the south-east of the house in order to make it more prominent. Attingham Park has been in the care of the National Trust since 1953.

Weobley, Herefordshire

Of all the small market towns in the Marches, Weobley is one of the most delightful. Weobley's attractions include a medieval castle site at one end of the town, a fine fourteenth-century church at the other, and a wide market place in between, and as such it conforms to classic Border market town plans. Broad Street lost its ancient Market House and middle row in the 1840s. In the Middle Ages the town boasted a market, two fairs and even a small jewry. There is an impressive range of half-timbered townhouses dating from the Middle Ages and later. These have many exceptional features, such as the massive medieval crucks of a small house in the *Red Lion*'s yard and a dragon-beam on the corner of the inn itself, which divided the jetties over both streets. Almost every kind of timber stud, post and panel can be found in Weobley's houses.

In 1533, Leland described Weobley as a 'market town when there is a goodly castle, but somewhat in decay'. There are seventeenth-century weavers' inventories from Weobley, but the town's chief manufacture was ale. Camden said that Weobley had 'more fair cellars than most market towns of its bigness in England' but 'with the increase for syder, this commodity hath declined'. In the 1830s, Pigot's *Directory* records a 'principal manufacture' of nails and malt. He lists seven tailors, six butchers, a watch- and clock-maker and a druggist, 'several shops having been opened in a very spirited manner'. The 1830s, however, were the days of Weobley's greatest notoriety as one of the 56 Parliamentary 'rotten' and 'pocket' boroughs disenfranchised by the Great Reform Act of 1832.

An as 'ancient borough', Weobley had sent two members to Parliament from 1295 to 1306 but their franchise, like that of nearby Bromyard, Ledbury and Ross, then lapsed. In 1682, the Tomkyns family, owners of the Garnstone estate and MPs for Leominster, successfully petitioned Parliament for Weobley's re-enfranchisement. For the next 100 years, the elections were contested successively by five local families — the Tomkyns and Birches from Garnstone, the Prices of Foxley, the Cornewalls of Moccas and Berrington and the Foleys of Stoke Edith, newcomers from the Black Country.

In 1717, Thomas Foley paid out £700 during a by-election which he lost because he claimed that Weobley voters were deemed to be unreliable 'unless someone spent more money on them'. From 1754 to 1832 Weobley was a typical rotten borough, in the hands of the Thynne family from Wiltshire, who were Lords of the Manor, and who had bought most of the towns burgage tenements. Weobley ceased to be a rotten borough in 1832, when it lost both its parliamentary representatives. A 1795 guidebook had described Weobley as consisting 'of a few small streets meanly constructed, without either market or traffic to establish its title to the rank of a town'. By the second half of the nineteenth century Weobley had lost all its crafts, such as nail and glove making. Yet today it has a small industrial estate and is a thriving community once again, thanks to the motor car and to tourism.

11 Industrial landscapes

The Welsh Marches are still essentially rural and even the relics of early industry are largely preserved within a rural setting. It is difficult today to appreciate that in the Roman period, *Ariconium*, in south-eastern Herefordshire, was an industrial town based on iron manufacture and called the Merthyr Tydfil of the Romans by one historian. During the eighteenth century Shropshire was the premier iron-producing county in the kingdom and the Industrial Revolution, if not born, was certainly nurtured in a small valley in central Shropshire — Coalbrookdale. It was here that in 1708-9 Abraham Darby first successfully smelted iron ore, substituting coke for charcoal, thereby heralding the introduction of a second Iron Age. Today Ironbridge and the Coalbrookdale have largely reverted to rural tranquillity, although many aspects of the Industrial Revolution have been excitingly re-established through the work of Ironbridge Gorge Museum Trust.

The wealth of mineral deposits in the Marches usually lie in reasonably accessible places near to running water and timber. This has made possible a long history of extractive and manufacturing industry in the region. These industries can be traced back to before the Roman Conquest, when much of the industry was of an itinerant nature, leaving little permanent impression on the landscape. Excavations at *Ariconium* have revealed rock-cut depressions containing remains of Romano-British iron-smelting furnaces and associated slag heaps; furthermore there is evidence to show that some of these slag heaps were reworked during the seventeenth century. Both the Roman and later iron workings are overgrown and indistinguishable without judicious exploration. Elsewhere only the occasional isolated row of cottages, derelict railway track, disturbed hillside, or unexpected nonconformist chapel tells of intense industrial activity in the past. The real impact on the landscape did not come until the sixteenth century and later. Even then, most industry was short-lived and evidence even of eighteenth and nineteenth-century industrial activity has, in some instances, merged back into the rural countryside. Today, apart from stone, sand and gravel quarrying, there is little extractive or primary industry in the Marches.

There are basically two types of Marcher historic industrial landscape. Firstly, there are the open upland areas where lead, ironstone, limestone and coal have been quarried for centuries. Such activities have left a scarred countryside of hollows and mounds, now overgrown and given over to rough grazing with scattered stone cottages straggling along the roads. Because of the comparatively small scale of activity in such areas, miners tended to follow industry, often building squatter cottages on common land close to where they worked. The miners were frequently part-time farmers and a tradition of small-holdings grew up in these parts of the Marches. The landscape they left behind is confined largely to such places as the Tanat valley, the Stiperstones, the Clee Hills, Bringewood Chase, the

85 Orleton Common on Titterstone Clee. The islands of enclosures on the commonland were created by squatters, many of whom worked in the nearby quarries. The fields on the right of the parish boundary were enclosed by an Act of Parliament in the late eighteenth and early nineteenth centuries, when the squatters in that area would have been evicted

Malvern Hills, and around the edge of the Forest of Dean. Industry in these areas was largely unplanned, working on a piecemeal basis to the capacity of the primitive mining equipment employed. Often a seam or deposit was abandoned long before it was exhausted. The mines were not served by any specialist communication system and as the work was constantly moving, there was little time for large settlements to develop.

The second industrial type was found mainly in eastern central Shropshire in the Shropshire coalfield, where the rural landscape has been completely altered by industry. This landscape was associated with the extraction of coal, iron and clay on a large scale and also with the manufacture of a wide variety of goods, principally ceramics and iron products. Industrial activity here declined during the latter part of the nineteenth and the early twentieth century, as new centres of manufacture were established in places such as the Black Country to the east. Since the late 1960s the main area of ancient industry, the Coalbrookdale coalfield, has been incorporated into Telford New Town. Prior to the building of the new town, open-cast mining was undertaken to clear up the coal seams, during the course of which many old shafts were uncovered. Before tracing the imprint of the iron industry, let us first examine two redundant industrial areas, where the scars of early industry have not yet completely healed.

The Shropshire lead mines

There are deposits of lead located in a relatively small area between the Stiperstones and Corndon. The lead is all to be found within a three-mile radius of the hamlet of Shelve, yet in the early 1870s, the 10 Shelve mines produced over 10 per cent of the country's lead ore.

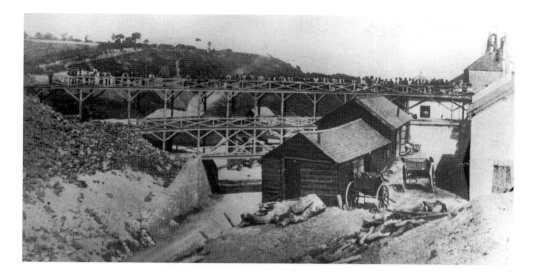

86a   A nineteenth-century photograph of lead mining in the Shelve district of Shropshire

However, the seams have now been exhausted or are so fragmented that mining is not profitable. The activities of the lead miners left a stark landscape of derelict engine houses, decaying chimney stacks, stagnant engine pools, and a maze of abandoned pits and shafts. The huge quantity of lead that was mined here in the past is demonstrated by the white tips of waste spar, which until recently could be seen for considerable distances in central Shropshire. The Romans began lead working here and pigs of lead stamped with the name of the Emperor Hadrian (AD 117-38) were found near Linley at Bishop's Castle in 1767. Other Roman remains found in the old workings include mining tools, notably wooden shovels and candles with wicks of hemp, as well as coins and pottery. Professor Barrie Jones has argued that an area of extensive earthworks in the vicinity of Linley Hall was created by Roman lead working, which used a system of artificial streams to wash out the ore in a process known as 'hushing'.

In north-western Shropshire, near Brompton, traces of lead and possibly silver working have been found in a number of early Roman military camps. The search for silver may even have been the reason for Roman involvement in the region in the first instance. During the early Middle Ages, Shelve was an important lead-producing area; Henry II laid down conditions governing the mining of lead in the Forest of Stiperstones and in 1180, the mines here were leased for £55. Lead was transported considerable distances to places as far away as Gloucester, Builth Wells and Wiltshire.

In more recent times the lead mines belonged to the ground landlords, principally the Earls of Tankerville and the More family. The former owned most of the northern and eastern parts of the orefield, which included the Tankerville, Pennerley, East Roman Gravels, Batholes and Roundhill mines. The latter owned most of the southern and eastern part of the orefield, including Roman Gravels, Ladywell and the Grit mines. Snailbeach, the richest mine in the orefield, was owned by the Marquis of Bath, and Bog mine, in the south, by the

86b A disused lead mining chimney at Shelve

Lister family, lords of Rowton. The chief ore, galena or lead sulphide, was originally smelted at Snailbeach and Pontesford, where tall chimney shafts with hundreds of yards of flues were erected to recover by-products such as arsenic. Later on, quantities of the ore were carried out of the region by way of the railway which ran from Minsterley to be smelted in Wales, Deeside and Bristol.

The first large-scale attempts at mining began in the mid-eighteenth century on the Grit sett (the term sett was used commonly in Shropshire to describe a mining property). John Lawrence, a local man, became a leading figure in large-scale mining in the area and by the end of the century had become so successful that he had gained a controlling influence over every major mine in the orefield, with the exception of Snailbeach. As the mines were not particularly deep, adits or tunnels dug into the hillside were used to extract the ore, although horse-powered winding engines or gins were used to raise water to the surface in barrels. Lawrence was one of the first in the region to experiment with steam engines, and bought several from Boulton and Watt in Birmingham, but he did not keep them in use for long and sold them to mines in other parts of the country.

At this time Lawrence also operated smeltworks on the coalfield, as did the Snailbeach Company, and with the high mineral prices enjoyed during the Napoleonic wars, it was a period of prosperity. In the 1820s, however, Lawrence lost possession of most of his mines which were leased by the surface landlords to companies from northern England, but his successors did not fare particularly well either, for lead prices fell steeply and by the mid-1840s all the new companies had abandoned their ventures.

In the 1850s the area experienced another substantial boom in which several new companies were established to work existing mines and sink new ones. The new companies brought Cornish engineers into the area, and it was they who constructed the typical Cornish engine houses whose prominent chimneys created striking landmarks. However, prices fell yet again and these ventures also failed. The mines passed back into local hands during the 1860s, but despite low lead prices it was again a time of relative prosperity, for two very rich deposits were discovered at Tankerville and Roman Gravels. Towards the ends of their working lives, many of the mines showed an increased output of zinc ore, first recorded in 1858, and of barytes, first recorded in 1860.

The mid-1870s were the years of maximum output from the Shropshire orefield, and the buildings erected during this period are largely those which remain as ruins today. In 1873 Shropshire produced 7600 tons of lead ore, but by the end of the decade lead ore prices had started to fall once more and this time did not recover. One by one the mines closed, as they could no longer cover their operating costs, and by 1895 Snailbeach was the only mine left working. This mine, once one of the richest in Europe, continued production until 1911, by which time it was almost completely exhausted.

Much of the lead mining in Shropshire was piecemeal, and miners tended to have to live in squatter cottages built on the edge of commonland with small pasture enclosures attached in order to supplement their incomes. Indeed the Earls of Tankerville encouraged miners to settle on the edge of the commons in the northern portion of Stiperstones. By the middle of the nineteenth century about 250 acres of common had been taken up by some 93 small holders, who created the communities of Pennerley and Perkins Beach. The hamlet of More had appeared by 1881, but by 1902 some cottages had already been abandoned in response to the decline in mining. The demise of the lead industry meant that the area was overpopulated, and the subsequent story of the region has largely been one of painful re-adjustment to marginal pastoral farming. The wealth made in the lead mines did not find its way back into the locality; cottages, churches and chapels are uniformly simple, roads are still only just adequate, and the single-track railway which served the region has long since been taken up. Until the 1970s the story of abandonment continued, but since then these roughly built dwellings and the plots of land attached to them have been increasingly in demand, and today they are eagerly sought after as retirement, commuter and holiday cottages. Like so many areas of the Marches it has become increasingly gentrified and its character subtly changed as newcomers have moved in and renovated the old industrial houses.

Lead is no longer mined in Shropshire, but for a century and a half the county was one of Britain's premier production areas. Working conditions were very dangerous, and mining associated diseases and death rampant, but the industrial remains have left behind a strange attraction and mystery. The most striking of the waste tips was the White Tip at Snailbeach; however, concerns about its toxic nature in the 1990s led to it being landscaped and grassed over.

The Clee Hill industries

It is surprising that the highest of the Marcher hills on the English side of the border, the Clee Hills, are amongst the least well known and the least visited. They consist of the Brown Clee, Titterstone Clee and Catherton Clee. Geologically they are made up of sandstone deposits, rich in minerals, but capped by a hard layer of basalt which gives them their distinctive flat-topped appearance. The Clee Hills contain a wealth of minerals — coal, iron, limestone, basalt and copper are all found there. The industrial activity associated with these rocks comes to a fairly abrupt halt in the south along the line of in the Teme valley, where the county boundaries of Shropshire, Herefordshire and Worcestershire converge and where the deposits of Old Red Sandstone begin to dominate. The relics of past industrial activity on the Clees merge with a landscape of pastoral farming; this too was a region predominantly inhabited by cottagers. The open heathland used for common grazing and the work in the collieries and quarries on top of the hill have been constant attractions over the centuries for men seeking work. As early as 1745

87 Deeply engraved industrial trackways on Brown Clee surrounding Nordy Bank Iron Age hillfort. In the foreground is a group of bell pit coal mines adjacent to a squatter enclosure

there were 49 squatter cottages on the wastes of the township of Smitton alone. According to the geologist Sir Roderick Murchison, writing in the nineteenth century, 'Some cottagers [kept] horses to carry lime and coal and were able to earn two or three shillings a day.' Other sources suggest that the miners were impoverished and were obliged to take on a variety of occupations including farming, as well as carrying lime and mining coal. Even today, when there is no longer industrial work on Brown Clee and quarrying on Titterstone Clee is limited to the supply of roadstone, the Clee Hill Commoners Association still thrives.

The Clees lie immediately to the south of Wenlock Edge, and the Corve Dale. The Brown Clee has an hourglass shape plan with two distinct summits, Clee Burf which rises to 1650ft, and Abdon Burf which rises to 1790ft — the highest point in Midland England. Such is their prominence that they are the only English hills to feature on the Mappa Mundi (*c.*1300), a unique medieval world map, kept in Hereford cathedral. Titterstone Clee has a distinctive profile, rather like a high-peaked cap, reaching up to just below 1750ft above sea level, and can be clearly identified for many miles from every point of the compass.

Today the landscapes of the two Clees are rather different from one another, although both have been deeply influenced by man's past activities. The hills boasted four major prehistoric hillforts until the nineteenth century, when three of them were severely damaged during a frenzy of indiscriminate mining activity. The fort which crowns the Titterstone Clee is one of the largest and highest in England. It is unusual because it has no ditch, although the ruins of a massive stone rampart which once surrounded it can still be clearly identified. The hillfort has been quarried away extensively on the south side and now houses a radar station. On Brown Clee the hillforts at Abdon Burf and Clee Burf are masked by the confused remnants of nineteenth-century industry. The third fort on the Brown Clee, however, at Nordy Bank, is both easily accessible and clearly identifiable on the ground, with a single bank and ditch.

At the end of the Iron Age the Clees seem to have been largely abandoned, perhaps until the late Anglo-Saxon and early Norman period, when, as noted in chapter 8, the

Brown Clee Hill formed the centrepiece of a Royal Forest. The Clee Royal Forest appears to have covered much of the Corve Dale and part of the Titterstone Clee as well. In the middle of the twelfth century the Forest was handed over to the Clifford family of Corfham Castle in the Corve Dale, who managed the area as a private hunting chase. During the later Middle Ages the exclusive rights of hunting claimed by the lords of Corfham over the old Clee Forest gradually lapsed; however certain common rights survived until recent times as a consequence of the area having once been under strict seigneurial control.

The inhabitants of all the settlements that originally lay within Clee Chase were allowed certain general rights of commoning on the summit of Brown Clee Hill and in particular within an area known as Earnstrey Park. The commoners who lived in settlements some way distant from the Brown Clee were known as 'strakers'. These commoners moved their animals by way of cattle drifts known as straker routes across the lands of other parishes until they reached common land. These old ways are still deeply engraved into the modern landscape, having cut their way down into the sandstone and are now often followed for short distances by local streams. The outcommoners, as they were known, held only restricted rights on the hilltop, compared to the inhabitants of townships immediately adjacent to the upland commons, who enjoyed a wider range of rights. Similar rights were to be found on a number of other common land areas in England, notably Cranborne Chase, where the two different types of commoners were known as inbounders and outbounders, and the outskirts of Galtres Forest, Yorkshire, and Duffield Frith, Derbyshire, where the commoners were called bounders. The Venville tenants of Dartmoor, as they were known, seem to have exercised customs very similar to those on the Brown Clee. Those tenants living within the old Devon Forest (later Dartmoor Chase) had the right to take anything from Dartmoor except green oak and venison. The method by which the Venville tenants were able to claim their animals and by which stray animals were impounded was called 'the drift'. According to this custom, the tenants were not informed until the morning of the rounding up that the drift was about to take place, so that interlopers would have no opportunity for removing their animals. Similarly, on the Brown Clee, the Clee chase keepers annually informed every township within the old Forest area that there was to be a drift the following day by the blowing of horns one hour before sunset. Every household was obliged to send a representative to the meeting at Botterell's Cross, an ancient stone high up on Brown Clee, within an hour of sunrise, and if they failed to report the household was fined 12 pence. The old straker rights operated on a restricted basis right up until the time of parliamentary enclosure, when they were extinguished. This did not stop a latter-day pretender to the lordship of the Clee Chase, Thomas Mytton, claiming the right to impound strays throughout the Clee Hills as late as 1809.

As early as the thirteenth century Wigmore Abbey was recorded as having taken coal from Titterstone Clee. In 1260 the lord of Corfham granted land with a licence 'to dig coals within the forest of Clee or to sell or give it away'. Piecemeal mining continued on the Clees for centuries and the summits of the hills, where the coal is most readily accessible, are dotted with bell-pit mines. Some of these are medieval, but as the bell-pit techniques continued until at least the eighteenth century, it is difficult to distinguish the earlier workings from the later. Bell-pit mines takes their names from the profile of the workings: the coal is reached from a central shaft which is dug into the seam from the surface, so that eventually a small underground bell-shaped pit is created. The coal which was produced was brought to the surface by the use of a simple windlass and bucket. When abandoned, the mines collapsed and filled up, leaving a circular mound with a central hollow around the former mine entrance. These mounds have the appearance of Bronze Age burial barrows and areas which have been intensely worked over, such as that lying immediately to the west of Abdon Burf and on Catherton Clee, appear 'pockmarked' particularly when viewed from the air. The surface of the Brown Clee is also scoured with remains of a multitude of former trackways which served the various industrial activities on the open upland summit of the mountain.

The antiquarian Leland, writing in the early sixteenth century, noted 'a blo shope on Titterstone Clee', perhaps a reference to a wind furnace. These consisted of piled-up stones, arranged to enable the dominant westerly winds which sweep across the Clees to fire the wood and smelt the iron ore. He also recorded that the Brown Clee 'is exceedyng good for Iyme, whereof there they make much and serve the countrie about'. Although ironstone quarrying for local furnaces continued, coal mining gradually became far more important and as early as 1727 coal produced on Titterstone Clee was valued at £1500; however, mining was still carried out in an erratic manner. Murchison commented:

> Coal has been wrought from these hills for time immemorial, and numerous old shafts attest the extent of the operations . . . as the ground, however, has never been allotted, each speculator having begun his work where he pleased, abandoned it when he saw a difficulty, it is impossible to say how much mineral has been wasted and what quantity remain in uncollected and broken masses.

One of the perennial problems of mining and quarrying on the summit of the Clees was that of transporting the quarried materials down the steep slopes of the hills. The coal and ironstone were carried down by pack-horse or even on the backs of cottagers' wives. Richard Jones of Ashford who attended the Titterstone Wake in 1846 recalled the young women 'fine and handsome upstanding wenches they were, and well dressed too; but you wouldn' not know t'em the next day with a bag of coal strapped to their backs, for in them days coal from the Clee Hill pits were carried down the hill on women's shoulders'. Close to one of the tracks leading to the summit of Titterstone Clee there used to be a large flat slab known as the resting stone. Here the women were able to rest without removing their loads from their backs. They then continued down to a mud track road where their burdens were lifted into horse-drawn carts and transported to places as far afield as Hereford. The Clee coal was of a good quality and as the nineteenth-century writer Plymley noted, such was the demand that 'the inhabitants [of south Shropshire and north Herefordshire] purchase at great expense the land carriage coal from the Clee Hills'. In the nineteenth century regular roads were constructed and later inclined planes were built from Bitterley to the summit of Titterstone Clee and from Ditton Priors to the summit of Brown Clee. Though long since abandoned, remnants of the steep access slopes used by these early railways can still be clearly identified.

The caps of the two Clees are made of basalt, known locally as dhu-stone (which means 'black' in Welsh), and there is a small industrial settlement on Titterstone Clee with the same name. This stone was much prized for both building and road construction in the past; Thomas Telford spoke highly of its qualities and used it extensively. Ironically, the very strength and resistance of the dhu-stone has made it less attractive as a road covering in recent years. Stones such as the 'greywacke' stone quarried at Sharpstones Hill south of Shrewsbury are preferred today as they break a little as they wear and provide a better surface for modern tyres, so now the use of Clee Hill stone is restricted to minor and estate roads. Some local villages, including the churches, are built almost exclusively of dhu-stone. When weathered, the stone turns a grey-brown colour, giving the villages and walled fields a rather sombre appearance, but like most local stone it blends harmoniously into the landscape.

The Clee Hill industries were relatively short lived, but during the late nineteenth century men came to work here from all over England, Wales, Ireland and Scotland and it is estimated that at the height of activity here there was a working population of 1500-2000. Once they arrived they were isolated because of the poor roads, and a journey to Ludlow and back, only 10 miles away, would have taken a full day. As a result, a particular Clee Hill dialect developed which was a conglomeration of dialects from various regions in Britain. Alfred Jenkins has produced a survey recording the dialect, at its richest between 1890 and 1939, but which has now all but disappeared.

The early iron industry in Shropshire

The development of the iron industry in the Shropshire coalfield began during the Middle Ages. Nevertheless it was coal which was the first of the mineral resources of east Shropshire to be exploited on a large scale. The Cistercian monks of Buildwas Abbey were granted rights to mine coal by Philip de Benthall in 1250, while the Cluniacs of Much Wenlock in 1322 allowed Walter de Caldbrook to mine coal at the Brockholes in Madeley parish. By the time of the dissolution of the monasteries the monks of Wombridge had an income of £5 a year from their mines on the coalfield. Later in the sixteenth century Leland noted, 'Coles be digged hard by Wombridge where the Priory was', and Camden regarded Oakengates as 'a small village of some note for the pit cole'. In Donnington township in Lilleshall parish there was a 'Colpytt Way' as early as 1592. By the late sixteenth century in the Severn Gorge, and particularly in the parishes south of the river, the coal industry had developed into a highly organised and well-capitalised enterprise.

It is recorded in 1397 that James 'Mynor' of Derbyshire obtained Crown permission to work a mine of copper and silver within the lordship (Wenlock Edge) of Wenlock Priory. In 1540 the Priory was working two iron foundries as well as the ironstone quarries in Shirlett Forest, and in 1559 it is recorded that a man was killed digging in the Shirlett mines. Wenlock Priory also had coal mines in Little Wenlock by the early sixteenth century. The monks of Buildwas Abbey had a small iron forge on their manorial property in the sixteenth century, possibly representing the beginnings of the

Coalbrookdale iron industry. At the dissolution these iron works were taken over and developed by families such as the Reynolds, the Baldwins and later the Darbys, all names central to the Industrial Revolution.

During the sixteenth century there was a burst of industrial activity in the Marches, starting near the River Severn and spreading westwards. This industry was based on charcoal blast furnaces, generally sponsored by local landowners. The blast furnace first appeared in England at the end of the fifteenth century, but it was almost a century before it completely replaced the ancient and unreliable bloomery process in the Marches, thus making way for later developments in the iron industry. Like most early industry, iron making was to be found on rivers and streams, generally close to the sources of raw material and power to work the bellows. Accordingly, we find the iron industry developing in comparatively remote places on the edge of the Shropshire Coalfield during the sixteenth and seventeenth centuries.

One of the first Shropshire blast furnaces was built on Shirlett Common in the 1540s, another was built by the Earl of Shrewsbury on the edge of the coalfield near Shifnal in 1564, and a third at Cleobury Mortimer was built by the Earl of Dudley, at about the same time. Others were built at Lilleshall (1591) and Bringewood (1601). The old blast furnace at Coalbrookdale, which may justly be considered the most famous in the world, was originally built by Sir Basil Brooke, lord of Madeley Manor, in 1638. Later furnaces were built at Bouldon (1644) and Willey (1658). The Shropshire iron works at that time formed part of a regional network of iron-making, in which iron was carried chiefly along the River Severn, to furnaces, forges and mills throughout the West Midlands and the Marches. The principal concentration of forges was in the Stour Valley in Worcestershire, but Coalbrookdale was the most significant iron producer of all.

The development of the charcoal-fired iron industry rapidly led to the exhaustion of the remaining supplies of local timber. As early as 1561 a licence was granted to Sir William Acton to fell trees necessary for making iron and to sell timber from Shirlett for his 'lately buylded and set up iron mills in Morveld [Morville]'. Because of the shortage of timber, Crown authority was required to clear woodland within 14 miles of the River Severn at this time. Supplies of accessible timber were also required for the emerging iron and glass industries and were largely provided from specially planted coppices. With the widespread creation of iron furnaces between Willey Park to the east and Bringewood in the west, the first attempts at controlled coppicing for industrial purposes were made. In 1550 Richard Minton and Richard Stokes coppiced an area of pasture in Shirlett Forest valued at £7. In 1583 a coppice in the Earl's Wood, Shirlett, 'was enclosed and fenced . . . and contained 1000 trees then standing and growing'; within 10 years the coppice had doubled in size. In the early seventeenth century the inhabitants of Ludlow complained bitterly about the clearance of wood on Bringewood Chase which was being used in the Bringewood furnace, since they claimed it was common land. By 1650 there were regular coppices throughout south Shropshire and northern Herefordshire, located mainly on the valley slopes and escarpments. From the mid-seventeenth century onwards charcoal, which was made from wood of up to 20 years' growth, was obtained from coppices where young trees were grown as a crop. There is an interesting description of coppicing at Gilbert's Wood, Abbey Dore, during the late seventeenth century, where it is recorded that it took three cords of wood to make a load of 'coal', and that the purchases of the wood must have 'reasonable and convenient wayes allowed . . . for the cariadge of the cole ariseinge of the woode . . . with libertie to take turf, buyld cabbeines, make coal pittes and such other necessaries for cutting of the said wood and makeinge of the said cole'.

As late as 1728 a survey of the manorial land in Ditton Priors was undertaken to determine how much coppice wood could be grown for the local iron furnaces, and by the mid-eighteenth century some 12 per cent of the parish was coppiced. Once established, the coppices became important not only for providing the fuel for the iron furnaces, but for other industrial processes, as well as for that perennial consumer, the building industry. An enquiry into the state of Shropshire woodlands in 1791 clearly demonstrated the exhaustion of other sources of woodland, even hedgerow trees, which led to an ever-increasing dependence on coppice wood. One remedy that seems to have been applied was to plant a number of different tree species in newly created enclosure hedges. Large areas of Shropshire's surviving woodland were originally planted for the iron industry, and paradoxically some of the most densely wooded parts of the county, such as the area to the south of Wellington, owe their tree cover to the former requirements of the charcoal blast furnace.

Many of the charcoal furnaces enjoyed only short lives, leaving few visible traces of their activity. The site of a small remotely sited seventeenth-century furnace at Abdon is represented today by overgrown trackways and a wooded dingle with a slag floor. However, the furnace footings are still there to be sought out, and the furnace pond and weir can still be identified. There is an abandoned road between the site and the deserted village of Abdon, which lies half a mile to the east. Abdon furnace was operating in 1654 when Sir Humphrey Briggs had 'liberty of getting and carrying away all mines of ironstone off the Brown Clee Hill', but by the end of the seventeenth century the furnace had ceased to function. There were other furnaces in the region, at Bouldon, Charlcotte, and Bringewood, the latter lying on the River Teme a few kilometres west of Ludlow. During the eighteenth century these furnaces were all operated by the Knight family of Downton. Some of the iron was treated in local forges such as those at Wrickton, Prescott and Cleobury Mortimer, but a considerable quantity was carried by cart to Bridgnorth and afterwards by barge to Stourbridge.

At its height, the Charlcotte furnace produced over 400 tons of iron annually, while Bringewood was making considerably more. Today Charlcotte is the best preserved of the three furnaces. The site, occupying a typical valley setting on the Clee Brook, consists of a fine stone-built furnace approximately 20ft square and 24ft high, with the foundations of an ore house to the north. Although the hearth has gone, the interior of the furnace is in good condition. Huge tree-covered mounds of charcoal furnace slag surround the site and give the farm its modern name of Cinder Hill. In the second half of the eighteenth century Charlcotte was required to draw upon coppice wood from increasingly distant parts but ultimately it was unable to compete with the coalfield furnaces, and closed at the end of the eighteenth century. Bouldon furnace appears to have stopped iron production at about the same time, when it was converted into a paper mill. Today there is little legacy of the iron works at Bouldon; only the formidable mill wheel from Coalbrookdale and the tree-covered slag heap behind the mill bear testimony to the former ironworks here.

88 Downton Castle at Downton-on-the-Rock, which was built by Richard Payne Knight on the proceeds of the Knight iron furnaces, sits at the centre of an area of extensive exotic landscaping

The same cannot be said of Bringewood, for although the furnace and its buildings are now largely gone, there remains the magnificent eighteenth-century bridge across the Teme as a monument to the early ironmasters. In this remote spot the Knight family developed as major ironmasters, making cannons during the Civil War and incidentally producing cast-iron tomb slabs, several of which are to be found outside the little church at nearby Burrington. This collection, the earliest of which dates back to 1619, is the finest of its kind outside the Kentish Weald. Elsewhere other subtle reminders of the early iron industry litter the banks of the Teme. Originally, the Knights lived at Bringewood Hall, but later moved to Downton, where Richard Payne Knight, virtuoso, archaeologist and poet, whose ideas on parkland landscapes are discussed above, designed and built Downton Castle (1772-8), one of the first romantic castellated buildings in England. Later an imposing church was built in the castle grounds and the northern banks of the Teme were extensively landscaped. Two bridges were built across the gorge to link the house with the iron works, one of which used to carry the Ludlow to Leintwardine road until it was diverted to avoid the castle. This fine, isolated bridge is one of the hidden marvels of the Borderland.

Close by, the school, chapel, houses and iron works are also deserted and are gradually sinking back into the tranquil wooded landscape. Below the bridge there is a small wharf and a little further downstream there are the remains of a tin-plating works; both are now completely overgrown and all but forgotten. Large quantities of exotic flowers and shrubs grow on both sides of the Teme. This part of the park has now run wild, and it is one of the most delightful and completely rural spots in the whole of the Welsh Marches.

Ironbridge, Coalbrookdale and the Shropshire coalfield

In his *History of Salop*, published in 1837, Charles Hulbert described Coalbrookdale as 'the most extraordinary district in the world'. Today Coalbrookdale and the Ironbridge still retain a charisma derived from their striking geography and their unique industrial history. The Ironbridge Gorge was formed by the River Severn cutting through the eastern extension of Wenlock Edge, revealing seams of coal, ironstone, clay and limestone in the process. The close juxtaposition of these resources, together with the potential for transport provided by the river, gave the area all the elements necessary for the industrial explosion which occurred during the eighteenth century. Such was the speed of industrial development on the Shropshire coalfield that by the late eighteenth century it was the premier iron-producing region in Great Britain.

89 The Ironbridge, which was opened on New Year's Day 1781, is Britain's outstanding industrial monument. It now forms the centrepiece of the Ironbridge Gorge Museum

To begin with, in the seventeenth and early eighteenth centuries, industrial activity concentrated on the Coalbrookdale, a narrow valley which runs north from the gorge, where the first Abraham Darby set up his furnace in 1708. The frenzy of activity that followed led to the area attracting numerous visitors both from Britain and abroad. In a very full description of Coalbrookdale written in 1801 by an unknown author, the Dale is described thus:

> The works and the vicinity are frequently visited by numbers of people, of most ranks and stations in life, who seem much astonished at the extensiveness of the Manufactory, and the regularity with which it is conducted, oft expressing their surprise that a situation so passing excellent, should be fix'd upon for the seat of so large a Manufactory, but these ideas generally vanish, when they are inform'd that they are situated amidst ev'ry requisite for the purpose of carrying them on, viz. Coals, Ironstone, Limestone and Water. Also the beautiful River Severn washing the bottom for the beneficial purpose of conveying the Goods to Market.

It was indeed the River Severn which provided the economic lifeline for the coalfield industries. For, despite the erratic and sometimes dangerous nature of the Severn navigation, the Shropshire coalfield was essentially part of a river-based economy until the coming of the railways. The Severn provided easy and direct access to markets as far away as Bristol, more than 80 miles from Coalbrookdale. Indeed as early as the seventeenth century the Severn had become the second busiest river in Europe (after the Rhine), carrying trows, wherries and barges as far as Pool Quay near Welshpool. The river carried Shropshire coal downstream to Tewkesbury and upstream to Shrewsbury and mid-Wales and was the principal means of communication between the many iron works of the Borderland region.

From the ports of the upper Severn, Uffington, Shrewsbury, Montford, Landrinio, Pool Quay and Clawdd Coch, road links extended into Wales, Cheshire and the north-west. Pack-horses and wagons with textiles from Manchester and earthenware from north Staffordshire came to the mid-Severn ports of Bridgnorth and Bewdley. Goods such as tobacco pipes from Broseley were distributed throughout the Midlands by barge, while mugs from Jackfield ceramic works gave their name to a number of inns along the length of the river. Often, however, cargoes could not be brought directly to or from the Severn Gorge itself because road access was so bad. Indeed, iron from Coalbrookdale bound for Stafford to the north-east was sometimes sent by road several kilometres south to Bridgnorth, before being offloaded onto barges to travel upriver to its final destination, passing through the Severn Gorge on the way. The carriage of wine, tea, spirits and tobacco also created important commercial ties between Shropshire and Bristol and the Americas. The Severn's tributaries extended the communication network, the Avon took Shropshire coal to Pershore and iron goods to Stratford, while the Wye conveyed a variety of cargoes to iron works near their mouths and the Vyrnwy took barges as far as Llanymynech.

The true beginnings of the Industrial Revolution in Shropshire date to 1708 when the Coalbrookdale blast furnace, which stood in ruins after an explosion, was leased by Abraham Darby. Darby had been born in the Black Country, but had moved to Coalbrookdale from Bristol where he had owned an iron foundry. He rebuilt the Coalbrookdale furnace and began to smelt iron using locally made coke rather than the conventional charcoal. Although the Coalbrookdale iron which resulted was suitable for making castings it did not produce good wrought iron. However, before he died in 1717, Darby had built a second furnace at Coalbrookdale and within a decade the Dale was producing a wide range of products which were distributed throughout the Midlands. Darby's successors continued to refine the iron-making process and the Shropshire iron industry was given a particular boost in 1756 with the outbreak of the Seven Years War. By 1760 there were nine furnaces operating in the region and Shropshire was well on its way to being the principal iron-producing area in Britain.

Although the Darby family acted as a catalyst for industrial innovation, there had already been important developments in Coalbrookdale and the Shropshire coalfield before their arrival. Wooden rails seem to have been used as early as 1605 at Broseley, when they were the objects of 'riotous behaviour', presumably in opposition to their use. In 1711 the Revd Francis Brokesby wrote about a sophisticated railway system at Madeley, where 'small carriages with four wheels' were 'thrust by men . . . along long underground passages to the boats on the Severn'. In the mid-eighteenth century a plan for a wagonway between Little Wenlock and Coalbrookdale was proposed in order that 'coals may be conveyed in the easiest and best manner, to make a wagonway and lay rails on sleepers in such a manner as is commonly used, and with coal wagons and horses and oxen to draw the same on or along the said railway to Coalbrookdale'. It was Abraham Darby II who eventually extended the railway system, cutting transport costs in the Dale significantly as a consequence. A little later Richard Reynolds began to replace the wooden rails with iron rails and between 1768 and 1771 it is reported that Reynolds was responsible for the laying of some 800 tons of cast-iron rails in the

90 *The Coalbrookdale warehouses linking Severn barges with a tramway from the Coalbrookdale Ironworks from a nineteenth-century photograph*

Shropshire coalfield. The new rails linked the iron-ore fields at Dawley with the coalfield and the furnaces, and by 1785 there were over 20 miles of rail in Coalbrookdale.

Among other innovations John Wilkinson launched the first iron boat called *The Trial* in 1787 and in 1802 Richard Trevithick built a steam railway locomotive. A little earlier, in 1784, Lord Dundonald made coke using enclosed ovens; this resulted in condensing the gases given off which were then used to produce tar and varnish. By the end of the eighteenth century there were proposals to diversify industrial activity in the coalfield by producing soda, glass, fertilisers, dye stuffs and soap. The first porcelain manufactury was established at Caughley in 1772 by Thomas Turner.

In 1773 Thomas Farnolls Pritchard, a Shrewsbury architect, approached the ironmaster John Wilkinson suggesting the building of an iron bridge in the Severn Gorge. Pritchard (born 1723) had already been responsible for several important buildings in Shropshire and neighbouring counties. In 1772 he had designed the bridge over the River Teme at Bringewood Forge, and in 1773-5 he designed a bridge over the Severn at Stourport. This bridge even appears to have used iron as a foundation for the masonry spans.

An act of parliament was passed in February 1776 to enable the building of the first iron bridge. Because of the various delays in implementing the act there is some confusion about precisely what role Pritchard eventually played in constructing the bridge. It does seem probable, however, that he contributed significantly to the design of the bridge as it was finally built. However, it was the iron founder Abraham Darby III who built the bridge and who also contributed to its design, and some sections of the bridge at least were fired in a modified version of the old furnace at Coalbrookdale. The Ironbridge was eventually opened on New Year's Day 1781, at a cost of £2737 4s 4d. This compared unfavourably with the more modest estimate of £550 put forward just five years earlier. However, the bridge rapidly became an attraction to sightseers. In October 1781 a regular stagecoach service, 'The Diligence', began to cross the Ironbridge on its way to Shrewsbury from London via Broseley and in the

91 A nineteenth-century photograph of the Coalport inclined plane, taken when it was still operating

nineteenth century several other stagecoach services including one from Liverpool to Bath used the bridge. One proprietor in the 1790s advertised his service by extolling 'that striking specimen of art and so much admired object of travellers', the Ironbridge, across which his coaches passed.

The little town of Ironbridge developed rapidly next to the new bridge on the eastern banks of the Severn. It lay a little further downstream from another new settlement at Coalport, which was the creation of William Reynolds, one of the most influential eighteenth-century Shropshire ironmasters. The town grew at the junction between the Shropshire Canal and the River Severn at the point that Reynolds brought china manufacturing, chain making and boat building. At Coalport there is another marvel of the coalfield, the Coalport inclined plane. This was the means by which canal boats were raised and lowered through a vertical height of 207ft between the end of the Shropshire Canal and the Coalport basin on the banks of the Severn. Tug-boats were floated onto cradles on wheels which were carried up and down the incline on rails. At the top of the incline a steam engine pulled the cradles and boats out of the water. Generally the heavier load from the top was used to draw up the lighter load from the bottom. When the load from the bottom was the heavier, the steam engine was used. The incline was able to lift a pair of five- or six-ton boats in three and a half minutes compared with the three or four hours that would have been required if conventional locks had been used. The incline was fully operational by 1793 and in use for about 100 years.

At the foot of the inclined plane, and driven under it, is the Tar Tunnel, begun by William Reynolds, who, unaware of the presence of tar, hoped to connect an underground passage with the lower workings of some pits at Blists Hill and so obtain easier loading into river boats on the Severn. The walls of this tunnel discharged a tarry petroleum substance which it was reported was 'exported in large quantities to all parts of Europe'. The Tar Tunnel was constructed about 1787 and soon after when the tar spring was located the flow averaged about 1000 gallons a week, although within a few years it had considerably diminished. The torch of industrial enterprise that had been ignited in rural Shropshire rapidly moved on to areas with richer mineral deposits and better communications, where increasingly specialised industries could be better served. In 1805 the Shropshire Coalfield was producing some 50,000 tons of iron a year, representing 20 per cent of the national output, but by 1869, the coalfield's peak year of production, its 200,000 tons of iron accounted for only two per cent the national output. This relative decline was followed by an absolute one, and although industries in the region continued to diversify, iron production had virtually ceased within a

century. The last iron was
smelted in Shropshire in 1959
and in the 1960s the coalfield
presented a sorry sight: waste and
slag tips, the unkempt ruins of
furnaces and kilns, dilapidated
industrial housing, the ceramic
manufacturing settlement of
Jackfield gradually sliding into
the Severn and the Ironbridge
itself breaking up. However, over
the past 30 years, a second
miracle has occurred. As part of
Telford New Town, the
Ironbridge Gorge Museum
Trust has energetically restored
the industrial monuments and

92 St Michael's Church, Madeley, built by Thomas Telford in 1796. Madeley now forms part of Telford New Town

buildings and has in the process again made this region one of the most interesting and
exciting in Europe. It is wholly appropriate that in November 1986 the Ironbridge Gorge was
designated a World Heritage Site by UNESCO.

Places to visit

Ironbridge and the Ironbridge Gorge Museum Trust, Shropshire SJ 673 034

The town of Ironbridge grew up at the eastern end of Abraham Darby's first cast-iron bridge
which was opened on New Year's Day 1781. It was a small industrial new town that profited
greatly from the Coalbrookdale and Ironbridge Gorge industries. During the twentieth
century, however, the little town, along with its associated industries, went into a steep decline
and was in a state of considerable depression until the late 1960s. It was at this stage that work
began on Telford New Town, with the intention of creating a completely new industrial
community on the ruins of the old. Since then the town of Ironbridge has revived
considerably as a tourist and educational centre, and the area around it has rapidly been
transformed into one of the most impressive open-air museums anywhere in the world.

The centre of the museum is at Blists Hill which was at the top of the inclined plane
carrying barges from the River Severn to the Shropshire coalfield. Here a considerable
number of major industrial attractions have either been restored or reconstructed. These
include the Blists H°ill iron furnaces and the Hay inclined plane. Also incorporated within
the museum are Abraham Darby's original Coalbrookdale works and the furnace where he
first successfully smelted iron ore, using coke instead of charcoal. In addition there are
numerous other attractions dating from the Industrial Revolution including the Coalport
china works, the Jackfield ceramic works and tile museum, the Severn wharf and warehouses,
and the world's first iron bridge. The Ironbridge Gorge Museum provides a welcome success
story against the background of a new town which is moving awkwardly into middle age.

12 Postscript

Agriculture and the landscape

Despite many changes, the Borderland remains essentially a rural region. Agriculture is still the dominant economic activity, although the agricultural depression of the late nineteenth and early twentieth centuries affected the Marches as it did the rest of the country. Rural depopulation was a problem, particularly in the more remote parts of the region, up until the 1960s. The rural population of Herefordshire dropped by 22 per cent between 1871 and 1931, and in the moorland areas of the Black Mountains this figure reached almost 50 per cent. Some upland farms were abandoned, as the height at which profitable agricultural activity could take place dropped, just as it had done during the later Middle Ages. This resulted in moorland which had been enthusiastically enclosed during the nineteenth century being left to revert to waste in many areas in the twentieth.

The mechanisation of agriculture since the First World War accelerated the process of rural depopulation and the 'ploughing up' campaign of the Second World War only partially halted the drift. After about 1960, however, the pattern began to change. A number of factors combined to make the rural Marches more attractive and to reverse the trend of depopulation. Improved communications through better metalled roads and universal motor transport meant that even the most remote parts of the Marches were within one hour's drive

93 Shrewsbury General Market built 1867-9 in Italianate style. Described by Nicholas Pevsner as 'the chief Victorian contribution to public architecture in the town, and not one to be proud of', it was demolished in 1965 and replaced by another less functional and less attractive Market Hall (see 96)

94 The M50 motorway under construction in western Gloucestershire. The road joins Ross on Wye with Tewkesbury and is one of only two stretches of motorway to cut across the central Marches

of a market town. The provision of electricity and piped water throughout the region led to an improvement in living conditions. Added to this the quality of the Marcher landscape has recently begun to be better appreciated. Many former agricultural and industrial labourers' cottages have been taken over as commuter, retirement, or holiday homes. Around the larger towns of Hereford, Chester, Shrewsbury and Telford many former villages now act as dormitory settlements for commuters working either in the region or further afield. In some cases this had led to insensitive house-building programmes which in places have compromised the visual attraction of some villages. On the Clee Hills former squatter cottages are now occupied by people who travel to work in the West Midland conurbation just 20 miles to the east, while even the remotest parts of the Forest of Dean have been 'discovered' and nowhere in the Marches is immune from gentrification. Such developments in the rural landscape may be viewed as a mixed blessing, but they are bringing life, money and interest back to many parts of the Marches which were in danger of dying.

The face of agriculture, too, has been changing. The Marches remain predominantly an area of mixed farming with an emphasis on dairy and sheep farming in the upland areas, but new crops and techniques have been introduced. Between the wars sugar beet was developed as a major cash crop, and since the 1970s the unpleasant yellow oil-seed rape has made a spirited entrance. Amongst the exotic newcomers to the Marchland livestock scene are the emu and the ostrich. Neither has the Borderland been immune from other worrying agricultural developments. The removal of hedgerows is common, and some parts of the Herefordshire plain and eastern Shropshire now have areas of prairie farming reminiscent of East Anglia. The EU farming policy has meant that large areas of permanent pasture have been ploughed up and planted with cereal crops, and wheat now grows at altitudes unheard of since the early Middle Ages. Because of its gentle aspect, Herefordshire has been particularly badly affected, but even in upland areas of Shropshire such as the Clun Forest,

95 A view of Sutton Hill housing estate in Telford New Town

valley sides with slopes that previously seemed quite impossible to plough are even now contributing to the European surplus. Policies designed to help poor European peasant farmers improve their land and yields are also being ruthlessly applied to precious and dwindling areas of marsh and moor. Since the Second World War, pressure on the upland areas has also come from the Forestry Commission, who have created dark coniferous deserts in areas of former moorland and mixed woodland.

At the time of writing farming in the Marches is facing its biggest crisis for a century. The globalisation of markets, together with other factors, has worked to undermine the viability of many farms in the region. As a consequence rural areas are looking to activities other than traditional farming to survive economically. Organic and specialist farming provide one possible alternative; the development of tourist-based activities such as farm museums or safari parks are others. The introduction of countryside stewardship schemes may however eventually prove of greater long-term value to a larger number of farmers. Some commentators believe that farming as a way of life in the Welsh Marches is in real danger of disappearing altogether. It is, however, difficult to imagine that a region which has lived by agriculture for at least 5000 years and has survived the Dark Ages and the Black Death will succumb. What is certain is that there will be further changes. Landscape is never static for long; it has always responded to changing economic and social conditions. The great danger in the Marches, as in other rural areas, is if there are sudden and dramatic changes brought about by a reaction to problems, which may well turn out to be relatively short term.

Quarrying and mining

Quarrying, which has been a feature of the Borderlands over many centuries, also presents a threat to the landscape, primarily because of the huge scale of contemporary operations. The eastern section of Wenlock Edge is being systematically removed, as are a number of other hills such as the Breiddens and the summit of Titterstone Clee Hill, while in Herefordshire the destruction of the interior of the massive hillfort at Sutton Walls by quarrying is a disgraceful story that has recently been emulated in some other places. At Sharpstones Hill, near Shrewsbury, a quarry almost a mile long produces high quality roadstone. The extraction of sand and gravel from the river terraces of the Severn and Wye has so far been only on a relatively modest scale, but needs careful monitoring if the mistakes committed elsewhere in the country are not to be sadly repeated.

The picture, however, is not completely bleak. Areas of former quarrying and mining activity, such as the coalmines of eastern Shropshire and the scarred lead mining district around Minsterley, are being either landscaped or allowed to heal themselves peacefully. In this context it is worth remembering that a quintessential feature of the Shrewsbury landscape, the Dingle, was originally a stone quarry. The Dingle is a delightful landscaped hollow at the centre of Shrewsbury's main park, the Quarry. In the

*96 Shrewsbury Market Hall built in 1965 (see **93**)*

sixteenth century the Quarry had been acquired by the Town Corporation and in 1585 it was 'agreed that the quarry of stone . . . behind the walls shall be reserved for the sole use of the Corporation'. Later the Dingle was used for bull baiting and for plays, and in the nineteenth century it was landscaped with pools and water features and incorporated into a fine riverside municipal park.

Towns in the late twentieth century

The fate of the Border towns during the last century mirrors that of the countryside on which they have depended so much. Until 1939 there was a general picture of stagnation or even decline, a decline that continued after the war in small western market towns such as Bishop's Castle and Kington, and which has only been reversed relatively recently. In the 1960s ambitious schemes for redeveloping the county towns were implemented. Hereford has lost more of its historical buildings than Shrewsbury and its geography has not proved to be a match to the penetrative power of the motor car. An inner ring road following the line of the city's medieval walls creates a *cordon sanitaire* between the mutilated historic centre and the suburbs. In Shrewsbury the cumbersome, but not unlovely, Victorian market hall was demolished and replaced by an equally cumbersome, but very unlovely, edifice. There were other casualties, including some fine half-timbered buildings which were demolished in order to provide what were perceived as 'improved' shopping facilities and to make motoring in the centre of town easier. Fortunately the complexity of the medieval road system, together with the virtually insurmountable

97 Rural diversification at Abbey Dore, Herefordshire. Llamas are being bred for wool and as a visitor attraction

98 Weobley High Street in 1933. This attractive village has altered little and is now prized both as a place to live and to visit

problems posed by the geography of the site on which Shrewsbury sits, have thwarted all attempts to bring more cars rapidly into the town centre by way of an inner ring road. At the time of writing, an uneasy truce prevails, with pedestrian precincts occupying the historic cores of both Shrewsbury and Hereford.

As yet the process of redevelopment has not penetrated far enough down the urban hierarchy to have done much serious damage to the smaller Marcher towns. However, despite strenuous efforts to achieve the impossible and damage Ludlow's matchless townscape, this gem of a town has survived largely intact. Even further down the scale there are some of the finest small towns or large villages to be found anywhere in Britain. High on the list must come Weobley, where not only has the town's medieval layout been preserved, but many fine half-timbered houses survive. Nearby Pembridge, with its detached belltower (one of seven in Herefordshire), runs it a close second.

The most dramatic urban development in the region has been the creation of a completely new city based on the debris of the Shropshire coalfield. Telford, which is now the most populous settlement in the Marches, was originally created in order to relieve inner city congestion around Birmingham and Wolverhampton and provide an alternative industrial base to the Black Country. The old centres of Dawley, Madely, Oakengates and Wellington have been welded together with their surrounding largely derelict industrial landscapes to make Britain's twenty-first post-war new town with a population of just over a quarter of a million. Since work started on the scheme in the mid-'60s, however, the economic climate has changed greatly, and not only is the West Midlands conurbation no longer seeking to accommodate its overspill, it is actually fighting for its own economic life. Industrial Telford has therefore suffered with the rest of industrial Britain, and in the 1990s had a very high level of unemployment.

99 The detached medieval bell tower of St Mary's church, Pembridge. Such bell towers are a curiosity of the Herefordshire landscape — there are six more in the county

Telford has also suffered from the traditional Marchland malaise of isolation — the M54 linking the town with the national motorway system was not opened until 1984. The only other stretch of motorway in the region, the M50, runs largely irrelevantly, as far as the Marches is concerned, across southern Herefordshire, joining the M5 to south Wales. Visually Telford suffers from the same problem experienced by similar developments elsewhere, and some of the early housing schemes were particularly unfortunate as they used cheap materials which deteriorated rapidly. But if Telford cannot be judged an unqualified success neither is it an unqualified failure. The town now boasts a wide variety of light industrial activity with a strong emphasis upon computer-based ventures. The Stafford Park Industrial Estate covers some 350 acres and houses hi-tech companies of virtually every description. The grain of the landscape on which the new town sits is being used to good effect to create spacious tree-covered vistas which are as pleasant as any to be found in a modern town elsewhere in the country. Ironbridge and the Severn gorge, which form Telford's southern boundary, are now as healthy as at any time since the nineteenth century, and certainly more attractive. Much of this improvement can be attributed to the work of the Ironbridge Gorge Museum Trust, which is conserving monuments of the Industrial Revolution, many of which would in the past have been discarded as worthless. This has resulted in the influx of tens of thousands of visitors to the area, justly making it one of the most popular tourist centres in the whole of Britain.

Conservation and tourism

Attitudes to the Border landscape and its past have changed markedly over the past half-century. This is particularly true in the towns, where a number of factors have combined to promote the preservation of historic buildings. Large-scale inner town redevelopment has become too costly and many have now come to question its desirability. The steady growth of tourism as a major source of income and employment has also encouraged preservation rather than destruction. Added to this, the changing national attitude expressed through legislation relating to historic buildings and conservation areas has worked towards the preservation of the historic heritage.

In Shrewsbury, for example, the restoration of the Bear Steps in the heart of the historic town in 1972 set a pattern for the adaptive reuse of historic buildings. Subsequently, new and profitable uses have been found for a variety of buildings, including the medieval timber houses in Barracks Passage, the medieval church of St Julian, and more recently the Victorian edifice which dominates the town's river view, the Royal Shropshire Infirmary. Rowley's Mansion (1618), the first brick building in the borough, and the adjoining Tudor building known as Rowley's House, have been restored to accommodate the town museum. Finally, the restoration of the Shrewsbury Library, formerly Shrewsbury School, was the largest, most ambitious, most expensive, and most successful conservation scheme ever undertaken in the town. Throughout the Marches similar, if more modest, schemes have been enacted. Another development which reflects the changed attitude to the past has been the creation of several new museums to add to those founded in the nineteenth century. Apart from the Ironbridge Gorge Museum, a section of the Severn Valley Railway has been reopened: some 13 miles of track between Bridgnorth and Bewdley carry steam trains through magnificent countryside down the Severn valley. A farm museum opened at Acton Scott and a museum of cider in Hereford. Along the western length of the Marches runs the Offa's Dyke Path which was opened as a long-distance footpath in 1971 and provides access to some of the wildest and most dramatic scenery in England.

The story of rural landscape preservation in the Marches is, perhaps inevitably, not such a happy one. Pressures on the countryside continue to take their toll on historic features and natural habitats. Nevertheless the Marches do have their share of Sites of Special Scientific Interest, which are part of an attempt to preserve a representative example of environments rich in both historical sites and flora and fauna. One of these is Moccas Deer Park to the west of Hereford, where a management agreement is working to maintain the balance between modern estate management techniques and the conservation of rare trees and insects within the context of an operational deer park.

Conscious conservation can only go so far; economic reality will ensure that the Marches do not become one great museum. It is up to all of us to make sure that any changes respect the integrity of the unique Border landscape. There has always been change and change there will always be.

> On Wenlock Edge the wood's in trouble;
> His forest fleece the Wrekin heaves;
> The gale, it plies the saplings double,
> And thick on Severn snow the leaves.
>
> 'Twould blow like this through holt and hanger
> When Uricon the city stood:
> 'Tis the old wind in the old anger,
> But then it threshed another wood.
>
> Then, 'twas before my time, the Roman
> At yonder heaving hill would stare:
> The blood that warms on English yeoman,
> The thoughts that hurt him, they were there.
>
> There, like the wind through woods in riot,
> Through him the gale of life blew high;
> The tree of man was never quiet:
> Then 'twas the Roman, now 'tis I.
>
> The gale, it plies the saplings double,
> It blows so hard, 'twill soon be gone:
> To-day the Roman and his trouble
> Are ashes under Uricon.
> (from *A Shropshire Lad* — A.E. Housman)

Index

Page numbers in **bold** denote illustrations